FOOD
FIGHT

FOOD FIGHT

From Plunder and Profit to People and Planet

STUART GILLESPIE

HarperCollins*Publishers*Ltd

For Lindsay, Ciara and Rory

Published by HarperCollins Publishers Ltd, by arrangement with
Canongate Books Ltd., Edinburgh

FIRST CANADIAN EDITION

How the Other Half Dies by Susan George, copyright © Susan George, 1976.
Used by kind permission of the author.

"A United Front Against the Debt" from *Thomas Sankara Speaks* by Thomas Sankara,
copyright © 1988, 2007 by Pathfinder Press. All rights reserved.

HarperCollins books may be purchased for educational, business,
or sales promotional use through our Special Markets Department.

HarperCollins Publishers Ltd
Bay Adelaide Centre, East Tower
22 Adelaide Street West, 41st Floor
Toronto, Ontario, Canada
M5H 4E3

www.harpercollins.ca

Typeset in Garamond Premier Pro by Palimpsest Book Production Ltd, Falkirk, Stirlingshire

Library and Archives Canada Cataloguing in Publication

Title: Food fight : from plunder and profit to people and planet / Stuart Gillespie.
Names: Gillespie, Stuart (Stuart R.), author
Description: First edition. | Includes bibliographical references.
Identifiers: Canadiana (print) 20250148285 | Canadiana (ebook) 20250149052 |
ISBN 9781443475297 (softcover) | ISBN 9781443475303 (ebook)
Subjects: LCSH: Food industry and trade—Health aspects. | LCSH: Food industry and trade—
Environmental aspects. | LCSH: Food industry and trade—Economic aspects. |
LCSH: Food industry and trade—Social aspects.
Classification: LCC HD9000.5 .G55 2025 | DDC 338.4/7664—dc23

Printed and bound in the United States of America
25 26 27 28 29 LBC 5 4 3 2 1

Contents

IV TRANSFORMATION

Introduction

Food is life but our food system is killing us. Designed in a different century for a different purpose – to mass-produce cheap calories to prevent famine – it's now generating obesity, ill-health and premature death. We need to transform it, into one that can nourish all eight billion of us and the planet we live on.

Right now, we're enmeshed in a cascade of overlapping crises. Obesity, undernutrition and the climate crisis are, in and of themselves, huge challenges. Things are made worse by the fact they overlap, they interact, and they share basic causes. And when COVID came along, a pandemic was added to the mix.[1]

Our current food system – which sits smack centre of the cascade – is no longer fit for purpose. It's a system that's now destroying more than it produces. Levels of hunger and undernutrition are rising again, while one in two adults are overweight or living with obesity. The 'double burden of malnutrition' affects most countries in the world now. By 2035, it will cost the global economy as much as COVID at its peak.[2] But this cost will be borne year on year, every year.

We are a species supremely adapted to forage, hunt, to find and consume food. Feasting in times of plenty allowed us to survive the more frequent times of want – a strategy dictated by the environment we lived in. But our food environment has changed in an evolutionary nanosecond. Most of us now rely on a diet of ultra-processed products. It's not real food; our bodies and metabolic systems can't handle it.

We're in a dangerous place, like dolphins in a desert. What used to be an advantage is now a liability. Transnational mega-companies have harnessed the biology of desire and used it to get us addicted to products that make them rich and us sick. A quarter of all adult deaths – over 12 million every year – are due to poor diets.[3] And it is still the poorest, the most marginalised, who are most likely to become malnourished, get sick and die too soon.

Like health, food lacks a specific, measurable dimension, because it is and it means so many things to us. Food is essential for our survival, though some makes us ill and can even kill us. It's a basic need, a source of pleasure, an object of desire. More fundamental than sex. But it can also generate stress, shame and fear. Food is identity, culture, celebration – a source of joy, friendship and love. Food brings people together; it can be a peace offering. But it can also be a source of conflict, even a weapon of war. Food is political, ethical, moral – a human right. And it's also an economic commodity with a price tag.

Through land, water and agriculture, food connects us with nature, animals and the environment. It works on many levels, at many scales, from the way nutrients affect our gut microbiome, our metabolism, even our mood, to the way food is provisioned and allocated within households and communities. Food is both a national concern and one of the most basic commodities in global trade and international co-operation.

Food systems encompass all steps from farm to fork, field to plate, seed to feed. The full chain of activities, the forces at play, the institutions and people involved, the outcomes and the web of connections between all these elements. Many food systems are small-scale and local, but there is one dominant global system that profits from products and practices that are not good for us.

The problem we face now is the simple fact that our global food system is an anachronism. In the last century it has performed miracles, but in this one it's a source of jeopardy. Over time, it has become sclerotic and it's now making us ill and destroying our planet. We should not speak of reform and repair, because it's not actually broken. The system we have is working just the way those who control it want it to work. For capitalism to sustain itself, it needs to generate profit. And in 2025, after nearly fifty years of neoliberalism, the most profitable food system is the one that manufactures ultra-processed products which are marketed aggressively across the world.

We have become hostages to this system.

But things are changing. People are educating themselves. We are increasingly fed up with the box of tricks that multinationals use to bamboozle us. Not just disillusioned, but angry, especially with governments that fail to act in our interests. We know enough now. It's time to harness this knowledge and power to drive the change that's needed.

In *Food Fight*, we go on a journey through time and place and across sectors and disciplines.

The first part ('Cascade') offers a snapshot of the food, nutrition and health situation in the world now. We look at the challenges we face, their manifestations, causes and consequences.

In the second part ('Regime'), we revisit the three food regimes that have most impacted how our food systems are structured today. Regimes are launched and sustained by power. Without learning from the past, we end up repeating it. In the three chapters in this section, we travel through three centuries of colonialism, followed by three decades of Cold War, and the last half-century of the neoliberal/corporate regime in which our current food system is embedded.

The third part ('Unravelling') is where we disentangle the structural drivers of the cascade and explore how they operate. We will see how the cascade involves vicious cycles in which the feedback amplifies or accelerates the effect. We will learn how the global food system has itself become a large part of the problem, having been captured by transnational corporations who profit from public ill-health while using an array of tactics to stop Government from getting in their way. We look at the environmental implications of this system, and the way it thrives on inequalities and health shocks, including pandemics like AIDS and COVID. These structural causes derive from our collective failure to rein in harmful industries, address food injustice and hold our elected leaders to account for their actions, or inaction. We unpack the different forms of power and the way they are used – because ultimately, to transform our food system, we need to make a radical shift in the balance of power.

The fourth part ('Transformation') shows how we can do this. We explore the roles of governments, civil society, citizens, researchers, journalists and company executives in transforming our food system into one that will see us through the rest of this century and beyond. We see how vicious cycles can be turned into virtuous cycles, how we can turn their connectivity into a positive multiplier, from adversity to advantage. The word 'crisis' after all comes from the Greek '*krisis*' which means, a separation, a turning point.

This is where we are right now.

INTRODUCTION

Food Fight shows how we got to this point and how, through a new set of collective and individual actions, we can drive a food revolution. As we move into the second quarter of the twenty-first century, it's clear we have enough evidence, experience and power. We can do it, together. We can create a better future for ourselves and our children. Especially our children.

I

CASCADE

1

Overfed, Undernourished

In the late Seventies, I became interested in nutrition because I wanted to understand why some people became malnourished and others didn't. Being malnourished meant being undernourished, being hungry. Obesity wasn't on the public health radar then.

Twenty years later, I led an initiative on the emergence of a 'double burden of malnutrition' – the co-existence of under-nutrition with overweight and obesity.[1] At the time it seemed more threat than reality. I was still focused on undernutrition because it was an outcome of deprivation. Until we started to look at the data, I thought obesity was a very different problem, down to individuals making bad choices.

I was so wrong.

Through the first quarter of this century, obesity has skyrock-eted in many countries of the world, in urban and rural areas, among both children and adults. Four out of ten adults (2.5 billion) are now overweight or living with obesity.[2] In the UK, it's closer to seven in ten.

Our team was trying to characterise the double burden at a population level, but over the years it became clear that it could exist in communities and even in households (stunted kids with overweight parents). This was more – not less – likely to happen in the poorest households in the poorest communities.

Later still, we realised it was happening *in the same individual*. A stunted child would grow into a stunted adult, who was then at greater risk of becoming overweight in an environment flooded by junk food.

The next big discovery was that the causes of undernutrition and overnutrition were similar. They weren't separate conditions, but overlapped in space and time, and they shared drivers that derived from disrupted infant feeding and care, and from dysfunctional food systems.

We need to return to a holistic focus on *mal*-nutrition (poor nutrition). In 2025, malnutrition in all its forms is by far the biggest cause of ill-health on this planet, affecting one in three people. Every country is affected.

The UK's double burden is world-beating. Hundreds of thousands of children in the sixth richest country in the world are simultaneously overweight and undernourished.[3,4] Preschool children in the UK are shorter than their peers in nearly all other high-income countries. For instance, five-year-old boys and girls are 7cm shorter than their Dutch counterparts. In 1985, British boys and girls ranked 69th of 200 nationalities for height. Boys are now 102nd and girls 96th.

Diet is the main driver of anthropometric outcomes (height, weight, growth), but it is not the only one. Many structural factors related to poverty, injustice and environmental disadvantage interact in their effects on nutrition and health. A child's height can be affected by illness, infection, stress, sleep quality, housing and living conditions – as well as diet.

Differences in the heights of young children between socioeconomic groups capture the effects of poverty and inequality. Data on the height of nineteen-year-olds in the UK, who grew up during the last fourteen years of Tory-led austerity, suggest economic factors contributed to the faltering growth of British children. We've become so focused on rising obesity that failing growth has slipped below the radar. A healthy diet is crucial for a sustained supply of the nutrients needed for growth, physical and cognitive development, and essential to avoid both under-nutrition and obesity.

In December 2023, *The Guardian*'s lead front-page article spelled out the growing crisis.[5] More than 800,000 patients had been admitted to hospital with nutritional deficiencies in 2022/23, a threefold increase on ten years earlier. Professor Kamila Hawthorne, Chair of the Royal College of GPs, said doctors were facing 'moral distress' because they couldn't help: 'It's not like you can prescribe money or food'.

Jan Jemson of Magic Breakfast (a charity providing free break-fasts to schoolchildren facing hunger) spoke of, 'children with teeth falling out ... with bowed legs.'[6] GPs in poorer areas reported a resurgence of Victorian-era diseases such as rickets and scurvy, caused by nutritional deficiencies. The highest rate of child undernutrition was found in Norfolk and Waveney, where one in twelve children were undernourished. The big irony here is that Norfolk is the breadbasket of the country and grows nearly a third of all edible crops and almost half of home-grown vegetables.

Meanwhile, obesity-related admissions to hospital have doubled in just six years. In the UK, one in three children are overweight or living with obesity.* By age ten to eleven, one in four boys and

---

* Overweight and obesity are differentiated using body mass index (BMI), a measure of body mass derived by dividing a person's weight (kg) by their height in metres squared (m^2). A BMI over 30 indicates obesity; between 25 and 30, overweight. <https://www.who.int/news-room/fact-sheets/detail/obesity-and-overweight>

one in five girls have obesity (30 per cent of all children in the most deprived areas compared with 13 per cent in the least deprived).[7]

Malnutrition is a global crisis. Undernutrition – in the form of stunting, wasting or micronutrient deficiencies – affects hundreds of millions worldwide, increasing ill-health and death, especially among young children and women, and generates a raft of consequences that play out at all levels from individual to national.

Stunting (low height for age) is the result of poor nutrition *in utero* and in early childhood. Around a quarter of all children under five years old on the planet (148 million) are affected, nearly all of whom live in Asia and Africa. Wasting (low weight for height) – a manifestation of acute growth failure caused by illness – affects 45 million under-fives.[8]

And then there are various deficiencies of micronutrients – essential vitamins and minerals – which afflict 2 billion people worldwide. More than 1.5 billion people are deficient in iron; in Africa and Southeast Asia, two-thirds of all preschoolers and half of all pregnant women are anaemic. Vitamin A deficiency affects 250 million preschool-age children, blinding up to 500,000 of them, half of whom will die shortly after losing their vision. A similar number of children are deficient in iodine, significantly impairing their cognitive development.

Some progress has been made in reducing stunting in children and underweight in women, and in tackling iodine deficiency. Anaemia in children and women and low birthweight rates however have not changed for decades.[9]

Turning to the other side of the double burden, obesity is now a global pandemic, affecting more than one billion people.[10] The United States led the way. Obesity among American adults nearly tripled in four decades (from 15 per cent in 1980 to 42 per cent in 2020).[11] In the UK, adult obesity has tripled in the last fifty years. One-third of all British adults now live with obesity, the highest proportion in Europe besides Malta and Turkey. Another third are overweight.

Looking ahead, the World Obesity Federation, predicts more than half the world's population (over 4 billion people) will be living with overweight or obesity by 2035 if current trends prevail, half of whom will have obesity. Childhood obesity could more than double by 2035 (in just fifteen years, from 2020 levels), affecting 208 million boys and 175 million girls.[12]

Of the ten countries with the greatest expected increases, nine are in Asia or Africa. Between 2006 and 2021 in India, for example, underweight among women halved (35 per cent to 18 per cent) as overweight doubled (12 per cent to 24 per cent) and it was a similar picture among men. The percentage of overweight or obesity among preschool children in India has now exceeded the percentage of undernourished children.[13]

This is not a sudden-onset disaster like a tsunami. The double burden is an unremitting landslide that's sweeping the globe. The good news is there is a lot we can do to turn things around, as we'll explore in the last part of this book. But first we need to dig deeper, to better understand what's going on . . . and why.

The life-cycle of malnutrition

I first explored the life-cycle dynamics of malnutrition in the mid-Nineties while developing a learning package for UNICEF staff. At that time, the focus was on undernutrition. The evidence was clear. If a mother is undernourished in pregnancy and her diet is poor, foetal growth and development will be compromised and the child will be more likely to have a low birthweight.

Effectively born undernourished, the newborn will have a

greater risk of dying in infancy and, if he or she survives, of acquiring developmental and health problems throughout childhood and into adult life. Any significant growth failure in this period will have irreversible consequences in later life.[14] Stunted children become stunted adolescents who have difficulties in completing their education and finding a decent job. This cycle is amplified among women who marry early, do not complete secondary education and are from poorer households.[15] Up to a third of children stunting at age five is due to this cycle. Undernutrition is thus not only one of the key manifestations of poverty, but also one of its key drivers in the future (both in adulthood and the next generation). Vicious cycles again.

Micronutrient malnutrition also travels through generations. A lack of essential vitamins and minerals can be devastating for a pregnant woman and her unborn child. The micronutrient-deficient mother is more likely to have complications in pregnancy and more likely to die giving birth. Iron-deficiency anaemia causes one in four maternal deaths around the world.[16] Her baby is more likely to be born prematurely, have low birthweight, suffer from congenital defects, be cognitively impaired by poor brain growth in the womb, and more likely to fail to develop and grow well in infancy.

Epigenetics and mismatched environments

In 1998, I met Professor David Barker of the University of Southampton. We were both in New York, working for UNICEF. Like many, I was intrigued (and a bit disturbed) by the groundbreaking 'Barker Hypothesis'. Barker was an epidemiologist who, in 1990, floated the notion that children born with low birthweight had higher risks of developing chronic diseases such as hypertension, coronary heart disease and diabetes, in middle age.

Since then, a wealth of literature has been generated on how early-life undernutrition (within the womb and the first year of life) reduces the capacity of developing organs to cope with stress. The result is a higher risk of cardiovascular and metabolic ill-health later in life. Historical studies of individuals who were *in utero* during the Dutch Hunger Winter (1944–1945), caused by the German blockade, confirmed an association between undernutrition in the womb and the development of obesity, heart disease and type 2 diabetes later in life. Babies in the womb during this famine were 30 per cent more likely to develop obesity in adulthood than other babies.[17]

Questions were in fact being asked a lot earlier. In the early Seventies, as a medical student in India, Chittaranjan Yajnik was bewildered by some of the diabetes patients at his hospital in Pune, India. They didn't look like type 2 diabetics. They didn't have obesity, they weren't old – they looked normal, some even quite thin.[18]

Twenty years later, he set up a cohort of mothers and their babies in six rural villages near Pune. The babies were small and thin but they had high levels of adiposity, especially around their waist – a predisposition to diabetes that they'd inherited at birth from their mothers whose diets during pregnancy were not nutritious.* The 'thin-fat baby' represents a mismatch of environments in rapid flux. As Bee Wilson eloquently put it: 'the story of the nutrition transition written on human bodies'.[19]

Epigenetics shows how where we live and what we do – our environment and our behaviour – can affect the way our genes work (whether a gene is expressed or not), which in turn can affect the health of our future children. If a woman is undernour-

---

* It was only when, in 2004, Yajnik revealed he had himself been a 'thin-fat baby' that he was able to get his work published – one of many examples of academic resistance to outlier ideas.

ished during pregnancy, her body sends signals to the foetus that the world is one in which it's hard to get enough calories. This triggers an adaptive response in the growing embryo in which the body stores more energy per calorie consumed, in preparation for this harsh outside world of scarcity. In genetic terms, these babies have phenotypes for hunger.

A problem arises when they are born into a rapidly changing world in which calories are no longer scarce, but rather flood the place in the form of cheap, energy-dense junk food. What was an adaptation is now a liability. This 'metabolic imprinting' makes it much more likely the child will develop obesity and chronic disease in later life.

Undernutrition in one generation causes overnutrition in the next one.

We used to speak of the life-cycle of malnutrition, but in reality, there are many cycles that spin around, generation after generation, each one influenced by the one before it. Nutritional disadvantage, driven by inequitable factors and processes, can last for decades.

This is a big deal. But it also gives us hope. Epigenetics is bad when the environment is bad. But it also means we can turn things around – from adversity to advantage – by protecting the nutrition and health status of women and by improving food environments.

Today, the more common situation is that of a mother being overweight during pregnancy. In the Global North more than half of all pregnancies are now in women who are overweight or living with obesity;[20] a third of these are also complicated by diabetes.[21]

Maternal obesity compromises the development of the unborn child's cardiovascular and central nervous systems, increases the risk of health problems at birth and beyond. Children born to mothers who have obesity during pregnancy are more likely to be born with a high or low birthweight and/or increased adiposity – either way putting them at greater risk of obesity later in life.[22]

If the expectant mother is hypertensive, babies may have low birthweight because of altered blood and therefore nutrient flow to the foetus. Rapid catch-up growth of a low-birthweight baby can amplify the effect of poor growth in the womb on the risk of metabolic and cardiovascular diseases later in life.[23] And a child who then develops obesity is five times more likely than healthy-weight peers to experience it as an adult.[24]

In essence, the period that extends from conception through nine months of pregnancy and the first two years of a child's life is critical for both child and mother. One thousand days. A period of vulnerability but also a golden window of opportunity when the greatest lifelong benefits can be set in motion.

2

Damage

Everybody, sooner or later, sits down to a banquet of consequences.
Robert Louis Stevenson

For two years in the mid-Eighties, I was a nutrition volunteer on a rural development project with Koya tribal communities in a teak forest in southern India. Child undernutrition was a big problem throughout the year, but especially in the rainy season. My job was to work with an inner circle of health-worker trainers to deliver a range of nutrition and health services to twenty-five hamlets.

To help us all figure what was happening, we set up a surveillance system that involved monitoring the growth of the youngest children. The first two years of life are crucial, as this is when they need the most care and when they're supposed to grow fastest.

Mothers did what they could, but they could barely cope. Everything went into overdrive during the monsoon, when armies of tribal women would work, bent double, dawn till dusk, transplanting rice saplings from the nursery beds into the main fields. This was also the time when diarrheal and respiratory disease peaked, when food stocks were lowest and the roads to clinics were impassable. When their parents were in the fields, kids were left at home, with siblings or grandparents. Infants would not be breastfed, or they'd be weaned abruptly onto formula feed which was often prepared with contaminated water. Many got sick, some died.

Around this time David Seckler, an American economist, thought he had a solution to India's malnutrition problem. He proposed waving a statistical wand to declare millions of stunted children to be perfectly fine.[1] They might be small, but that didn't mean they weren't healthy. He speculated that short stature was an adaptation to environmental stress. This was the 'small but healthy' hypothesis – a smaller child has lower nutrient requirements and can therefore survive on less food. This gives them a better chance of survival.

His article in the *Economic and Political Weekly* (*EPW*) infuriated me. Things looked very different in the forest. Stunting was not a slow incremental process of disease-free slowing of growth. It was savage. Some kids managed to catch up some of their lost growth later, but then they would get hit again. A brutal roller coaster. This wasn't adaptation, it was a desperate struggle. If they survived, they'd become small adults. We did not know then what the long-term implications were for their brain development, their employability, their future. That evidence came later.

I was blown away by the arrogance of economists who thought they had the answers to the world's nutrition problems. Three decades later, in 2013, Arvind Panagariya, a leading Indian economist, became convinced, like Seckler, that the nutritional status of Indian children should not be judged using international reference standards. (This, despite the fact that Indian children were among a pool of children used to define the standards.) He believed that Indian children (and presumably adults) were genetically different to children from any other country. This time, an entire issue of *EPW* had been devoted to the debate. I wrote a rebuttal ('Myths and Realities') as did others, including Jean Dreze and Angus Deaton who had just won the Nobel Prize for Economics.[2] A few weeks later, India's Prime Minister, Narendra Modi, appointed Panagariya as Head of the Planning Commission, the leading civil servant post in the country.

The problem is not 'being small' – it's *becoming* small'. The process of growth failure is bad for the child in the present (illness, lack of psychosocial care, etc.) and it has long-term costs. Adults who failed to grow well during childhood are disadvantaged in manual work that requires strength. Much more damaging than that are the long-term implications for cognitive development, which in turn affects learning in school, employability and their future lives.

The consequences of malnutrition are massive and pervasive. But they're also often hidden. The bulk of the iceberg is below the waterline. Four types of damage – relating to survival, health, social and economic effects – are key.

Survival and health

Malnutrition kills millions and erodes the potential of billions. It is by far the biggest cause of ill-health and premature death globally, contributing as much disease burden as the next two to three leading categories combined (hypertension, tobacco, high glucose).[3] One-quarter of all adult deaths each year – more than 12 million – are due to poor diets and malnutrition.[4]

Undernutrition causes 45 per cent of all deaths of children under five years of age in low- and middle-income countries.[5] These deaths are preventable.

Malnutrition stunts growth and impairs development. These children may never attain their full possible height and their brains may never fully develop. They will begin their lives at a marked disadvantage, they will face learning difficulties in school and earn less as adults.[6] Associations between early nutrition and human capital – a concept that includes skills, health, knowledge and resilience – have been shown repeatedly in cohort and intervention studies. As we saw earlier, consequences persist through the life-cycle and across generations.

Obesity arises when the genes with which you were born clash with the food environment in which you live. People have obesity just like they have cancer or diabetes. It's not their identity.*

The World Health Organization (WHO) and the European Commission, whose primary concern is the prevalence of disease in a population, recognise obesity as a disease. The medicalisation of obesity at individual level, however, can drive weight stigma and fatphobia against people of higher weight. The reality is, having a high BMI or higher adiposity is *not* a disease in itself. Not every person whose BMI is over 30 is unwell. High BMI is a *marker* of risk, it's not the disease itself (just as nicotine-stained fingers of smokers is not a disease).[7] The dysregulation of dietary intake and related metabolic dysfunction is the disease. Tackling obesity therefore is not about 'making fat people thin', it's about improving people's health.

People with higher levels of adiposity are at much greater *risk* of becoming unwell, even if they are metabolically healthy in the present. Fat cells are like balloons: they expand when you gain weight and shrink when you lose it. Unlike balloons, however, they don't pop when they get too big, they start to leak.[8] Spillover

---

* Just as a person with dementia is not a *demented* person, a child with cancer is not *cancerous*, a person with obesity is not *obese*. As with any disease, we use person-first language.

fat ends up in our muscles and liver which, over time, can lead to lipotoxicity (fat poisoning) and then later, type 2 diabetes, heart disease and certain cancers.

Obesity is the leading risk factor for type 2 diabetes which affects half a billion people worldwide. In the US, seven out of every ten adults are overweight or have obesity, four of whom have 'metabolic syndrome' which ramps up the risk of heart disease, stroke and type 2 diabetes.[9] One-third of the USA population is pre-diabetic, most of whom don't even know it. Every year in the USA, 73,000 lower limbs are amputated.

Four countries have more diabetes deaths than the US: India, China, Indonesia and Mexico.[10] In India, in just one decade (2009–2019) the proportion of deaths and disability caused by diabetes grew by a staggering 60 per cent. More than 100 million Indians now live with diabetes, and another 136 million have prediabetes.

Globally, one in eight people will have diabetes by 2050, if obesity and dietary trends continue. This would be the biggest pandemic in human history. The effect for countries in the Global South,* especially Africa and South Asia, would be catastrophic.[11] Taken together, all obesity-related conditions account for about 18 per cent of all healthy life years lost.†

Social stress
Vicious cycles play out within the life-cycle and across generations. Malnutrition leads to illness which affects the ability to work, to hold down a job, to raise an income and avoid poverty.

---

* Global South: https://worldpopulationreview.com/country-rankings/global-south-countries
† Time lost (of an expected lifespan) due to premature death or ill-health associated with a disease or condition.

Poverty in turn causes stress, disordered eating and disrupted sleep, which leads to malnutrition and ill-health which affects the chances of holding down a decent job.

And so the cycle turns . . .

As paradoxical as it may sound, food *insecurity* is strongly linked with obesity. Uncertainty of access is insecurity. We store more fat per calorie consumed when access to food is unpredictable, to buffer ourselves against future shortfall.[12] The cost of this 'adaptation' is an increased risk of obesity. Uncertain access to food can also generate anxiety, stress and depression, which lead to binge-eating of cheap, energy-dense comfort foods, packed with sugar, fat, salt and additives, that have short-term, stress-alleviating effects.[13] Ensuing 'feast-and-famine' cycles lead to increased body fat and faster weight gain when food becomes plentiful.[14]

Beyond food and nutrition, stress and anxiety is a virtual pandemic, especially among teenage girls. In 2023, a quarter of a million children in the UK were on NHS waiting lists because of mental ill-health. Status anxiety fuelled by social media can lead to disordered eating and sleeping patterns. We've become hybrid beings, with dual online–offline existences. The digitalisation of society and increases in daily screen time are associated with reduced physical activity, a more sedentary lifestyle and increased stress.[15]

Obesity travels through social networks via social media, through junk- and fast-food posting and by facilitating access to it.[16] Time online shapes eating behaviours. This includes mindless overeating while viewing, exposure to junk food and drink ads, reduced sleep, as well as via bodily dissatisfaction and physical inactivity.

Obesity also leads to stigma which has psychological, behavioural and social effects.[17] Stress engages the hypothalamus-pituitary-adrenal axis – a central mechanism that drives obesity via appetite, food preference, sleep duration and physical activity.[18] Children with obesity are double victims as they are at risk of the compounding effects of both physical ill-health and social discrimination.

Fat-shaming and weight stigma are abhorrent. The body-positivity movement advocates the acceptance of all bodies, regardless of size, gender, race or appearance. Where things become tricky is the extension to the notion that you can be healthy at any size – that obesity does not confer health risks. This is simply not true. The notion of 'health at any size' is a fallacy. Living with obesity is not healthy, but the individual is not to blame.[19] We need to make this distinction.

The price we pay

In 2019, the *Lancet* Global Syndemic Commission reported the annual global economic costs of obesity are about US$2 trillion, representing nearly 3 per cent of the world's gross domestic product (GDP).[20] Roughly equivalent to the impacts of smoking or armed conflicts.

In the two continents housing the most malnourished people (Asia and Africa), the annual GDP losses due to malnutrition average 11 per cent. Greater than the loss experienced during the 2008–2010 financial crisis (and this is an underestimate as it doesn't capture lifelong and intergenerational effects).

The total cost to the global economy of malnutrition in all its forms is around US$3.5 trillion a year – a cost that derives from poor school performance, diminished labour productivity, increased health-care costs, foregone economic growth, preventable child deaths and premature adult mortality. This will rise to US$4.3 trillion annually by 2035 if prevention and treatment measures don't improve. At almost 3 per cent of global GDP, this is comparable with the impact of COVID in 2020, year on year.[21]

In the UK, where more than one in four adults have obesity, 30,000 deaths, 80 per cent of illness treated by GPs and 18 million sick days each year are caused by obesity. An Imperial College study found that the UK National Health Service could save £14 billion per year if everyone had a healthy weight.[22] The study tracked 2.8 million NHS patients for at least ten years. Those with a BMI over 40 were found to cost the NHS £1,400 per year compared to £638 for those with a healthy weight. By far the largest cost was hospital admissions, which had risen sixfold in just a decade.

Office for National Statistics (ONS) data show that 2.8 million workers (one in thirteen, an all-time high) are on long-term sickness, mostly due to poor diet. This reduces the country's GDP by 3.8 per cent. The UK Government is forcing its citizens to pay an extra £409 in taxes every year for its own failure to do anything about this crisis.

In November 2024, the Food, Farming and Countryside Commission released a report that ended up on the front page of *The Guardian*.[23] Groundbreaking new analysis showed that the UK's addiction to junk food cost £268 billion a year – far outstripping the entire NHS budget. Of that, £67.5bn was picked up by the NHS, £14.3bn by social care services and £10.1bn by the welfare system. The other £176bn represented the indirect cost of lost productivity from people who are too sick to work due to diet-related illness (£116.4bn) and 'human costs' including pain and early death (£60bn). This is the price tag for decades of governmental inertia in the face of a food industry that puts profit ahead of people. A cost that we, not the industry, pay for.

II

REGIME

Food is both essential to life and a monetised commodity which means its production, ownership, use and consumption has always been governed by relations of power. Most developments in the professional disciplines of food policy and nutrition have happened in the last 100 years, but we need to go much further back to understand how food systems co-evolved with wider systems of slavery, colonialism and capitalism.

If we look at contemporary food history through a power lens, we can see three distinct regimes: Colonial (1655–1943), Cold War (1943–1976) and Corporate (1976–present).[1]

Regimes, not eras, because they evolve and are sustained by power. The third regime in which corporations hold sway is the one in which our current food system is embedded.

3

Colonial

Sugar started it all. In 1493, Christopher Columbus stashed a bundle of sugar cane in the hold of his ship as it made its second transatlantic crossing from the Canary Islands. He also carried bananas. The sugar was to seed plantations, the bananas were to seed small plots of land to provide cheap calories for enslaved Africans who would grow and harvest the sugar.

The first colonised country was Jamaica, which the Spanish ruled for a century and a half until they were defeated by the English in 1655.

Sugar slavery hinged on a triangular trade in which manufactured goods were exported from Britain to Africa, exchanged for enslaved people, who were taken to plantations in the West Indies, where they were traded for sugar, tobacco and cotton that were shipped back to Britain.[1] In three dimensions, this would be a pyramid, with profit concentrated among a small number of British slave-owners at the apex, built off the back of hundreds of thousands of enslaved Africans at the base.[2]

Four times more profitable per acre than tobacco, sugar was the Empire's cash cow. It took just two years to make enough profit to cover the original cost of land purchased for the plantation. Sugar slavery fuelled the Industrial Revolution in Britain (1760–1840), it bankrolled Britain's expanding empire (including the North American colonies) and it enabled major scientific advances in medicine and health.

The West Indies became a patchwork of sugar plantations. Britain was responsible for 50 per cent of all enslaved Africans – around 3.4 million people – shipped from Africa to the Americas between 1662 and 1807. Every week, around 500 Africans had chains clamped around their ankles, before being lined up side by side, in layers in the hold. Week after week, for 150 years. Those who died would be cut free and thrown overboard. Sharks followed the ships.

Sugar was changing the world. In the four centuries that followed Columbus's arrival, millions of Indigenous lives were destroyed and nearly 11 million Africans were enslaved – and this isn't counting the hundreds of thousands who perished at sea.[3] As it drove the most hideous migration in history, sugar transformed the physical and environmental face of large expanses of the planet.

The first country to abolish slavery was Saint Domingue (now Haiti) in 1804, when enslaved workers expelled the French and declared independence. French sugar plantation owners and enslaved workers poured into the US state of Louisiana. Five decades later, over 125,000 enslaved people in Louisiana were producing one-quarter of the world's sugar cane. As Khalil Gibran Muhammad says: 'New Orleans became the Walmart of people-selling'. Work was extremely dangerous – boiling kettles, open furnaces, grinding rollers, all operating 24/7. Exhausted workers could easily lose an arm to the rollers or be flayed for a drop in productivity. Life was brutal and short.

Meanwhile, in the land of the coloniser, sugar had gone from being a luxury item to a major source of calories in the British diet. In 1800, 2 per cent of calories came from sugar; by 1900, this had risen to 15 per cent.

Sugar has always been associated with strength and vitality. Our sweet tooth was an evolutionary advantage for our hunter-gatherer ancestors, who would seek out ripe fruit which had the most concentrated micronutrients. Sweetness meant health then. In ancient medicine, sugar was prescribed as a treatment for various illnesses, from the thirteenth through to the eighteenth centuries. The expression 'like an apothecary without sugar' meant 'useless'.

In 1881, Abram Lyle built a refinery on the Thames to process the white gold. Lyle's Golden Syrup still has the picture of a dead lion covered in a swarm of bees above the line '*Out of the strong came forth sweetness*', connoting the biblical story of Samson who kills a young lion. He later sees the carcass infested with bees and scoops out honey to sustain him. Power brought sweetness, which fuelled power.

Sugar continued to drive the imperial project. Our craving for sweetness is a product of empire that is still embedded within the annual ritual for Christmas pudding, in which numerous ingredients came together from different colonised countries. Sultanas from South Africa, raisins from Australia, Canadian apples, eggs from Ireland, cloves from Zanzibar, demerara sugar from the West Indies, cinnamon from India and brandy from Palestine. Only the breadcrumbs were home-grown.

Tea took over from textiles as the main import from the East India Company in the eighteenth century because it was an acceptable vehicle for sugar. A link to diabetes was made later, and by the nineteenth century, the renowned American nutrition scientist, Wilbur Atwater, claimed sugar was an inferior source of calorific energy. In the early twentieth century, the upper classes started to replace sugary foods with protein, although sugar continued to figure prominently as a cheap energy hit for workers, for whom meat was too expensive.

The British Empire abolished slavery in 1833. Three decades later, at a critical juncture in the American Civil War in 1862, Lincoln declared the emancipation of enslaved people. The end of slavery, however, did not mean the end of unfree labour. Plantation owners resorted to coercive measures to prevent 'freed people' from leaving, including tenancies where rents were deliberately set above earnings to shackle workers in permanent debt. In addition, 1.5 million Asians migrated abroad as indentured labourers throughout the nineteenth and early twentieth centuries.

The plantation model continued to be used to develop new commodities, and it continued to wreak environmental havoc, as gangs of labourers burned their way through the natural habitat to clear land. The British Empire abolished indentured labour in 1917.

The empire that sugar built was the largest in history, both by population (531 million in 1938) and by area (34 million km^2 in 1922), but it was a small citrus fruit that enabled its expansion. Britannia ruled the waves because it kept large stocks of limes and lemons in the holds of its ships. Scurvy due to vitamin C deficiency was so prevalent that shipowners and governments assumed a 50 per cent death rate from it for sailors embarking on any long-distance voyage. More than 2 million sailors worldwide died of scurvy, from the time of Columbus's transatlantic voyage at the end of the fifteenth century to the mid-nineteenth century.

When the American Revolution (1765–91) disrupted the lucrative triangular trade in the West Indies, Britain turned its focus to India. Another colonial raid, but this one also gave birth to international capitalism. Elizabeth I's original 1600 charter for the East India Company was for fifteen years, but her heir, James I, extended it indefinitely. With one stipulation – to keep turning a profit. The historian Alex von Tunzelmann wrote: 'Thus a beast was created whose only objective was money . . . pure capitalism unleashed for the first time in history ... a private empire of money, unburdened by conscience, rampaging across Asia.'[4]

The East India Company pioneered the shareholder model which led to an explosion of new corporations in Europe and the USA in the last third of the nineteenth century, as growth was no longer restricted by family wealth.

In the early days of empire, it was companies, not countries, who had colonies. Kojo Koram captured it well: 'rather than saying Britain had an empire, it would be more accurate to say that the empire had Britain.' Britain was sustained by imperialism.*[5]

Occupy, subdue, control, exploit, extract – colonialism created the cash-cropping economy (including tea, coffee, maize) and paved the way for twentieth-century capitalism that revolved around economic extraction, the manufacture of desire, and the oligopolistic control of food and health systems by a handful of large companies.

Companies drove the colonial project as they took over ownership and control of large swathes of the world. The power of empire, and its underlying racism and violence, derived not from sovereignty, but from a form of capitalism sanctioned by legal agreements drawn up to coat acts of coercion with a sheen of legitimacy.[6] As Lewes Robert wrote in 1671, in *The Merchants Map of Commerce*: 'It's not our conquest, but our commerce, it is not our swords, but our sails, that first spread the English name over and about the world'.

Famine, war and colonial nutrition
Against the backdrop of the colonial-capitalist rampage, food became a lucrative commodity, ripe for plunder and profit. Let's

---

* During the week I read his book, I saw this graffiti under a bridge in east London: 'We did not come to Britain, Britain came to us'.

look at the connected history of famine, hunger and the emerging discipline of nutrition. Food is sustenance but who gets to eat? Who does not?

In the late eighteenth century, two classical economists were shaping policy in Britain. In his *Wealth of Nations* (1776), Adam Smith saw free markets as the means to prevent famine, unrestricted by a 'nanny state'.[7] Two decades later, in *An Essay on the Principle of Population* (1798), Robert Malthus argued famine was a 'natural condition' to arrest population growth and keep it in balance with food supply.[8]

Famine-prevention policy didn't exist at the time of Ireland's Great Hunger. The last major peacetime famine in Western Europe, between 1845 and 1850, led to the deaths of 1.5 million Irish citizens from outright starvation or from diseases caused or exacerbated by acute malnutrition. Another 2 million emigrated. The famine was precipitated by the arrival of a potato fungus for which there was no antidote. *Precipitated* . . . not caused. The effect of the fungus was merely a symptom. The actual cause of the famine was the existence of a colonial power that exploited Irish tenant farmers who worked the land snatched by the English. Their diet consisted of potato. That was it. Up to 15 pounds in weight each day, enough to fill a stomach.

Diversification is insurance, but for these farmers it was a luxury they didn't have. They had just one variant – a tasteless watery potato called Lumpers. When this was wiped out, they had nothing to eat, no money to buy food from the market, and in any case, most foods – livestock, fish, peas, beans, oats, honey – were still being exported to Great Britain. When the famine started to bite in western Ireland, farmers left the land and headed to the workhouses of Dublin or Belfast.

Studying this at college in 1978, I started out believing in the myth of natural causes before digging deeper into the darker colonial connections. Four years later, while staying with a family on Lake Titicaca in Bolivia, I was blown away by the variety of potatoes that were being grown and harvested at different times of the year. Multiple colours, sizes, tastes. Blight would occasionally hit one variant, but there were always others, ensuring survival.

A few decades after the Irish famine, another British colony – India – was hit by a huge famine in 1877, caused by prolonged drought and failed governance by the colonial power. Up to 10 million died.[9] For the first time, the atrocity was covered by journalists and the British belatedly accepted responsibility. By 1880, detailed 'famine codes' outlined systems for early warning, activation of relief, use of public works for agricultural improvement and free food distribution. Famine came to be seen as a failure of economic and political systems rendering it morally imperative for states to respond, and to make investments to prevent famine (including irrigation and strengthened rail networks.)

Famine is the terrible tip of a very large iceberg of hunger and undernutrition that hits societies' most vulnerable – women and children – hardest.

As a discipline, nutrition only started to be taken seriously after the second Boer War in 1902, when the UK Government appointed the dramatically titled Interdepartmental Committee on Physical Deterioration to figure out why so few young British men had been fit or strong enough to be recruited.[10] Those that did fight tended to be smaller than the Dutch settlers they were fighting. Two years later, it announced its findings. Industrial pollution and ignorant, lazy, frequently drunk parents were blamed. But above all, weak soldiers were seen as a consequence of a working-class diet of white bread, tea and jam.

Food Fighter: Eglantyne Jebb

Eglantyne Jebb was one of the world's first and certainly the most vocal advocate of children's rights. She had seen photos in a newspaper of children starving due to Allied troops' blockades of Germany and Austria. Incensed, she had to act. She printed leaflets with the photos ('Our blockade caused this') and handed them out in Trafalgar Square. Although she was arrested and fined, the judge was so impressed by her that he paid the fine. This was the first donation to Save the Children. Many asked, 'How can you help enemy children?' One of Jebb's supporters, the great George Bernard Shaw, responded, 'I have no enemies under six'.

In 1921, Jebb chartered a ship, filled it with 600 tons of food and medicine and sailed to Russia, where she saved thousands of lives. Three years later, she attended the 1924 League of Nations convention in Geneva. There, she presented her Declaration of the Rights of the Child to world leaders, asserting that every child had human rights ('The child that is hungry must be fed, the child that is sick must be nursed'). The declaration was adopted a year later and in extended form by the United Nations in 1959. It later inspired the 1989 UN Convention on the Rights of the Child, a landmark human rights treaty championed by UNICEF.

Inspired by Jebb, a group of Americans established Save the Children in the USA in 1932, where they helped struggling families during the Great Depression. Over ninety years later, it's still active.

Years later, concern ramped up following large-scale starvation in post-First World War Europe. Even then, the motivation was not ethical or altruistic. It was utilitarian, driven by growing knowledge of the damage caused by a poor diet to the health and productivity of colonial workers. The science of nutrition was needed to keep workers alive and keep the Empire afloat.

To this end, nutrition scientists were asked: how much muscle and tissue is burned by manual labour? What must the worker eat (and, consequently, be paid in food) to be able to work and to raise children – the future colonial workforce?

This coincided with the rise of eugenics – the white supremacist theory of perfecting human genetic stock by 'better breeding', which led to programmes of forced sterilisation. The development of nutritional science was informed and facilitated by racist, colonial beliefs.[11]

Nutrition emerged as a global challenge in 1935, when the League of Nations Health Organisation (LNHO) published 'Nutrition Considered in Relation to Public Health and to Economic Conditions'. The report identified 'thoroughly deficient' diets in Asia as a problem to be addressed by nutrition professionals with technical know-how. In 1939, at the outset of the Second World War, the Colonial Office issued its first comprehensive review that indicated widespread malnutrition across the British colonies. No mention was made of wider structural drivers, including colonialism itself.

Meat, Mania and Cornflakes

Meat was believed to be necessary for bodily strength and was linked with desirable psychological traits like bravery and rationality, when it was found that certain populations (e.g. USA, Australia and Germany) had very high intakes of meat whereas many Asian and African populations hardly ate it at all. This offered nineteenth-century academics one possible explanation of imperial power and domination as a consequence of natural law ('the effeminate rice-eaters of India and China have again and again yielded to the superior moral courage of an infinitely smaller number of meat-eating Englishmen').[12]

Dr John Henry Kellogg (1852–1943) argued that consumption of meat led to bodily pollution, spiritual temptation and the unfortunate urge to masturbate. This, he explained, was due to its protein content. The idea that high protein consumption was dangerous was common among Christian denominations. Kellogg invented corn flakes in 1894 to wean the population off its usual breakfast of meat and coffee. In 1914, an advert for shredded wheat biscuits masquerading as an article on prison reform was published in a range of Christian publications in the USA. The advert suggested that an excess of high protein foods poisoned the blood, disturbed mental equilibrium, caused a 'quarrelsome temperament' and might lead to 'more heinous crimes.'

By the dawn of the twentieth century, John and his brother William were making US$3 million per year from their cereals. In later life, they fell out over sugar. William was keen to add it to Cornflakes to make them more palatable; John wouldn't have it. William won, John left and they didn't speak to each other for the last thirty years of their lives. As William became very rich, John dabbled in eugenics, founding the 'Race Betterment Foundation'. Kellogg's remains the biggest cereal company in the world with a 30 per cent market share and sales in excess of US$15 billion per year. We will hear more about this company later.

In May 1982, I was sitting outside a small *albergo* in Peru sipping coca mate tea, and chatting with the owner, Guillermo. I had been hit by altitude sickness (*siroche*) after the train ride from sea level in Lima up to Galera, the highest railway station in the world at 4,781m, in the Andes.

Peru seemed like two countries with two peoples. I could see the stark inequality in Lima, but the bigger gap was between the urban coastal lowlands and the rural highland, between the mixed-race *mestizo* urban-dwellers and the Andean Quechuan communities. Indigenous highlanders were shorter, squatter, poorer.

I asked Guillermo about these two countries, connected by the railway. He told me the railway had been built eighty years earlier to connect Lima and its port with the silver mines in Cerro de Pasco, the highest city in the Andes: 'The wealth was really sucked out then'.

Agriculture had always been tough, he said, but it became harder in the Seventies due to population pressure and land sub-division. Men were pulled into the mines, or they migrated to the cities on the coast:

> Everything we have here is taken away . . . eventually. The railway just made it easier. Silver, alpaca wool, food – all extracted. Even people . . . kids would go to work in the *haciendas* on the coast, picking sugar cane for a few *sole* per day, or they'd head inland to the jungle to harvest coca leaves.

Then he told me about the *pishtaco*.

In Quechuan, '*pishtay*' means 'to behead or cut into slices'. A *pishtaco* is a bogeyman, who dated back to the time of the conquistadores. A white man from the world below and beyond, the *pishtaco* cut up locals and sold their flesh as *chicarrones* (fried meat). The Spanish colonial invaders were said to have killed Indigenous peoples in the Andes and boiled their corpses to produce fat to grease their muskets and cannons. Locals also feared missionaries were *pishtacos* – in this case, the fat was used to oil the bells in the lavish churches they built. And then it was capitalists, who used human fat to grease sugar-mill machinery. The common thread in all these stories was the outsider coming in to brutally extract something of value, including the human body itself.

A few weeks later, I heard a story from a US aid worker, about food aid being rejected in a cluster of villages in the mountains because it had been seen as an attempt to fatten up children for the *pishtaco*.

Colonial extraction has had many manifestations and given rise to countless stories across cultures. In India, colonialism didn't end with national independence, it just took on a different form. As in Peru, Indigenous peoples continued to be exploited. In southern India, the Koya ('hill-dwellers') started as a semi-nomadic tribe practising shifting cultivation. Later, due to pressure on the land, they turned to settled agriculture and collection of produce from the forests they inhabited.

During my time there, I learned a lot from Joggaya, a Koya with animal tattoos on his arms and long hair pulled into a ponytail. His father, the local healer, had died a few months before I arrived, from snakebite. Joggaya was my age, early twenties, but he had a gravitas that belied his years. In my first few months, as the summer heat was building, we'd go on treks in the forest.

He'd point out the trees – tamarind, teak, ebony, mahua, neem, gulmohar, sag – most of which had multiple uses. The mahua was the most versatile. Its flowers could be eaten raw, baked into cakes or fermented to make a spirit that tasted like triple-strength vodka. Oil extracted from its seeds could be used for cooking, lighting or as soap. Then there was the dodgy tamarind whose trunk harboured malevolent spirits ('never fall asleep under *their* branches'), the ebony tree whose leaves were used to make *bidi* cigarettes, and neem which was both anti-malarial and a perfect toothpaste.

He told me how this life, his forest, was disappearing:

> It was always common land. We didn't know about land deeds
> – *pattas* – we never needed them. My brother's land was stolen
> five years ago – a Hindu landlord from Kothaguddem just
> came in and started farming it. He'd bribed the forest guards
> to get *pattas*. The land's gone now.

The forest was being chipped away by non-tribal outsiders from the plains, who knew how to work the system, who to bribe and how to set themselves up as moneylenders. If the high-interest loans they offered could not be repaid, Koya children would become bonded labour – effectively enslaved – well into adult-hood. If they survived that long.

But it was worse. The slash and burn of the forest that followed these land grabs – as tribals sought new land to farm – changed the pattern of the monsoon rains, made them less predictable. The seasons started to change, Joggaya said, and life in the forest became more precarious for the Koya. This in turn made them more dependent on the moneylenders to help them out. This is what a poverty trap looks like.

With this rising stress, the fault lines between the two tribes were deepening. 'We always used to get along fine,' he said. 'But now there are flashpoints every year over water – fights over who controls the run-off to whose land, when.' It was getting harder to farm the land. The last two years had been drought years, so food stocks were already way down. Families without land had migrated to mines, building sites or brick kilns.

'When I was a kid, we didn't need to leave in the dry season,' Joggaya said, 'We'd just go further into the trees to collect timber, berries, leaves. The forest would feed us. But it's dying now.'

4

Cold War

The seeds of our increasingly dysfunctional food system were sown in the last century. The second food regime that emerged at the end of the Second World War was driven by two factors. The first, after the Great Depression in the 1930s, was the US policy to stabilise staple-food production by subsidising wheat and soy. Too much was produced, so the administration channelled the surplus to key strategic Cold War allies, such as Japan, Korea, Mexico, Israel, Pakistan, Egypt and Colombia at knock-down prices, or as food aid. The goal – to feed their growing workforces and act as a buffer against Communists in China and Russia. The first wave of philanthropists – Rockefeller, Ford and Kellogg – emerged at this time and together with the US Government, pushed for population control in the 'Third World', again to avoid Communist uprisings being sparked by a food crisis.

The second element comprised a new bundle of agricultural technologies, developed in Mexico in the 1940s, by American agronomist Norman Borlaug and his team of crop breeders. This package started to be exported in the 1960s, mainly to Asia, using agribusinesses set up in Europe to help the war-ravaged continent get back on its feet. Agricultural research led to new hybrid seeds (maize, soy, wheat) engineered to take advantage of improvements in irrigation and soil fertility, while a chemical revolution generated an array of fertilisers, pesticides, fungicides and herbicides.* Large agribusinesses like Bayer, BASF, John Deere, Dow and Dupont capitalised on this 'Green Revolution'.

The Green Revolution prevented Malthus's predictions from materialising. World grain output more than doubled between 1950 and 1980, as did yields (output per acre), which meant there were more than enough calories to feed the growing population without major increases in farmed land.

By the end of the Second World War, the USA was the world's military and economic superpower. Between 1947 and 1952, the US Marshall Plan pumped US$13 billion into Europe – much of it American food, animal feed and fertiliser – pulling the continent back from the brink, while propelling American corporate power to global dominance. European governments prioritised national food security by subsidising staple-crop production. Food became available and producers made a lot of money. Half a century after the war, these supply-side subsidies were still in existence, creating havoc with global trade and global health, as we'll see.

In the mid-twentieth century, the complexities of postwar reconstruction and an increasingly globalised world gave rise to the modern field of international development aimed at improving the lives and economic prospects of (what were then termed) 'underdeveloped' or 'Third World' countries.

---

* Possibly the greatest single technological innovation of all had been made at the beginning of the twentieth century when German electrochemist Fritz Haber figured out how to synthesise ammonia by combining atmospheric nitrogen with hydrogen. This discovery was later industrialised by Carl Bosch, working for BASF, who worked out how to mass-produce this new fertiliser using fossil fuels.

The first United Nations conference on food and agriculture (held in Hot Springs, Virginia, in April 1943) drew on the League of Nations' work and Theodore and Eleanor Roosevelt's conviction that freedom in the postwar period should start with 'freedom from hunger'. The focus was on food production, while access to food was highlighted in the statement that, 'poverty is the first cause of malnutrition and hunger'. Placing explicit responsibility on countries themselves to 'develop a food and nutrition policy . . . drawn up to suit the particular circumstances of each country', the conference concluded with a call for action.

A few months later, the Bengal famine started. Driven by wartime measures and the indifference of British rulers, it lasted for several months, killing 3 million Bengalis. The UN had to step up. In 1945, the Food and Agriculture Organization (FAO) of the United Nations was established in Rome to facilitate international collaboration. The UN International Children's Emergency Fund (UNICEF) was then launched in 1946 to provide aid to hungry children in Europe, before expanding into other regions and other types of nutrition and health support. Two years later, in 1948, the World Health Organization (WHO) was founded in Geneva. Each agency had a nutrition department. Serious efforts were made to foster collaboration among these various agencies, but often with tensions about mandates and priorities that remain to this day.*

Throughout this time, the colonial elephant in the room – the number one international structural driver of malnutrition and

---

* Forty years later, in 1989, my first job with the WHO, Geneva, was with a small team charged with bringing together the various UN agencies – by that time, there were eleven – to address malnutrition. No one wanted to be co-ordinated of course, and we could only encourage harmonisation, not enforce it.

ill-health – was ignored. The United Nations Charter of 1945 did not address colonialism – all it asked of the colonisers was to look after the colonised.

The Universal Declaration of Human Rights, the first document to list the thirty rights to which everyone is entitled, was adopted by the UN General Assembly on 10 December 1948. To compose and agree across countries on the text of the declaration, at a time when the world was divided into eastern and western blocs, was a monumental achievement. The pivotal Article 25 read:

> Everyone has the right to a standard of living adequate for the health and wellbeing of himself and of his family, including food, clothing, housing and medical care and necessary social services, and the right to security in the event of unemployment, sickness, disability, widowhood, old age or other lack of livelihood.[1]

The US institutionalised food aid for development and famine relief via the creation of the UN World Food Programme (WFP) in 1961 – the fourth UN agency (after FAO, WHO and UNICEF) directly responsible for food and nutrition support. Using early-warning systems, logistics, and cash and food-aid grants, WFP became the global leader in famine prevention, and was awarded the Nobel Peace Prize in 2020.

Famine relief also stimulated the emergence of national and international NGOs to distribute food aid. Oxfam (originally, Oxford Committee for Famine Relief) and CARE (originally, the Cooperative for American Remittance to Europe) were established for relief operations during and after the Second World War, decades after Eglantyne Jebb had launched Save the Children.

In the 1950s, the global community looked at the challenge of increasing the supply of basic food staples. This shift away from the broader view of malnutrition espoused in the Hot Springs conference was the result of alarming new evidence of accelerating population growth globally (from 10 million per year in the early 1900s to 27 million per year by 1950).[2] Such rapid growth, unprecedented in world history, triggered widespread Malthusian pessimism about the ability of food production to keep pace with population, let alone increase energy intake for the large share of the world's population that was already undernourished.

White saviourism was rife in the 1950s. *The Lancet*, for example, recommended the Colonial Medical Service:

> to those who are smitten with wanderlust, or who are imbued with a spirit of adventure, or who are interested in trying to help the less developed members of the British Commonwealth to attain a higher standard of living and health.[3]

Myths and legends

It was also during this time that the nutrition community became fixated on the 'protein gap'. Protein malnutrition had been first identified by a British-West-Indian nutritionist, Cicely Williams, in the form of the disease – kwashiorkor – through her field research in the Gold Coast (now Ghana). History, however, has glossed over the insights Williams gained from the local Indigenous peoples, the Ga, who had named the disease.

By the 1950s, a joint FAO/WHO report identified protein deficiency as the major problem, and the UN promoted interventions with protein-dense foods targeted at infants and children, including large school feeding programmes based on donations of food aid, especially dried skimmed milk.*

International agricultural research centres became obsessed with 'filling the protein gap', spending two decades developing protein concentrates and increasing the protein content of conventional foods. As the Green Revolution spread to Asia in the 1960s, cereal production kept ahead of population growth. Food energy supply grew from 2,200 kilocalories per person per day in 1961 to 2,880 kcals as the new millennium dawned, during which time per capita arable area halved. Much of this growth was in Asia where energy supply increased 30 per cent from 1970 to 1995.[4] The United States' hegemony on the global food system, driven by trade, subsidies and Green Revolution technologies, continued until the 1970s.

There was a dark side to this hyper-concentration of agricultural policy on just three staples (rice, maize, wheat) and on calories, as opposed to nutrient diversity. The Green Revolution has become an 'epic narrative' where repeated stories, no matter how misleading, are reproduced over time to influence the future. In reality, as wheat production soared, diet diversity declined as nutrient-dense crops like pulses, fruits and vegetables were marginalised. Inequalities rose as only the larger farmers could fully avail themselves of the new technologies, and mechanisation removed a large source of employment from the rural economy.[5] Levels of hunger barely changed – rising production means nothing if you can't afford it. Millions of smallholders, who

---

* In March 2023, an exhibition at the Wellcome Institute in London entitled *Milk* included a letter to UNICEF from the UK Foreign Office in 1954. The letter conveys an offer to provide surplus milk products to UNICEF for distribution overseas so long as these are recognised as 'contributions in kind' (substituting for financial aid) and accompanied by publicity celebrating the largesse of the UK Government.

produced food but were still net buyers, dependent on the market, were hit by sharp price hikes.

In addition, the fact that crop-yield increases were dependent on extensive use of agrochemicals and unsustainable ground-water extraction was kept hidden. Chemical fertilisers and pesticides that doused the land generated a raft of environmental hazards.

The Alliance for a Green Revolution in Africa (AGRA), funded by the Gates Foundation, subscribes to this epic narrative, as do many agricultural scientists and technologists intent on preserving their power in the food system. Social innovations don't see the light in this world, national priorities take precedence over local ones and traditional approaches are ignored. Food cultures, and their linked knowledge systems, start to wither away. Decades of 'betting on the strong' (the larger, richer farmers) meant that nothing much was done to address deep-rooted inequities in food systems. Criticism of the Green Revolution and the neoliberal model of agriculture and trade laid the foundation for the food sovereignty movement led by La Via Campesina.

La Via Campesina

Founded in 1993, La Via Campesina is an international organisation of farmers, peasants, small-scale producers and farm workers who advocate for food sovereignty – the right of nations and peoples to determine how their land is used and to control their own food systems and food cultures. A fundamental pushback against the neoliberal commoditisation of food towards alternative agricultures such as organic farming and agroecology. Food sovereignty places a special focus on the rights of Indigenous people to healthy and culturally appropriate foods produced through traditional practices. It's since become institutionalised in a number of countries, including Bolivia, Ecuador and Mali. France and Senegal have ministers of agriculture and food sovereignty.

By the 1970s, the development community had realised the need for a reset – a move away from the mono-focus on increasing the 'pile of food' towards a more balanced focus on ensuring *access* to food. An increased priority was attached to reaching small-holders in drought-prone areas, who had been bypassed by the Green Revolution.

Around this time, nutrition scientists began to challenge the notion that protein deficiency was the main nutritional problem. In India, Professor P.V. Sukhatme showed that if people's diets were adequate in calories, then their protein intake too would be adequate.[6] Then, in 1974, Donald McLaren published 'The Great Protein Fiasco', which finally blew the protein obsession out of the water.[7] In a classic example of a collapsing paradigm, solutions to malnutrition began to be sought in the wider social and economic arena, well beyond technical nutrient fixes. Nutrition became everybody's business but nobody's main responsibility.

In the middle of the 1973–75 food crisis, following an unprecedented spike in global cereal prices, the World Food Conference (hosted by FAO in Rome in 1974) focused on issues of distribution and access to food, as these became increasingly perceived as drivers of hunger and undernutrition. One line in the concluding statement was reiterated thousands of times and is still a historical benchmark of the profession:

'Every man, woman and child has the inalienable right to be free from hunger and malnutrition'.

To this day, countries and organisations routinely invoke human rights while continuing to practise capitalism that pays little attention to marginalised populations who cannot access the food that their labour produces.

In 1976, the World Bank published a pivotal study showing that reliance on economic growth alone to assure dietary adequacy among the poor, would take too long.[8] Social protection to ensure access to food was promoted and some countries (e.g. Sri Lanka) with long experience with targeted food subsidies and food-for-work programmes had tangible impacts on nutrition and infant mortality.

Nineteen seventy-six was also the year that French American political scientist-activist, Susan George, published *How the Other Half Dies*, a book that had a major impact in development discourse in the late Seventies, a book that changed my life.

5

Corporate

If it takes you six hours to read this book, somewhere in the world 2,500 people will have died of starvation or of hunger-related illness by the time you finish. Not because there are too many passengers on Spaceship Earth, not because of bad weather or changing climate, but because food is controlled by the rich.

Susan George, *How the Other Half Dies*[1]

I read these words on the back of a paperback, while sheltering from a heatwave in a bookshop in Cambridge in the summer of 1976. George eviscerated multinational agribusiness corporations, Western governments with their food-aid policies and the 'supposedly neutral multilateral development organisations' who, she argued, all shared responsibility for these deaths. At sixteen, I didn't have a clue, but I wanted to learn how this was happening. Looking back to that year it was around this time that food systems started to change for the worse, as the graph in Figure 5.1 shows.

Since the 1950s, farms had been growing in size, becoming more specialised, more mechanised and more dependent on fossil fuels. Improvements and economies of scale in transportation, manufacturing, processing, preservation and packaging led to power becoming concentrated in a few large food and beverage companies. Machines displaced farm workers who then left rural areas and headed into cities. Production subsidies, granted after the Second World War, created enormous surpluses of staple crops.

From the ashes of empire, a new ideology was emerging. Neoliberalism was characterised by trade liberalisation, deregulation, private property rights, low tax, minimal welfare – with the role of the State pared back to ensuring the functioning of the market. Neoliberalists considered health – and anything that determines it, like diet – to be the responsibility of the individual. Structural and commercial drivers of malnutrition were ignored.

This was the birth of the third food regime – the era of massive transnational food corporations ('Big Food'). Neoliberalism provided the perfect enabling environment. Unlike the previous two regimes that were led by nation states – the UK and USA respectively – the third regime came to be governed by large corporations, later facilitated by the World Trade Organization (WTO).

The launch of the WTO in 1995 was supposed to end producer subsidies and remove trade restrictions. What actually happened was the World Bank and the International Monetary Fund (IMF) put 'developing countries' under pressure to open their markets, while richer countries availed themselves of the same monster subsidies. This was nothing remotely like a level playing field of free trade. Poorer countries were overwhelmed as major corporations in the USA and Europe profited from what was effectively a massive programme of corporate welfare.

But it was worse than that. Much of the excess production caused by these subsidies was dumped in developing country markets thus undermining local producers. In 2004, Tate & Lyle received £227 million in export subsidies whereas Nestlé was paid to export milk (on top of their US$60 billion food sales). EU sugar-dumping lowered prices across the developing world, devastating countries like Mozambique, where it was the largest source of employment.

It was a similar story with milk. In 2002, subsidised powdered milk from the EU (at 60 per cent of the international price) put the Jamaican dairy industry out of business. In 2004, Oxfam's Make Trade Fair campaign ('Ever Felt Dumped On?') enlisted celebrities like the REM singer Michael Stipe to draw attention to the harmful dumping of surplus milk, wheat and coffee. North America, Europe, New Zealand and Australia all disposed of surplus milk through foreign-aid programmes and exported it to low-income countries, undercutting local farmers and creating a dependency on imported foods. Surpluses of milk and sugar – the most profitable foodstuffs in history – were being used against those who would benefit from supplying them. Dumping continues to this day but affected countries are fighting back, as we'll explore later.[2]

Milk Oppression

Of all foods, milk is the most politicised. It symbolises both power and care. As demand grew in the nineteenth century, many people died after drinking contaminated milk. The dairy industry responded with pasteurisation, led by large corporations. Milk's whiteness was symbolic and promotional campaigns invariably used white, middle-class, nuclear families in adverts. Professor Andrea Freeman's extraordinary history – 'The Unbearable Whiteness of Milk: Food

Oppression and the USDA' – shows how this played out in the USA.[3] Over a hundred years ago, the US National Dairy Council launched a promotional initiative with these words:

> The people who have achieved, who have become large, strong, vigorous people, who have reduced their infant mortality, who have the best trades in the world, who have an appreciation for art, literature and music, who are progressive in science and every activity of the human intellect are the people who have used liberal amounts of milk and its products.

When the United States Department of Agriculture (USDA) reacted to evidence of the links between saturated fat and heart disease by encouraging Americans to avoid dairy products, milk sales dropped. At the same time, the US Government continued to provide huge production subsidies to the dairy industry. To handle the surplus, the USDA created Dairy Management Incorporated (DMI) in 1995, to promote consumption of dairy products, including cheese. DMI partnered with fast-food companies to create and market new products, such as Domino's Seven-Cheese American Legends pizzas and Taco Bell's steak quesadilla, which contain a huge amount of cheese. It created the award-winning advertising campaign 'Got Milk?' which featured an array of biddable celebrities with milk moustaches.

By 2010, Americans were eating an average of 33lbs of cheese a year, nearly triple the 1970 level, and cheese had become the largest source of saturated fat. DMI continued to promote cheese-laden products to restaurants while arguing that Americans could lose weight by consuming more dairy products.[4]

The USDA was in a quandary. How to continue to protect the dairy industry, by allowing it to continue to overproduce, and at the same time fulfil its other mandate and reduce the harm to the US population? In a classic case of what Freeman calls 'food oppression' it chose to target poor people in disadvantaged neighbourhoods, where a much higher proportion of African Americans and Latina/os lived – ethnic groups who cannot digest dairy products due to a deficiency in the enzyme lactase. Junk food makes you sick eventually, but you become sick immediately if the only products you can afford to eat are indigestible.

This is nutritional racism.[*]

The USDA also disposes of surplus milk in the form of free formula to mothers in the Special Supplemental Nutrition Program for Women, Infants and Children (WIC) and to public school students who qualify for free lunches – again, both groups disproportionately represented by people of colour.

Milk-drinking fitted into a racist-colonial view of the world in which white people were physically superior due to, or evidenced by, their drinking milk. The importance of milk for infant nutrition and its alignment with cultural superiority has for decades been exploited by the infant formula industry.

*

---

* Even the phrase 'lactose intolerance' reflects a cultural bias. Northern Europeans and Scandinavians developed the enzyme after drinking their herds' milk at times of food scarcity, but they're the global exception. Why don't we refer to this minority as *lactose persistent* instead of pathologising the lack of the enzyme?

After Big Food had figured out how to develop ultra-processed products that were three times more profitable than healthier, less processed foods, the new global food system started to bed in. Hyper-capitalism took off.

An increasingly globalised focus on economic growth (measured solely through gross domestic product – GDP) was both unsustainable and damaging to people and planet. Capitalism revolves around profit that is privatised whereas external harms are socialised, for someone else (us) to pay for. On top of the massive injustice, this ignores the fact that such 'externalities' will come back to bite us all. Widespread human and environmental ill-health and growing inequalities are slowing economic growth across the world, diminishing returns as the blow-back builds.

Neoliberalism has been especially disastrous for countries in the Global South, driving a growth in asset wealth that far exceeds rises in salaries and wages and a major upswing in inequalities within and between countries. In *Edible Economics*, Ha-Joon Chang explodes the myth that Britain and then the USA became global economic powerhouses because of their free-trade and free-market policies.[5] Both countries had, in fact, led the world in protectionism to develop their national industries. Similarly, any fledgling economy in the Global South needs space and time for local producers to develop and acquire the capabilities to engage in higher productivity industries. As was done with the UK, USA and most of the Global North, this requires initial trade protection, subsidies, regulation of foreign investors and other proactive governmental measures.

Let's look again through the power lens. In the last few decades of the twentieth century, power started shifting from nation states and the multilateral system (UN) to transnational corporations, aided since 1995 by the World Trade Organization (WTO).

Free-market zealots defended capitalism using the language of freedom – invoking the 'nanny state' argument to justify a laissez-faire approach to the food industry. Less Government means more freedom for the consumer, they proclaim.

Sounds reasonable. But freedom comes from the power to control one's environment. Are citizens/consumers in control? Or does the industry control the food environment and people's access to affordable healthy food? Who really is free? Light-touch or absent Government means more freedom for companies to produce and sell whatever's most profitable – which means less freedom for individuals to avoid ultra-processed foods that are flooding our high streets. If other freedoms – political or social – clash with economic freedom, free marketeers will always fight for the latter, and they almost always win.

Power is different from income. In any circumscribed space, like a country or a food system, we cannot grow power. It's zero-sum, a cake that needs to be divided. If one person or organisation gains more power, then others lose some. Income is different because it's possible for income to rise for everyone. So, the challenge then becomes how to correct imbalances to spread power around, more equitably.

People are poor largely because of historical, political and technological forces over which they have limited (if any) power to influence. Not because of their individual shortcomings. Not because of their unwillingness to work hard. And because they're poor, they are more likely to live in a junk-food swamp, with little physical or economic access to healthy food (we'll explore food environments shortly).

Similar imbalances in power and freedom exist at the global level. The rules of international trade are set and administered by stronger countries in the WTO, who retain the power to shape and manage the system in their interests. These countries also made trade liberalisation a key condition for their support to low-income countries. If a Global-South Government chooses to protect its emerging economy, it risks foreclosing options of foreign-aid and low-interest loans from the World Bank and the IMF. A monumental injustice given the history of plunder and protectionism that sucked wealth from these countries and then blocked them from growing.

Ghanaian independence leader and first Prime Minister, Kwame Nkrumah, coined the term 'neocolonialism' to capture the ways European and Western powers continued to exert economic, political and even cultural power over former colonies after independence.* In 1965, he wrote:

The 'end of empire' has been accompanied by a flourishing of other means of subjugation. The British Empire has become the Commonwealth, but the proceeds from the exploitation of British imperialism are increasing. [...] A recent survey made plain the plunder of British monopolies. It listed 9 out of 20 of Britain's biggest monopolies as direct colonial exploiting companies.[6]

Neocolonialism is the terrible twin of neoliberalism. The East India Company was the first but there's now a cabal of multi-national organisations with complex and overlapping interests with state governments.

When the Portuguese started shipping Africans to the Americas,

---

* In Nigeria for example, British Petroleum and the Royal Dutch Company continued to control most of the oil reserves in the Niger Delta a long time after independence. Britain imported cotton from India and exported it back as clothing. Cost efficiencies of British industrialisation meant these products were cheaper than those produced at home, undermining India's own industry.

they provided bananas as cheap, portable calories on slave ships. On the plantations, enslaved people were encouraged to plant bananas on the small plots given to them, to supplement their meagre rations. The banana is the most productive fruit in the world and that productivity was being used to keep enslaved people alive at minimal cost to plantation owners.

Multinational corporations now operate like that in low-income countries. Global-North countries perpetuate extractive relationships with former colonies through trade that caters to their market at the latter's expense. Big Food uses Global-South nations as a supply bank of cheap labour, land and resources. With host-government complicity, these corporations cause irreparable harm to the environment and the local population. Only when there are public policies to ensure maximum transfer of technologies, worker skills and management practices will host economies truly benefit from the presence of multinational corporations.

Transnational sugar companies have, throughout history, been major beneficiaries of protectionism. Like Britain and France before them, the USA in the early twentieth century viewed sugar as an important element in the way it defined its power. Sugar became a major preservative and – as we now know – one of the main drivers of the obesity pandemic.

Behind the curves

In the last half-century, transnational food corporations have grown at an astonishing rate. Investments in research and development have driven an ever-expanding range of ultra-processed products that tick all the boxes of being convenient, tasty, time-saving and long lasting. The fact they're also of low nutritional quality, energy-dense and unhealthy doesn't impinge on marketing which only serves the profit god. Their aggressive marketing by parent companies has propelled a shift from home-prepared meals to pre-prepared, ready-to-eat meals which we'll explore later.

Against the backdrop of this recent history, we can see something dramatic happening to rates of obesity. In the USA and UK – two countries with the best available data – as the share of dietary calories deriving from ultra-processed foods grew, obesity rocketed.

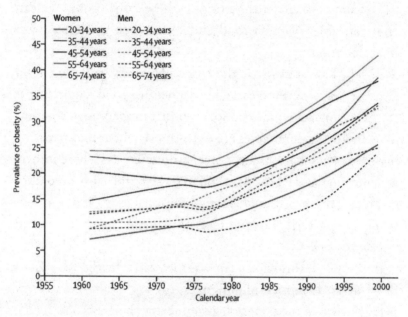

Figure 5.1. Trends in US adult obesity (1960–2000).[7]

Figure 5.1 depicts an epidemic. Genetics can only determine where any one individual sits on a normal population distribution of weights. It cannot explain why an entire population changes weight, shifting to the right on the normal distribution graph. Nor are these curves caused by a mass failure of willpower, given that it occurred at the same time in many countries and across every single demographic – children, adults, men, women, in every ethnic group. Whatever caused this ongoing epidemic must have had mass exposure across the population across the board and it must have been fast-acting.

In other words, it must have been something in our environment.

Global food corporations have an assured market – humans don't need to smoke tobacco, but everyone needs to eat food. But even in the 1980s, it had already become clear that market growth was hitting the ceiling of our biological capacity to consume. Satiety was getting in the way of profit. We can only consume so much food and we tend to get bored with the same food.

Engel's Law states that the share of income spent on food decreases as income increases, in part because food requirements are physiologically limited. So, even in a burgeoning economy, food and drink companies are much more reliant on increasing their market share than other industries. As shareholders demand increased profits, companies respond with predatory marketing campaigns to displace traditional foods and by developing a wide variety of products that can be easily consumed in excess of need.

In the USA, this expansion was facilitated by the 1973 Farm Bill which paid farmers billions of tax dollars in subsidies to grow as much corn as they wanted, guaranteeing them a profit. By the late twentieth century, US granaries were overflowing, and production and consumption of carbohydrate-rich sweeteners was off the scale. Back in 1957, Richard Marshall and Earl Kooi – two American biochemists working at the Corn Products Company – had hit upon a process for making a sweetener (high-fructose corn syrup) from the excess corn produced. The only problem then was it was too expensive to produce. The 1973 bill suddenly made it commercially viable.

The Farm Bill was rocket fuel to the obesity epidemic. Staple-food production increased, portion sizes became larger and the marketing of energy-dense junk foods more aggressive. Other countries did not have the US Farm Bill, but, by this time, these trends – like the corporations driving them, and the foods and sugary drinks they marketed – were global, so it was only a matter of time.

The rise of sugary-drink consumption thanks to Coca-Cola, PepsiCo, among others, is another driver of the dramatic upswing in obesity. During the 1970s, the percentage of calories coming from fizzy drinks tripled. Correlation is not causation, but the timing maps directly onto the timing of the spurt in obesity, and just like the curves, the effect was felt by men and women, all ages and in every ethnic group. Liquid calories are especially dangerous as they're calorie-dense snacks capable of slipping under our satiety radar. Our brain simply doesn't recognise them.

On top of this, Big Food companies were searching for yet more ways to keep growing profits. The industry ramped up its 'innovation' budgets leading to myriad new products, all variants on the original junk flagship. Food scientists were tasked with innovating and diversifying portfolios to 'add value' to their products. 'Value' here has nothing to do with human health – it's a cosy industry term to describe what is simply yet more profit for the manufacturer. More 'value' means we now have 172 flavours of Pringles.

Then, in the 1980s, the convenience food market took off, including microwave meals, TV dinners, more eating out, more between-meal snacking. During the fifty years of this corporate regime, the amount of food consumed as convenience/take-out meals by an average person in the UK has gone up by a factor of ten!

Onwards, upwards, outwards . . .

A few visionaries, like Barry Popkin, had seen it coming. A nutrition professor from the University of North Carolina, Popkin had been a key member of our 'double burden' team back in 1999. Five years earlier, in 1994, he had seen an unusual shift in the data from national nutrition surveys in China. He coined the term 'nutrition transition' to depict this new trend – as under-nutrition was in decline, overweight and obesity were accelerating, albeit from very low levels.[8]

He started to notice the same pattern emerging elsewhere. As economies grew, countries were moving from rural, low-produc-tivity agricultural systems focused on staples (e.g. much of sub-Saharan Africa) to more diversified systems including legumes and micronutrient-rich foods (e.g. Asia) and on to increasingly commercialised systems (e.g. Europe, North America) in urban contexts, flooded with ultra-processed foods.

This agricultural shift maps onto a dietary transition. As incomes rise, the urban poor and emerging middle class reduce their consumption of cereals, roots and tubers while increasing demand for refined grains and flours, sugar, salt and fats. Demand for ultra-processed foods at supermarkets, restaurants and street vendors rises. For the middle class, demand for fruits, vegetables, dairy, poultry, eggs, meat and fish strongly increases. But so does the demand for junk food.

The Global North started to move through the nutrition tran-sition in the middle of the last century. It's taken us seventy odd years to get to where we are now – the best part of three gener-ations. Not only is the transition happening so much faster for countries in the Global South (what's disturbing is that cities and towns of middle-income Asian countries including Thailand, China and India have made the same journey in just one gener-ation), it is happening at a much earlier stage of economic and social development. Both these trends – the speed of change and its earlier onset – are rendering these countries more vulnerable to the harms.

Beyond increasing consumption in existing markets, another way for companies to increase profits is to enter new markets and displace traditional foods. Transnationals owe no loyalty to any particular state. Once high-income country markets are saturated, they simply move their money and plant to low-income countries, where labour is cheaper and regulatory systems (both human and environmental health) weak or non-existent.

Following the 1970s oil and debt crises, countries of the Global South opened their doors to foreign investment, just as Big Food embarked on its search for new untapped markets. An early sign of the nutrition transition is the rise in the supply and consumption of cheap vegetable oils, especially soybean oil.[9] In the 1980s, the Brazilian Government, for example, lowered import taxes on fertiliser, removed restrictions on foreign investment in agriculture and scrapped its soybean export tax. Within a few years, global markets were awash with cheap soybean oil.

Even as far back as 1971, more than half of Coca-Cola's profits were generated outside the USA. Coca-Cola had for decades benefited from US aid. This funded overseas projects, allowing the company to grow sugar and citrus fruits and establish new bottling plants in the Caribbean, Africa and Asia.* Bottling Coca-Cola requires massive volumes of water, the extraction of which has a huge environmental impact.

As transnationals captured ever-larger shares of global markets and junk food spread across the world, obesity rates accelerated.

---

* During the Second World War, Coca-Cola received a giant boost after the US Army persuaded the US Government to exempt the company from sugar rationing and have supplies sent to all army bases around the world.

Way more than a dietary transition, this started to look more like a heist.

In 2010, the world's largest food manufacturer, Nestlé, issued a press release announcing the launch of a 'floating supermarket' stocked with Nestlé products on the Amazon River. A boat stashed with ultra-processed sugar, more than 500 years after the one laden with sugar cane, captained by Columbus. This grotesque project was touted as an 'unprecedented business model [that] will extend the company's presence in Brazilian households.'[10]

Then, in April 2024, Public Eye (a Swiss investigative organisation) and the International Baby Foods Action Network (IBFAN) released a report showing how Nestlé was adding sugar and honey to infant milk and cereal products sold in many poorer countries.[11] Not only did this run completely counter to international guidelines aimed at preventing obesity and chronic diseases, it also encapsulated the gross hypocrisy and double standards of the corporation. Similar products in Global-North countries contained no added sugar. The highest amount found – 7.3 grams per serving (nearly two whole sugar cubes!) – was detected in the Philippines in a product targeted at six-month-old babies.

The policy response
Through this last half-century of corporate conquest, what happened in the parallel world of food and nutrition policy? What were nutrition professionals thinking? More to the point, what were they doing?

In the late 1970s, the perception of hunger had begun to shift from the supply side to the demand side. In 1981, Amartya Sen published *Poverty and Famines: An Essay on Entitlement and Deprivation*, in which he argued that famines were man-made, and malnutrition was due to poverty and inequality, not a lack of food.

He had been just nine years old in 1943 when 3 million people died in his home state of Bengal – the last famine to strike India, the last famine driven by Empire. There was plenty of food around then, but most people could not afford it. Food prices had soared, driven by Churchill's move to provision British and American troops, and the rich were hoarding food. After digging deep into the origins, Sen went on to develop a theory of development that focused on freedom and capability – a person's ability to be or do something. The people Sen saw starve to death in the street outside his home were not free to act, to nourish themselves. His work had a huge impact and he went on to win a Nobel Prize as the food supply paradigm crashed to the floor. The World Bank began to support poverty reduction, while the World Food Programme scaled up food-for-work programmes. The focus however was still on undernutrition, with food viewed as a source of calories, not nutrients. No one had a clue that overweight could ever become a problem.

Iringa's Triple A

In the mid-1980s, Iringa was the poorest region of Tanzania, one of the poorest countries in sub-Saharan Africa. Most children were seriously underweight. It was here that the Tanzanian Food and Nutrition Centre – with support from the Swedish International Development Authority, UNICEF and WHO – sought to turn words into action. Vertical, top-down interventions were out. Iringa revolved around local problem assessment by affected communities, social mobilisation and tailor-made combinations of nutrition and food-security interventions. Community workers monitored child growth to identify vulnerable families and then worked with them to analyse causes and draw up an action plan. The local government committed to support the plan.

The 'Triple A Cycle' was born. Assess, Analyse, Act, then go again. Depending on causes, interventions ranged from face-to-face counselling to health service referral, livelihood-development schemes, microcredit or social protection schemes.

Iringa was a dramatic success. In just five years, severe child malnutrition was eliminated and moderate malnutrition halved.[12] The programme was scaled up to cover more than fifty districts in Tanzania by 1989. But its impact went much further – the Iringa story was foundational in the development of UNICEF's first comprehensive global nutrition strategy, launched in 1990 and still the most widely used by nutrition professionals today.[13]

Despite Iringa's shining star, most international development organisations were not prepared to devolve power to communities. Too much was riding on their retention of control. In the early 1990s, nutrition professionals simply defaulted to their comfort zone. The profession of nutritional science had always been structured to favour single-nutrient explanations of problems, since individual scientists tended to be experts in a specific nutrient, and because such explanations were easier to explain to policymakers and easier for them to address.

Micronutrients had the additional advantage of having the energetic support of companies who were set to profit from the roll-out of global programmes of supplementation. In this way, the nutrition profession started to play directly into the hands of the large corporations who welcomed a curative, biomedical or nutrient-centric perspective that steered well clear of wider action on the harms their products and practices were causing.

In 2013, Professor Gyorgy Scrinis of the University of Melbourne, coined the term 'nutritionism'.[14] A predatory ideology, nutritionism drives the framing of both corporate strategies and public policies in terms of nutritional disease. Top-down technological tinkering with food composition (reformulation) is its modus operandi. Politics and governance are ignored.

In the mid-2020s, nutritionism still holds sway, aligning with food engineering (especially by the ultra-processed food industry) and the nutri-centric approach of setting national dietary guidelines. A long, long way from a community-driven approach that seeks to understand and address the challenges of people who cannot access a healthy diet.

But let's return to Iringa for a moment.

Two luminaries shaping the world of nutrition back then were a garrulous Swede called Urban Jonsson and a dynamic Tanzanian, Olivia Yambi. Urban and Olivia cut their teeth in Iringa. With colleagues, they came up with the Triple A Cycle which, to me, was brilliant in its simplicity and utility. Faced with a big complex challenge, like child malnutrition – as they were in Iringa – they figured they needed to collect as much data and information on the problem, how it had evolved over time (Assess), what's known about its causes and the capacity to respond (Analyse). Then, and only then, would they collectively figure out the right strategy (Act). Every step was done with the full, active involvement of the local community.

In 1989, Urban was appointed Global Director for Nutrition, UNICEF New York. I worked with him on Triple A workshops in several countries in the years that followed. Urban was always adamant on one thing. There needed to be two *separate* workshops. In the first, the focus was solely on the problem and its causes (the first two 'As'). Any talk of action was banned until a clear consensus had been reached among all participants on the nature of the challenge. The second workshop then picked up from the first and focused purely on developing an action plan. This prevented any premature jumping to conclusions on solutions before the problem had been properly described.

This book follows the same path. We have just done the Assessment stage. Part III, 'Unravelling', which follows now, is Analysis, and Part IV, 'Transformation', is the Action stage.

III

UNRAVELLING

You cannot cross the sea merely by
standing and staring at the water.
Rabindranath Tagore

We need to move into a new era, one based on a common vision of human and planetary health, in which power is better balanced. But before we figure out how to get there, we need to unravel the structural drivers of the crisis cascade we're currently enmeshed in. By shining a light on the dynamics of the corporate food regime in the twilight years of neoliberalism, we start to see the entry points, the levers and drivers of change. Unpacking the cascade enables a comprehensive view of both causes and solutions, enabling disparate actors (individuals, organisations) to unite towards a common goal.

This is where we're going now. Chapters 6 and 7 focus on the ultra-processed products around which our current food system revolves, before we turn in Chapter 8 to consider the places where we access food – our food environments. Chapters 9 and 10 then look at external shocks and stresses (pandemics, climate, environment) that become entangled with our food system. Chapter 11 then turns to people at the end of the line – workers and consumers who are most vulnerable to malnutrition. The last three chapters (Chapters 12–14) focus on the big two powerhouses (corporations and governments), the nature of their power, the different forms it takes and the way they use it.

Part III is the middle stage of the Triple A Cycle – the Analysis stage. After this we will be better equipped to act, to play our part in the food revolution that will propel us forward into this new era.

6

First Food Fight

June 1984, Laknavaram forest. The monsoon brought life, but it also brought death. Like everything else, bacteria were on a roll, which meant epidemics of diarrhoea and pneumonia. Mothers were out in the fields, transplanting rice for up to fifteen hours a day. The youngest kids were left with their siblings – six-year-olds looking after two-year-olds.

At our late July growth check, one month after the rains had started, I was stunned to see that nearly all of the under-twos had just stopped growing. For a child so young, this was a big deal. It wasn't a lack of food, it was a lack of time to care and to feed. When there's a terrible time crunch, choices have to be made. Some families had back-up from grandparents, but the youngest who were still being breastfed would either be taken to the field and left under an umbrella, or weaned abruptly onto mushy foods or formula feeds, often made with contaminated water.

Bagyama was typical. Five months old, she was severely underweight at just 4.5kg. She wasn't growing. Her chronic diarrhoea was the tipping point at the end of a cascade of hardship and struggle. As her parents, Lunawaht and Bodri, barely out of their teens, worked full-time, she was left with her grandmother.

Lunawaht had half an acre of scrubland. With no land deeds,

he was ineligible for a commercial loan. To buy fertiliser, he needed to hit up a local loan shark who charged 40 per cent interest. The family could only eat twice a day. He told me he needed to take loans to buy food: 'If we don't eat, we get weak, we get sick which means we can't work . . . then we starve.'

Bodri weighed just 37kg – the weight of an average ten-year old in the UK – and she was severely anaemic. Somehow, she managed to keep working – sowing, transplanting, weeding: 'I tie a cloth tight around my waist, so I don't feel hungry'. While she was in the fields, baby Bagyama was left with her grand-mother who couldn't cope. She'd make up some Amulspray – formula feed picked up from the clinic. Ellama, our lead health worker, was sure this was the main cause of Bagyama's illness: 'It's overdiluted or made with dirty water – probably both. Either way she'll get sick'.

What enraged Ellama more than anything was the way that clinics would sow doubt among mothers about their ability to breastfeed, and then provide them with free Amulspray samples that the company had urged them 'to try out'.

It's not hard to find images to illustrate this. On my course, back in London, a year earlier, one session had started with a slide showing the August 1973 cover of *The New Internationalist*, alongside the editorial:

> On the cover of this issue is a photograph of grave no. 19232. It is the grave of a Zambian baby. On it, the mother has placed a feeding bottle and an empty tin of milk powder. They are symbols of infant death and of the mother's attempt to do her best for her child during its short life. What the mother does not know is that the way in which she used that same milk powder and feeding bottle was also the main cause of her baby's death.[1]

During the 1970s, multinational companies (and Nestlé in particular) were driving high infant death rates in Asia and Africa by the way they were marketing infant formula foods.[2] By 1981, the World Health Assembly passed the International Code of Marketing of Breast-milk Substitutes ('The Code') that banned any form of marketing that implied that breastfeeding was not the best way to feed and nurture an infant.[3]

Ellama knew all this. She also knew little was being done to enforce these rules. 'Companies know how to find loopholes, they just change their name, change the product description,' she told me, 'They still bribe clinic managers to keep handing out samples. Most mothers can't read the label anyway.'

Over the last four decades, evidence on the benefits of breast-feeding and breast milk – 'first food' – has piled high.[4] Breastfeeding prevents babies from dying, from getting sick, from failing to grow. Exclusive breastfeeding for the first six months is associated with higher intelligence, strengthened immunity and a lower risk of overweight and diabetes. Great for the mother too: it reduces her own risk of diabetes, heart disease, breast and ovarian cancer. Optimal breastfeeding prevents 820,000 child deaths and 20,000 breast cancer deaths each year and saves US$300 billion from reduced health-care costs for children given breast milk.[5] There's probably a lot more – we're only beginning to learn about the role of breast milk in fortifying the infant's microbiome. Fewer than half of all babies, however, are exclusively breastfed.

Infant formula is crucial for babies who don't have access to breast milk and for mothers working outside the home, who are unable to pump or store breast milk, or who lack family support. But aggressive marketing that revolves around misinformation on the nutritional value of formula and limited information on the myriad benefits of breastfeeding, have distorted decision-making for many young mothers.[6]

Nestlé is the world's largest food company. It owns more than 2,000 brands, 450 manufacturing facilities in around 80 countries, with sales in 186 countries, and employs 276,000 workers. In 2023, Nestlé reported US$103 billion in sales (that's $200,000 every minute, round the clock) and US$18 billion in global profit.

The story started in 1867 when Henri Nestlé developed a 'formula' to alter the fat, protein and sugar in cow's milk to mimic human milk. In 1905 his company merged with the Anglo-Swiss Condensed Milk Company to form the Nestlé Group.

Fast-forward three decades. In 1936, Dr Cicely Williams (one of the few female British colonial medical officers, who we met in Chapter 4) was transferred from the Gold Coast (now Ghana) to Malaya. Here she came face to face with Nestlé's predatory advertising of condensed milk as 'ideal for delicate infants'. In 1939, she was invited to address the Singapore Rotary Club, chaired by the president of Nestlé. She called her speech 'Milk and Murder':

> If you are legal purists, you may wish me to change the title of this address to 'Milk and Manslaughter', but if your lives were embittered as mine is, by seeing day after day this massacre of the innocents by unsuitable feeding, then I believe you would feel as I do that misguided propaganda on infant feeding should be punished as the most criminal form of sedition and that these deaths should be regarded as murder.

This was the start of the fightback against corporate malpractice that was killing babies. After the Second World War, Nestlé felt it needed to seed new markets. The company approached India's newly independent Government in 1947 and started production in Punjab shortly after.

By the 1970s, Nestlé was active in many low-income countries. Dressed as nurses, Nestlé reps hung out in hospitals where they promoted formula foods as a replacement for breast milk.[7] Mothers were provided with one free can when they left the hospital – a potentially lethal freebie. Most mothers lived where water was not safe, where the feed could easily be contaminated in preparation leading to diarrhoea, dehydration and often death. Bottles were not sterilised due to lack of time and fuel to boil water. Women would overdilute the formula (to eke it out), which meant the newborn was not able to absorb the nutrients. Once they had started to use formula, they couldn't switch back to breastfeeding – it was too late in the lactation cycle.

Nestlé targeted hospitals with offers to build or renovate facilities for newborn care or to subsidise office furnishings. 'Nurses' would drop by new mothers' homes unannounced and question the mother's ability to start or sustain breast-feeding before handing out baby formula. Instructions were in English which the mother could not read, and even if they could, they'd be reading lies about the content's superiority over breast milk. Hundreds of thousands of babies died every year from diarrhoea and dehydration from contaminated feeds.[8]

Then in the summer of 1973, *The New Internationalist* published its 'Baby Food Tragedy' story with its chilling graveside photo on the cover.[9] This became a lightning rod, not only regarding the role of the formula industry, but also on the wider issue of commercial drivers of malnutrition and the role of transnational corporations in public health.

Over fifty years later, it still is.

In 1974, another report 'Nestlé Kills Babies', led to a mass boycott. Nestlé denied responsibility, claiming that the real problem was access to water. At the same time, the company was seizing and bottling the public water supply, reducing the water table and starting a wave of plastic pollution that is now worse than ever.

In 1978, Senator Edward Kennedy held a series of US Senate Hearings on the industry's unethical marketing practices. International meetings with the World Health Organization, UNICEF and The International Baby Food Action Network (IBFAN) followed. In 1981, the World Health Assembly launched the Code. Advertising of formula in hospitals and clinics was banned, and it was up to countries to monitor the Code implementation.

A recent analysis has calculated that Nestlé's entry into low- and middle-income countries caused 212,000 infant deaths per year where clean water was not available at the peak of the controversy in 1981, and around 11 million excess infant deaths between 1960 and 2015.[10]

This was not the end of the story. After the Code was launched, the Reagan administration threatened to pull US funding from UNICEF if it continued to fight Big Formula. UNICEF's director, Jim Grant stood his ground. Shamefully, the US held out for thirteen years before, in 1994, becoming the last country to endorse the Code.

The Code has made a big difference, despite being voluntary. The industry had to find different ways to make profit from formula, or to ditch it. Most companies chose the former. One key move was to widen the boundaries of formula markets to target older children, promoting formula products for older infants, young children and even pregnant and lactating mothers.*

A multibillion market has since developed for ultra-processed products designed to circumvent the Code. Unnecessary and dangerous products that continue to damage child health, fuel obesity and pollute the environment.

In 2017, IBFAN published a report *Breaking the Rules, Stretching the Rules*, in which it highlighted multiple Code violations.[11] Five years later, the World Health Organization and UNICEF reported how formula marketing continued to be pervasive, personalised and powerful. Companies were using manipulative marketing tactics that exploited parents' anxieties and aspirations, distorting science and medicine to legitimise their claims and systematically targeting health professionals to encourage them to promote formula milk products.[12]

In 2023, the *Lancet* Series on Breastfeeding highlighted the ways in which the formula food industry and powerful exporting states

---

* New digital technologies have greatly increased the reach of marketing in ways that blur the lines between advertising and nutrition and care advice. Algorithm-driven digital marketing targets mothers when they are most concerned about breastfeeding. Industry-paid influencers discuss difficulties of breastfeeding as preludes to formula marketing. Parenting apps with round-the-clock chat services enable product placement and offer free samples or deals. Breastfeeding advocacy is framed as judgmental and anti-feminist, formula as empowering. Online regulation is scant. Governments don't get involved and the gaps are filled by the formula industry. Words like 'brain', 'neuro', 'IQ' on product labels – often linked to images of happy bouncing babies – violate the 1981 Code, so the industry has had to become more sophisticated in finding loopholes and exploiting grey areas. One of these is dark 'neuromarketing' in which AI (social listening, facial recognition, augmented or virtual reality) is used to target women when they are at their most vulnerable/receptive. Pregnant women are targeted on social media with ads about infant formula that mysteriously pop up a month before their due date.

were using weak Codex Alimentarius trade standards in their attempts to stop governments bringing in marketing controls.

In the 2018 World Health Assembly in Geneva, a resolution by Ecuador encouraged countries to strive to 'limit the inaccurate or misleading marketing of breast-milk substitutes'. The US delegation promptly objected, demanding that language asking governments to 'protect, promote and support breastfeeding' be removed, as well as a request that policymakers 'restrict the promotion of food products that can have deleterious effects on young children'. When Ecuador refused, US officials threatened trade tariffs and withdrawal of military aid to Ecuador, as well as slashing its contribution to the WHO if it didn't get its way.

'We were astonished, appalled . . . and saddened,' said Patti Rundall, the Policy Director of Baby Milk Action. 'What happened was tantamount to blackmail, with the US holding the world hostage and trying to overturn nearly 40 years of consensus on the best way to protect infant and young child health.' More than a dozen other countries declined, citing fear of economic retaliation. In the end the Russians stepped in to introduce the measure, and the Americans backed off.

The US Government has been waging battles like this for years across the world, according to a recent ProPublica investigation.[13] In Thailand, in 2017, when health experts tried to stop aggressive advertising of formula, US trade officials challenged the Thai Government on the floor of the World Trade Organization. Thai officials argued the new regulation would protect mothers and babies. In the end, they were bullied into backing down. ProPublica's exhaustive investigation in nearly two dozen countries showed the US Government repeatedly fighting the industry's corner, advancing commercial interests as Global-South countries sought to safeguard the health of their youngest children.[14]

Big Formula has huge economic (and as we've just seen, political) power. In the forty years since the Code's adoption, the industry has grown almost fortyfold to US$55 billion a year.[15] On marketing alone, it spends more than US$3 billion a year.

Seventy per cent of all countries (136 of 194) that report on the Code have adopted at least some provisions into national law, but just 18 per cent have adopted all provisions while 30 per cent have no legal measures whatsoever.[16] Breastfeeding is still threatened by the industry and its hostile marketing practices, and violations of the Code are widespread across the world.

While infant formula was created to replace human milk, there are many other ultra-processed products that have been created to replace foods in general, for all age groups. The purpose is simply to maximise profit for the creators and those who hold shares in their companies. This 'nutrition transition' is the lifeblood of the corporate food regime, its entire *raison d'être*. Let's travel now to South America to learn how this unfolded.

7

Fake Food Flood

At the end of the last century, Brazil's nutrition transition went into overdrive. Between 1975 and 1989, rates of child underweight more than halved at national level (from 18 per cent to just 7 per cent). Even in the poorest region in the north-east, rates dropped from 27 per cent to 13 per cent. Undernutrition was being brought under control.

One person who was in the perfect position to track these changes was Professor Carlos Monteiro from the University of São Paolo. I first met Carlos in Geneva in the early Nineties when he contributed a case study for a multi-country series – 'How Nutrition Improves' – that I was coordinating for the UN.[1] He told the story of Brazil's success in reducing child stunting. But he was already becoming aware of something ominous looming on the horizon.

As diets were changing fast, with highly processed foods and sugary drinks crowding out other foods, the challenge at the dawn of a new millennium was shifting from undernutrition to *over-nutrition*. Carlos could see the tsunami building. He figured there needed to be a system to differentiate healthy from unhealthy foods. Without this, there could be no guidance for citizens, no regulation by Government or other policies to shift the balance towards healthier diets (nutrient-rich, with limited saturated fat, sugars and salt and minimal ultra-processed foods).

In 2009, Carlos floated the idea of the NOVA system that delineated four groups of food products with regard to their degree of processing. Group 1 were unprocessed and minimally processed foods. Group 2 included oils, butter, lard, sugar, salt derived from Group 1 foods or from nature by pressing, refining, grinding, milling or drying. And Group 3 were processed foods made by adding Group 2 ingredients to Group 1 foods.

The fourth group (NOVA 4) comprises *ultra*-processed food and drink products extracted from foods, or derived from food constituents, with little if any intact food. Industrial formulations with five or more of the following myriad ingredients – sugar, fats, salt, antioxidants, stabilisers, preservatives, hydrogenated oils, interesterified oils, hydrolysed proteins, soy protein isolate, mechanically separated meat, maltodextrin, invert sugar, high-fructose corn syrup, dyes, colours, colour stabilisers, flavours, flavour enhancers, non-sugar sweeteners, carbonating agents, firming agents, bulking agents, anti-bulking agents, defoaming agents, anti-caking agents, glazing agents, emulsifiers, sequestrants, humectants . . .

Here's a shorter definition: industrially produced foods wrapped in plastic, containing ingredients not available in the home.* Ultra-processed food (UPF) is formula food for all ages. NOVA 4 products are high in both sugar and fat – a combination

---

* NOVA 4 includes ready-to-consume products like fizzy drinks; sweet or savoury packaged snacks; chocolate, confectionery; ice cream; mass-produced packaged breads and buns; margarines and other spreads; biscuits, cookies, pastries, cakes; breakfast 'cereals', 'cereal' and 'energy' bars; 'energy' drinks; milk drinks, 'fruit' yoghurts, 'fruit' drinks; 'cocoa' drinks; instant sauces. Many pre-prepared ready-to-heat products including pies, pasta and pizza dishes; chicken nuggets, burgers, hot dogs; powdered and packaged instant soups, noodles and desserts. NOVA 4 also includes infant formulas, follow-on milks, as well as 'health' and 'slimming' products such as meal replacement shakes and powders.

rarely found in nature. Energy-dense, they're low in fibre, protein, micronutrients and phytochemicals. Michael Pollan calls them 'edible, food-like substances'.[2] Most products now bear little resemblance, in fact, to food.[3] It's fake food. Like Prince becoming a symbol, or Twitter becoming X, we could perhaps add the qualifier, 'formerly known as . . .'

Fake food is designed to be cheap, convenient, long lasting, hyper palatable, ready to eat anytime, anywhere. And it's designed to hook us. Sugar, salt, fat and carbs are combined with additives in a secret alchemy. Bliss point, mouthfeel, flavour burst – a whole new vocabulary has emerged to describe their seductive powers. UPF manufacturers spend a fortune on research to optimise the way these products crunch, ooze and melt in the mouth, to make us eat more of them, more often. Fake foods are developed in a similar way to addictive drugs, comprising a big hit of fast-acting, rapidly absorbed ingredients, enhanced by additives. Consumers crave them, and they lose control over intake.

The NOVA classification includes, as part of the definition, the *purpose* of the processing. The purpose of NOVA 4 products is not to nourish people, it is to displace other foods and make a lot of money for the corporations who manufacture and market them.

Our basic biology evolved over 100,000 years to keep us healthy. It's taken a few decades – an evolutionary nanosecond – to subvert it for profit. We are programmed to eat high-fat, high-sugar and salty foods (HFSS for short) in order to store energy for periods of scarcity – and we have an instinct to eat these types of foods whenever we can, wherever we find them. By developing a global panorama of such products, the industry has monetised this compulsion. Alongside them, there's a whole range of drinks which bypass normal satiety feedback loops, so we can just keep swigging away.

Ultra-processing widens the scope for the manufacturer to alter the product in different ways to create profit. Reliance on a few crops is not a barrier when they can be transformed into a kaleidoscope of products with different shapes, size, colours, tastes, flavours, smells, textures.

The global reach of these corporations helps them source ingredients from around the world. In Chapter 3 we heard about Christmas-pudding ingredients from different corners of the Empire. Now we have a new form of colonialism that permits similar international extraction of ingredients to be baked into synthetic products: palm oil from Asia, cocoa from Africa, soy from South America, wheat from the USA, flavouring from Europe, and so on.[4]

Ultra-processed foods are two to three times cheaper per calorie than healthier foods.[5] But the main cost – in ill-health, early death and a trashed planet – is being borne by us and by future generations.

Giant companies have giant global markets which mean they prefer shelf-stable products that travel well. Fake food is far more profitable than other foods; additives save money (stabilisers prolong shelf life, flavours are cheaper than fruit). Ultra-processing involves adding more and more steps to the 'value chain' to add more and more profit.[6] UPFs are really profit-generators disguised as food. We're eating more of it because the market has been cornered by a handful of mega-companies (Big Food) who, because they're all publicly traded, have a fiduciary responsibility to deliver maximum value to their shareholders who demand continuous growth and higher profits.

Where is the incentive to benefit the nutrition and health of consumers? So long as huge profits can be made, there is little incentive. The industry will continue to 'privatise the gain, socialise the cost'; the way capitalism has always worked.

History, biology and business all combine in what Henry Dimbleby has termed the 'Junk Food Cycle' – a reinforcing feed-back loop which operates as follows: our biological predilection for calorie-dense foods is exploited by companies who invest time and money to create and market such products, which enhance sales and consumer demand for more, which boosts profits, which leads to more investment in more products to reach yet more consumers, across the world.

This vicious cycle not only traps the consumer, it traps food companies too. If one company breaks from the pack and stops making UPFs, another will march right in and occupy the vacated market space. The healthy-food innovator will lose shareholders as its profits drop. This is why it's essential for Government to step in to make the rules clear to all. Companies will never regulate themselves for public health, they exist to drive the bottom line.

Dangerous diet

In 2021, I met Chris van Tulleken at University College, London. He was interviewing people for his forthcoming book: *Ultra-Processed People*. Chris's groundbreaking documentary *What Are We Feeding Our Kids?* had recently aired on the BBC and he had a best-selling podcast on junk-food harms. The documentary followed him for a month during which he ate a diet of 80 per cent ultra-processed food, similar to one in five people in the UK. After a month, he reported poor sleep, heartburn, depression, anxiety, sluggishness, constipation and a low libido. He became miserable. The 6kg he'd gained made him feel 'ten years older'. His appetite hormones were all over the place – large meals didn't make him feel full.

Most disturbing was a real-time segment in the documentary when he's given the results of a brain scan. After a month on this diet, structural changes had occurred in his brain that – the doctor told him – may, or may not, be reversible. Later, in his 2023 book *Ultra-Processed People* he elaborated: the wiring in the brain was the same, but the information flowing through it had changed. Over time, this causes a change in structure as new connections grow to deal with the traffic.

In the 2010s, studies started to use the NOVA system to differentiate food products. Now, hardly a week goes by without another study associating UPF consumption with disease or death. There are hundreds of studies linking diets high in UPF with increased risk of a panoply of chronic diseases.*

In 2024, the *British Medical Journal* published a systematic umbrella review of forty-five pooled meta-analyses from fourteen reviews of studies of associations between exposure to ultra-processed foods (as defined by NOVA) and adverse health outcomes.[7] The review captured findings from studies covering 10 million participants, all published since 2020, none of which were funded by a UPF company.

Evidence was graded. The authors found 'convincing evidence' that higher ultra-processed food intake was associated with a 50 per cent increased risk of cardiovascular disease-related death, a similarly elevated risk of anxiety and common mental disorders, and a 12 per cent greater risk of type 2 diabetes. They also found 'highly suggestive evidence' of a 21 per cent greater risk of death from any cause, a 40–66 per cent higher risk of heart disease-related

---

* Including obesity, cardiovascular disease, type 2 diabetes, colonic, ovarian and breast cancers, fatty liver disease, gall bladder disease, inflammatory bowel disease, irritable bowel syndrome, kidney disease, dental problems, asthma, depression, insomnia, dementia, gout, osteoarthritis, frailty, auto-immune disease, thyroid dysfunction, eating disorders and premature death.

death, obesity, type 2 diabetes and sleep problems, and a 22 per cent increased risk of depression.

Yes, most of these are observational studies that show correlations not causation, but there are a lot of them (most of which control for the influence of participants' overall dietary intake, BMI, and other factors). The evidence is consistent – higher UPF consumption is associated with many adverse health outcomes.[8]

UPFs are especially bad for infants and children, including those consumed by their mothers before and during pregnancy. High UPF consumption of the mother during gestation can lead to oxidative stress, slowing of growth of the embryo and later, to a reduced ability of the child to process verbal stimuli and verbally express thoughts at four to five years of age.[9]

In 2021, an association was found between diet quality in mothers and children, and a child's ADHD diagnosis and symptoms.[10] Microbes in the large bowel of pregnant mothers and infants when they're born influence immune development and brain development. Poor diet reduces the diversity of the microbiome. Could this be driving part of the rising incidence of neurodevelopmental and mental health disorders in young children? We just don't know . . . yet.

Following birth, high UPF consumption by mothers during the child-rearing period was also associated with a higher risk of overweight or obesity in the infant as UPF-dense diets 'track through' to the infant's diet. Increased UPF consumption among infants is associated with increased weight gain, decreased height growth, increased risk of tooth decay and poorer cardiovascular health.

Ultra-processed food is deliberately designed to displace other foods, to be overconsumed and to hook the consumer. Displacement, overconsumption and addiction – three purposes that overlap. Let's look at each one and see how this plays out:

1. Displacement

Ultra-processed foods would not be such a big problem if we didn't consume so many of them. UPFs displace diverse whole foods from the diet, especially among children and low-income groups. In a recent analysis of over 35,000 products manufactured by the top twenty global food and drink companies, 89 per cent of sales derived from unhealthy products.[11] Every single company made at least 75 per cent of its total profits from the sale of unhealthy foods – and two (Red Bull and Ferrero) made *all* their profits from such sales. Less than 5 per cent of total sales of Mondelēz, Mars and PepsiCo were healthy. In 2022, Nestlé acknowledged that most of its products weren't healthy and they never will be.[12] In April 2024, nine out of ten shareholders at the annual general meeting in Lausanne voted to continue to prioritise unhealthy foods.[13]

Less than 10 per cent of the UK population meet the World Health Organization dietary recommendations and 70 per cent adhere to four or fewer of the nine dietary recommendations set out in the UK's dietary guidelines (the Eatwell Guide). Real food has been relegated – it's now the optional side salad to the junk main course.

The UK has the third-highest volume of UPF sales across eighty countries globally,[14] accounting for over 60 per cent of food intake,[15] and 73–78 per cent among schoolchildren.[16] It's happening all over the world, including Africa and South Asia – two continents that have only just started to make inroads into undernutrition and hunger. From 2002 to 2016, sales of ultra-processed foods *doubled* in South and Southeast Asia. Up to a half of all calories in the diets of preschool children in Nepal now comes from these products.[17] In Ghana and Vietnam, more than 60 per cent of the energy adolescents consumed came from foods obtained out of the home, which are invariably less micronutrient-dense and more ultra-processed.[18]

A bizarre example of displacement emerged in February 2024 in a perfect 'let them eat cake' re-enactment by the CEO of Kellogg's, Gary Pilnick. In an interview on CNBC, Pilnick (who earns up to US$5 million per year) suggested that struggling families eat 'cereal for dinner' despite prices having risen by 28 per cent in the last four years. Kellogg's started its 'give chicken the night off' campaign in 2022.

2. Overconsumption

Why are we overeating? A lot of the focus of research has been on the unnatural synergy of the high fat, sugar and salt (HFSS) content of junk food. But something else is happening under the radar, beyond the mix of nutrients in the food. Ultra-processed foods appear to have other characteristics (or have lost some) that may make them detrimental to health. Is there something in the way these products are made which makes them unhealthy?

Professor Kevin Hall, Nutrition and Metabolism Researcher at the US National Institute of Health (NIH), didn't think so, but he decided to test this hypothesis. In 2019, he ran a gold-standard randomised controlled trial. For one month, he kept twenty people locked up at the NIH in Bethesda, outside Washington DC. He split them into two groups: one group ate UPFs for two weeks; the second group ate a diet with an identical nutritional profile, but minimally processed. They were told they could eat *ad libitum* – as much or as little as they liked. Then they switched.

Results showed that energy intake was far greater with the ultra-processed diet – on average, 508kcals more per day – a huge difference, which led the UPF group to gain around 1kg in weight in two weeks. When they went onto the minimally processed diet for two weeks, they lost it. Other studies have pointed to significant differences conferred by ultra-processing.[19,20] Both ultra-processing and the high concentrations of fat, sugar and salt are harmful. Any approach to improve diet should therefore address *both* dimensions.

But what is it about ultra-processing that's causing people to overconsume? Well, we just don't know yet. It's likely to be some combination of several physiological, biological and social mechanisms. The top ten candidates include the following:[21]

1. UPFs are very energy-dense because they're dry, low in fibre, high in fat and sugar.

2. UPFs are engineered for overconsumption – purposively designed to be hyper-palatable by modifying the mix of fats, carbs and sodium. As well as overeating, this may lead to a form of addiction (see below).

3. Food intake is normally guided by the balance of nutrients, flavours and bioactive compounds. This is disrupted by ultra-processing. The mismatch between the taste signals from the mouth and the nutrition content in some UPFs alters metabolism and appetite in ways we don't yet understand.

4. Ultra-processing disrupts the natural matrix of the food, changing its texture, resulting in a soft product that can be eaten quickly and mindlessly to excess, long before the satiety response kicks in. More calories per mouthful, more calories per minute, more calories before your brain signals you've had enough.

5. Nutrients from UPFs (because they're so low in fibre) are absorbed higher up in the gut, which may reduce the diversity and health of the microbiome and affect gut–brain signalling and appetite regulation.

6. We have not evolved to metabolise artificial additives such

as emulsifiers, stabilisers, thickeners, preservatives, solvents, carriers, waxes, protectors – some of which are derived from petroleum. Any of these in and of themselves may damage the microbiome over the long term, even before potential 'cocktail effects' due to their mixing. The International Agency for Research on Cancer recently classified the non-sugar sweetener aspartame as 'possibly carcinogenic to humans'.[22]

7. Flavour enhancers, like glutamate, trick the body into thinking the product is healthy and nutritious.

8. Junk food has a peculiar quality that it can make you simultaneously overweight and undernourished. Along with high energy density, UPFs have low concentrations of protein and micronutrients. This may drive us to eat more, as we've evolved to eat until we get the protein and nutrients we need to function.

9. Intensive industrial processing produces potentially harmful substances (e.g. acrolein, acrylamide, industrial trans-fatty acids).

10. Plastics in packaging (especially drinks) alter the endocrine system and act as obesogens. Endocrine-disrupting chemicals affect adipose tissue formation, appetite control and weight gain.[23]

Another big issue with UPFs is the fact they are often consumed with sugar-sweetened drinks which bypass satiety feedback mechanisms. Drinks like Coca-Cola and Pepsi are snacks, but our bodies don't register them as such. They can be extremely calorific, and yet appetite-reducing hormones (that normally register fullness and stop you consuming more) are not triggered. We have a weak satiety response to clear drinks regardless of how many calories they're laden with. We just keep on drinking, especially when the beverage is ice-cold, laden with sugar or sweeteners and fizzing away. We know that sugary drinks rot teeth and make you eat more food than you need. Randomised controlled trials have shown that sweeteners can impair glycaemic response in healthy adults – the 'Coke plus burger' fast-food meal deal is there for a reason.

This is why liquid calories are the best profit-generators of all, and why Coca-Cola and PepsiCo are two of the biggest food and beverage companies in the world (Coca-Cola's retail sales in 2020 were US$227 billion; PepsiCo's were US$160 billion).[24]

Our hunger for sweetness is a liability in a world flooded with sugar and chemical sweeteners. British children now consume, on average, *thirty times* the volume of soft drinks that their counterparts did in 1950. For many, this is like an extra meal each day, one that the body does not recognise as a meal. This is one of the starkest mismatches between our biology and our food environment – one that the industry falls over itself to sustain.

Research continues to try to disentangle the key mechanisms causing the damage. But we don't have to wait for this – we know enough to act now, to develop policies to regulate UPFs.[25]

3. Dopamine delight

UPFs may be bad for us but are they addictive, like tobacco? Using the Yale Food Addiction Scale,* an analysis of two systematic reviews comprising 281 studies from thirty-six different countries found the average level of UPF addiction to be 14 per

---

* The scale assesses all eleven symptoms of substance-use disorder in the Diagnostic and Statistical Manual of Mental Disorders (DSM-5), including loss of control over intake, cravings, withdrawal symptoms and continued use despite adverse effects.

cent in adults (similar to alcohol and tobacco), 15 per cent among youths and 12 per cent in children (which is unprecedented). Among individuals with obesity, rates are higher (28 per cent adults, 19 per cent youths).[26]

Dopamine is a neurotransmitter and hormone that floods the brain in times of excitement and desire, especially in relation to the four Fs: fighting, fleeing, fornicating, feeding. When the craving for something is about to be sated – when you smell the burger and fries in front of you – dopamine is cascading over your cerebral neurons. As Kingsley Amis said, it's not about *being* drunk, it's about *getting* drunk. This moment when anticipation and reward are in perfect balance is marketing gold dust.

The rapid speed at which UPFs deliver their unique combinations of refined carbohydrates and fats to the gut – the hit – drives addiction. The industry has effectively harnessed the biology of desire to make products that exploit the impulsive traits of our dopamine-wired brains. The Pringles ad is spot-on: '*once you pop, you can't stop*'. Pringles are not crisps – they're made by mixing dehydrated potato, rice and wheat along with a cocktail of sugar, fat, salt and multiple flavourings into a gloopy paste which is then baked, sliced and bent to fit onto the human tongue to optimise the first hit. The manufacture of desire, followed by its easy consumption. So much easier, as an eating disorder expert said to me, to 'press the fuck-it button' and take another mouthful or six . . .

Satisfying an addiction becomes harder over time. More is needed to get the hit, and cravings intensify, as they become less enjoyable. Addiction is a problem of outsized 'wanting' despite reduced 'liking' – one that becomes less controllable over time.[27] Prioritising the short term over the long term means quitting is postponed indefinitely. Yes, you have agency, but it's compromised.

What you eat makes you feel sick, reduces quality sleep, makes you irritable, 'hangry' and more vulnerable to cravings.

Individual self-regulation does not work, just like industrial self-regulation. It ignores everything we know about human behaviour. Urging individual responsibility in an environment flooded with harmful products is bound to fail.

Big Food has learned a lot about all this from the masters of addiction – Big Tobacco. A 2022 study by Tera Fazzino and researchers at the University of Kansas published in the journal *Addiction* shows 'substantial tobacco-related influence on the U.S. food system.'[28]

Tobacco companies had a vast library of colours, flavours and additives, developed for cigarettes, that could be repurposed for food products. Between 1988 and 2001, foods produced by tobacco-owned companies, like Kraft, General Foods, Birds Eye (owned by Philip Morris) and Nabisco and Oreo (owned by R.J. Reynolds), were 29 per cent more likely to be classified as hyper-palatable (due to high fat and sodium content) and 80 per cent more likely (due to high carbohydrate and sodium) than foods produced by other companies.[29]

As concern around the amount of sugar in the American diet grew in the 1990s, the companies pivoted to promote foods that could be enhanced with sodium. Tobacco companies pulled out of the US food system in the 2000s, but their addictive products remained.

Recent research by neurologist Sharmili Edwin Thanarajah has shown that, like addictive drugs, habitual exposure to junk food can rewire brain circuits and induce neurobehavioral adaptations that lead to overeating and weight gain. If further research confirms UPFs are addictive, governments will be impelled to act to improve food environments – just as they (eventually) did with tobacco.[30]

The food industry will find itself in a legal minefield unless it admits culpability, refrains from predatory marketing, stops interfering in policy processes and reduces the harms of its products.

Now we'll sell you the cure

Companies keep driving profit margins by seeding new markets across the world and by endlessly diversifying product lines. But there's a third route to new markets: when a company creates the antidote to its own toxic products.

Big Food started buying diet companies a long time ago. Heinz bought Weight Watchers in 1978 for just US$72 million. Unilever were a bit slow off the mark: they had to pay US$2.3 billion in 2000 to buy SlimFast. Nestlé then bought Jenny Craig in 2006 in what the Nestlé chairman cited as a landmark in their transition into a 'nutrition, health and wellness company'.[31] Ultra-processed 'slimming foods' had names like 'Lean Cuisine' and 'Hot Pockets'. Nestlé now sells chewable multivitamins to be taken after bariatric surgery for obesity.

The British diet industry alone is worth £2 billion a year – about the same amount the NHS spends on A&E. This is dwarfed by the US$60 billion annual revenues of the US diet industry. Then there are all the foibles, fads and fears to be catered to, each a new opportunity for companies to grow market share. Low-fat, low-carb, high-protein, gluten-free. Health scares are both threat and opportunity for the food industry.

In 2021, after more than a century of promoting its sweet products, Coca-Cola advertised its new flagship 'Zero Sugar' by highlighting something it no longer has. In 2024, its big rival PepsiCo decided it was time to launch an electric blue cola that looked like anti-freeze. The junk-food cycle continues to spin inexorably, as transnational titans exploit any new chink of competitive advantage they can find to grow their bottom line.

In August 2024, the investigative journalist platform Follow the Money published a deep-dive into this booming 'double agenda', highlighting recent Big Food investments (especially by Nestlé) in 'nearly 100 healthcare companies'.[32]

The stratospheric popularity of the GLP-1 agonist weight-loss drugs Ozempic and Wegovy has provided yet another example of industry capturing new markets created by the harms of their products.[33] As users report cravings for protein-rich products in smaller portions, tailored to reduce gastrointestinal side effects, the industry is 'innovating' to provide them. A brand-new market estimated to reach 15 million people, or 13 per cent of the US population, by 2030. In May 2024, Nestlé announced Vital Pursuit, a new line of frozen, high-protein foods. 'We want to be there for every moment in our consumers' lives – today and in the future,' said Steve Presley, CEO, Nestlé North America.

8

Swamps and Deserts

Having investigated food products, we now need to look into food environments – the places where the food chain meets us. Food environments comprise the physical, economic, policy and socio-cultural surroundings, opportunities and conditions that determine whether we consume healthy or less-healthy diets.[1]

We are not free to choose what we eat. Food environments are created and curated by food and drink manufacturers and retailers, who decide what they will produce, market and sell, at what price, when and where.

We cannot blame individuals for their choices, as they are so heavily constrained by the obesogenic environment in which they live.[2] Of course, the food environment does not actually *cause* malnutrition. It's the collision between the environment and our genetic predisposition that nourishes or malnourishes us. If the environment is flooded with ultra-processed food, more people are at risk, especially people who can't afford to buy healthier foods which are a lot more expensive.

Obesity is so widespread now that the response needs to be large-scale (population-level) prevention, which means it needs to be led by Government. Prevention has to address the environment in its broadest sense. We cannot easily eliminate either the disposition to overeat when food is widely available nor the quasi-addictive effects of certain foods, unless and until we regulate them.

But one thing is certain – we can change the environment to make it less obesogenic. We will come to this later, but first we need to get a better handle on the four factors that shape our food environments: affordability, access, convenience and desirability of food. Let's look at each of them in turn.

1. Can you afford it?

Income growth enables individuals and households to access more food and better food. Food poverty on the other hand is caused by insufficient income, delays and changes to benefits, debt and the increasing cost of living. The human face of food poverty has changed. Fifty years ago, we would see images of hungry, energy-deprived children. Now it's more common to see stigmatising (headless) images of people with obesity.

One of the major effects of the 2022–23 food price hikes was a sharp shift towards even greater reliance on cheap, ultra-processed foods than in the past. The junk-food cycle accelerated – as purchasing power dropped, more work was needed to provide for families, and with less time to prepare meals, snacks and junk became the easiest affordable option. Food spend is elastic, which means people compromise on dietary quality and/or go hungry when times are hard.

On average, around the world, a healthy diet of nutrient-dense foods is four times more expensive than a calorie-sufficient basic diet.[3] In 2022, one third of the world's population (about 2.8 billion people) could not afford a healthy diet.[4] Shocking in itself, but the global figure masks huge regional variation: 72 per cent of residents of low-income countries were unable to afford a healthy diet, compared to just 6 per cent of residents of high-income countries.[5]

The average share of income that households in low-income countries spend on food is 52 per cent. If we use this as a threshold, we see numerous countries where the vast majority of the population cannot afford a healthy diet (for example, 96 per cent households in Nigeria, 87 per cent in Ethiopia, 81 per cent in Kenya, 71 per cent in India, 74 per cent in Bangladesh, 69 per cent in Indonesia).[6]

At the global level, in addition to the double burden of malnutrition among children and adults, the crisis cascade led to up to 757 million people worldwide (nearly one in ten) facing hunger in 2023, an astonishing rise of 144 million since 2019.[7]

Meanwhile, in the UK – the sixth richest economy in the world, with the second-worst income inequality in the G7 – nearly 10 million adults and children were food-insecure in June/July 2024, a week before the general election.[8] The poorest fifth of the population would need to spend at least half of their disposable income to afford the Government-recommended healthy diet. Completely unrealistic, which is why they consume 37 per cent less fruit and vegetables, 54 per cent less fish and 17 per cent less fibre than the richest fifth.*[9] The gap between the cost of healthy and unhealthy diets mirrors other inequalities that we'll explore later.

---

* The gaps are widening. Between 2021 and 2023, 60 per cent of food-insecure households cut back on purchasing fruit compared to 11 per cent of food-secure households (in month before survey). It's the same pattern with vegetables (44 per cent of food-insecure households cutting back compared with 6 per cent of food-secure) and fish (59 per cent vs. 15 per cent). During this period, the cost of healthier foods per 1000kcal increased by £1.76 compared with an increase of just £0.76 for less healthy foods, making the healthy option even less affordable for families.

2. Can you find it?

While income is critical in shaping economic access to food, physical access is determined by the proximity of shops and what's actually in them. Fresh markets in developing countries used to be the primary source of food, but many have been overtaken by supermarkets, full of ultra-processed foods.

When the first supermarket (King Cullen) opened in Queens, New York City, in 1930, it stocked 200 items. Now supermarkets carry up to 40,000 items and out-of-town hypermarkets, up to 50,000. Psychologist Barry Schwartz speaks of the 'paradox of choice' wherein too many options bring stress, making us less happy, not more. Option paralysis.

But that's hyper-capitalism. Diversification is a big profit-generator that demands ever more products, more shelf space, bigger supermarkets, more outlets. It's the same with fast food: McDonald's menus increased from 85 to 145 choices between 2007 and 2013. The biggest sellers are still the high-fat/salt items but there are many ways to enclose these combinations in food-like products, and there are many ways to market them.

In 1999, I joined the International Food Policy Research Institute (IFPRI) and moved to Washington DC. On my second day, I joined friends on their 'regular' six-weekly supermarket shop. We spent an hour in one (appropriately) called Giant. I wandered around, dazed and confused, in the land of Big Food. Entire aisles were dedicated to one type of food: one for chips (crisps), one for sodas (Coke, Pepsi), one for jelly (jam). There didn't appear to be much for a lone, single human. Everything came in monster-sized family packs. I saw croissants the size of dinner plates, bags of popcorn the size of pillows, and hundreds of different combinations of microwaveable ready-meals, shrouded in dayglo plastic. Checking the ingredients, I noticed that pretty much everything contained one or more of the following: maize, wheat, soya, palm oil and something I'd never heard of before – high-fructose corn syrup.

I asked about fresh groceries, which piqued my American friends' interest: 'Oh, so you shop European style . . . every day?' Grocery shopping in DC then mostly involved stocking up on giant boxes of mac 'n' cheese, pasta, saltina crackers, sugary cereals, multiple tins and jars. 'Healthy' options were in the Health Aisle – mainly cereal bars. Supermarkets did have 'fresh produce' aisles, but these were invariably pushed to the back of the store, out of the way of time-frazzled customers. Many people had basements, where supplies were stashed – tins and jars mostly, as rats or racoons would get the rest.

Supermarkets bring big benefits – they make shopping more efficient and they increase choice. But they are the endpoint of a supply chain that's become warped due to hyper-concentrated power. Supermarkets pay farmers less than it costs to produce the food, which means they go out of business and we have to import more . . . now much harder in the UK because of the lunacy of Brexit. As food journalist Jay Rayner pointed out: 'There are numerous people working for major supermarkets who are eligible for working tax credits. In effect the Government (and thus us, as taxpayers) provides a subsidy to these huge companies, by topping up the income of their low-paid employees.'[10]

Supermarkets and convenience stores have been proliferating across the world for decades and have reached out well beyond big cities now. Their use is strongly associated with increased purchase of ultra-processed foods. One-quarter of household food spend in low- and middle-income countries is on food prepared outside the home (mainly fast food, street food), and some segments of urban populations depend entirely on street foods.

Over the last few decades, as governments in the Global South have sought out new investors to propel their economies forward, the food industry has been more than eager to help out. From 1980 to 2000, direct investment from the USA into food processing overseas quadrupled. New factories were opened by Nestlé, PepsiCo and others. In the last century Latin America was targeted; in this one it is South Asia and more recently, Africa.

Sales of snacks and soft drinks have tripled over the past decade in India, for example, exceeding US$30 billion in 2022. 'India's on fire . . .' said Hanneke Faber, outgoing Head of Nutrition at Unilever, '. . . it's a fantastic growth engine!'

'Food deserts' are places where finding any healthy food is a challenge: 3.3 million people in the UK live in areas where no fresh produce is available within fifteen minutes by public transport. Forty per cent of the poorest households don't have a car so getting to a supermarket is hard.[11] Healthy eating is made even more difficult when the same ingredients from small convenience stores cost 10 per cent more in deprived areas than in affluent areas.

Another type of food environment – 'food swamps' – are places inundated with outlets selling calorie-dense, ultra-processed junk or fast-food takeaways. A UPF swamp is often a healthy-food desert. More than one in four places to buy food on the UK high street are fast-food outlets.[12] People living in the most deprived areas have double jeopardy, with more than twice the density of food outlets (than the least deprived), most of which are selling unhealthy foods.*[13]

---

* A study from the University of Cambridge examined menus from almost 55,000 food outlets on Just Eat, an online food ordering and delivery platform. Each menu was given a score between 0 and 12, with 12 being the healthiest. To extrapolate the data, the researchers used artificial intelligence to predict the

Recent research in Mexico and the USA has highlighted the strong links between food swamps, poverty, social inequality and higher death rates from obesity and other chronic diseases.[14]

It's not just the density of these outlets, it's the suffocating ubiquity of ads, physical and digital. The poorest half of the population in England and Wales is home to 63,000 outdoor billboard ads (82 per cent total), compared with just 13,000 in the more affluent half.[15] Aggressive marketing and ready availability of UPFs heightens chronic stress which is endemic in inner-city food swamps. If you live by a fast-food restaurant, you're much more likely to have obesity. Opening a fast-food restaurant within 0.1 miles of a school gate has been found to be associated with more than 5 per cent increase in child obesity rates.[16]

When we consider physical access, there's also a within-store dimension. The choice architecture of supermarkets is designed to maximise overconsumption. Snack foods are placed by checkouts, ultra-processed products aimed at kids are placed at the end of aisles at their eyeline height.*

3. Do you have time?

Food choices are affected not only by availability and access to foods but also by convenience and desirability. Over the last two decades we've witnessed a seismic shift in food culture. The nutrition transition changes not only what we buy but also how we eat it. Age-old rituals that revolve around commensality – sitting as a family or group to eat at the same table – have been obliter-

---

healthiness of almost 180,000 menus across the UK.

* In 2023, the UK sought to ban the lucrative end-of-aisle promotional deals that were almost invariably UPFs. Not to be deterred, several supermarkets decided it was a good time to scatter a few pallet stacks around – these weren't *aisles*, so they were exempt, albeit ideal for piling high with junk.

ated from many households and communities. As we've become more digitalised, we've become atomised. No matter how much time we interact with others online, we're physically more isolated. Sharing and bonding over a leisurely meal at a table (slow food) has become a rarity. Food is snatched on the run, throughout the day and consumed mindlessly, alone in front of a screen. One study of American teenagers found that those who use screens at mealtimes were less likely to eat green vegetables or fruit, more likely to drink sugary sodas and less likely to talk.[17]

For the commercial food sector, in the 1990s this opened up a whole new arena for profit – anytime, anywhere snacking. Convenience foods were easy to buy, to store, to open, to prepare, to eat. Companies exploited the fact we like variety and convenience. That was good for them too, as it increased sales.* Humans became grazing animals, as snacks every couple of hours replaced three set meals per day. A third of all calories consumed by the average American adult now come from snacks. Bee Wilson calls them 'salty ghosts of the meals of their grandparents.' Snacks are a big part of the reason obesity co-exists with deprivation.

Pre-prepared sandwiches became a booming industry in the UK, as supermarkets again capitalised and set up 'meal deals' that included bonus cans of Coke or Pepsi and/or bags of crisps. Across the Channel, in France, it was a different story – until 2021, eating at your desk was illegal.[18] Later, as snack sales started to plateau in the Global North, Big Food looked elsewhere to new untapped markets, like India.

Convenience also means extending shelf life as much as possible. Products are designed to last forever. I remember

---

* Mondelēz's 2023 *State of Snacking* report noted a big increase between 2020 and 2023, adding US$15 billion to the company's market capitalisation in this period.

opening a friend's fridge in the USA and finding stacks of McDonald's boxes – a full shelf and a half of Happy Meals. She told me they kept really well. They looked like grave goods.

When saturation is reached, a new uncharted territory is opened up. The next big diversification, the ultimate in convenience, is 24/7 room service, wherever you are, whenever you like. Meals, snacks, drinks brought to you in polystyrene cartons, pre-cooked, ready to eat. You just need to walk a few paces to open the door of your apartment. Food brought by tapping a screen and consumed half an hour later in front of it, still tapping away. You don't need to chew much either.

There were 7.4 million monthly users of Deliveroo in 2022, less than a decade after it started. Many other companies have since popped up, including Seamless and Uber Eats. Hundreds of thousands of delivery riders zipping around cities so we can stay glued to our screens. The packaging involved in all this is off the scale. Delivery riders are underpaid with no safety nets. New markets, new profit.

4. What do you *really* want?

After affordability, physical access and convenience, the fourth factor shaping our food environment is what the food industry is really manufacturing – desire. MBA courses across the world start by posing questions like: What are we selling? What does it cost? Where do people find it? How do we catch their attention and get them to buy it?

Desirability increases demand for a product, which increase sales, which means more profit. We've looked at three of the four Ps of marketing: product, price and place. The last pillar – promotion – involves advertising, sponsorship, labelling, all targeted to manufacture desire via multiple channels, including social media, music streaming, TV and online media. Only the car industry spends more money on advertising than the food industry. Fake food and sugary-drink promotions have become wallpaper.[19] Children in the UK were exposed to 15 billion junk-food adverts online in 2019, a twentyfold increase in just two years.

The industry routinely shoots down the argument that marketing changes consumption as they want to avoid Government stepping in to restrict it. This is total nonsense: marketing and advertising are incredibly successful which is why so much money is spent on them. A review of twenty-two studies found that children who were exposed to TV or internet adverts for unhealthy food consumed more afterwards – both in quantity and calorific load – than those in control groups.[20] Marketing aims to create allure, to glamorise and normalise the purchase and consumption of unhealthy products. In a survey by Cancer Research UK, 40 per cent of respondents aged eleven to nineteen said they felt pressured to eat unhealthily by ads, rising to 52 per cent of people with obesity.[21]

Food and drink had the fifth largest worldwide advertising spend in 2016, costing over US$23 billion, with Nestlé having the third-highest spend of any company.[22] In the UK, three food chains were among the top five spenders on UK outdoor advertising in 2023: McDonald's £81 million (by far the highest), followed by KFC and Coca-Cola at £31 million each.[23] A third of food and soft-drink advertising spend in the UK goes on confectionery, snacks, desserts and soft drinks, compared with only 1 per cent for fruit and vegetables.[24]

In the UK, the youth activist movement Bite Back 2030's report, *Fuel Us, Don't Fool Us*, made disturbing reading.[25] In 2022, the UK food industry spent £55 million on online adverts for unhealthy products, leading to 6.5 billion advertising exposures. 'Kidfluencers' (children with a high social media following) are wooed and sponsored by the industry to amplify messaging.[26] Digital marketing, including algorithmic targeting, is becoming ever more sophisticated. In one creepy incident, Alice Mazon, aged eighteen, Co-Chair of the London Youth Board, was congratulated by Domino's Pizza on receiving her exam results before her mother even knew.[27]

Just five companies – Haribo, Mars, Mondelez, PepsiCo and Kellogg's – are responsible for over 80 per cent of TV ads aired in the UK, before the watershed for snacks and confectionery. This, despite all of them claiming not to advertise to children.[28]

9

Carbon and Plastic

Not only is the industry hurting us, it's also hurting the planet. Food systems are major drivers of climate and environmental crises which, in turn, exacerbate food insecurity and malnutrition. The interactions are two-way, intertwined within the cascade. Let's look at how this plays out.

How food systems drive climate and environmental crises
Food systems generate one-third of all man-made greenhouse-gas emissions – the second biggest emitter after the fossil-fuel industry.[*1] Food emissions alone will take us beyond the 1.5°C rise in temperature by the end of this century, unless we radically change our food system.[2]

Manufacturing and packaging are energy-intensive and highly polluting. Soaring global demand for cheap ingredients leads to rapid deforestation, soil degradation, massive biodiversity loss, species extinction and air, water and plastic pollution.[3]

Agribusiness derives its power from the mass production of a

---

* 13 per cent of emissions come from agriculture and livestock (most from producing red meat and milk), 11 per cent from land use change and 10 per cent from transport, processing, packaging, retail and waste (see note 22: Romanello, M. et al. 2023).

handful of crops on land that used to be forest, much of which is the ancestral land of Indigenous peoples. Nearly a billion people in the world don't get enough to eat, despite the fact the world grows twice as much as we need. Of the 3 billion tonnes of cereals produced every year, less than half goes directly to humans, 41 per cent goes to livestock and 11 per cent is used for biofuels which end up in cars (the US puts 50 per cent more maize into its cars than Africa produces). One-third of the global crop harvest is wasted. That's around 3 trillion meals per year – the equivalent of all India's food emissions in 2019.

Ultra-processed foods account for 30–50 per cent of diet-related energy use, biodiversity loss, greenhouse-gas emissions, land use, food waste and water use.[4] Emissions from UPFs increased by 245 per cent between 1987 and 2018.[5] Nestlé's emissions are three times those of its host country, Switzerland.[6]

The Green Revolution was never really green. To maximise yield, land is doused in fertilisers, pesticides and herbicides made from fossil fuels. These synthetic chemicals contaminate the soil, water and the food it produces before breaking down into nitrous oxide which drives climate change. All of this is subsidised by governments, which means taxpayers . . . which means us.

We can begin to understand the true cost of our food system by focusing on three foodstuffs (meat, palm oil, soy) and three consequences (agrobiodiversity loss, water and plastic pollution).

Three foods
First, meat. Beef emits over thirty times more carbon dioxide per calorie of food than tofu or lentils. A meat-eating family of three, consuming 1kg per week, would generate more greenhouse gas from their diet than from the electricity they use, or the car they drive. In cooking so many cows, we're cooking ourselves.[7] Making meat from plants is extraordinarily inefficient. Three-quarters of

the world's farmland is used for cattle and yet meat and dairy only provide us with 18 per cent of the calories we need and 37 per cent of the protein.[8] For every 100 calories of cereal that we feed cows, we get just 3 calories back as beef (4 for lamb, 9 for pork and 13 for chicken). Most of the meat we eat is ultra-processed (like nuggets and burgers). Our meat habit leads to tropical forests being cut down, which drives pandemic disease, as well as climate change. Antibiotic use in factory farms leads to resistant bacteria in animal faeces, which eventually find their way into the food chain. The looming threat of antimicrobial resistance is a lot more serious than the occasional viral pandemic.

Second, palm oil. Much of the calorific load of UPF derives from refined vegetable oils, mainly palm oil. Since 1970, more than half of the virgin rainforest in Indonesia has been destroyed for oil palm.[9] The World Bank and IMF promoted palm oil as a way for Indonesia and Malaysia to clear their debt. Nestlé was caught buying palm oil from dodgy mills that were responsible for the displacement of Indigenous peoples, the decimation of forests and their biodiversity.[10] After a Greenpeace campaign in 2010, Nestlé promised to change, but seven years later, the corporation admitted that nearly half of its palm oil still came from these same plantations.

A third environmental destroyer is soy – used to feed livestock and make UPFs. At over 40 per cent protein, soy is ideal for bulk-feeding animals. Soy protein isolate is used to improve 'mouthfeel' in UPFs and to allow the product to be marketed as high in protein.[11] In the meat, fish, cheese, eggs and milk we eat and drink in the UK, we're effectively consuming over 60kg of soy every year that comes from a Wales-sized chunk of land carved out of the Amazon rainforest.[12,13] Many UK supermarkets use soy suppliers that have been linked to over 27,000 hectares of deforestation threatening the land of over 650,000 Indigenous peoples in Brazil. In the 2010s, production of staples in Brazil dropped (rice by 43 per cent, beans by 30 per cent) as soy production increased 70 per cent. The chemicals used to grow soybeans pollute lakes and rivers.

Three consequences
The loss of agrobiodiversity caused by Big Food's concentration on a handful of crops (wheat, soy, maize) has drastically undermined the resilience of food systems. Crop diversity has always been an insurance against climate change and a coping mechanism in times of scarcity (remember the Great Hunger in Ireland). When this is taken away, agriculture becomes more vulnerable to shocks, food prices rise, which makes people even more reliant on the cheapest foods – unhealthy UPFs.

Access to water is a human right, but Big Soda has been turning it into a private good for decades. Water has been drawn from aquifers, springs, rivers and lakes, put in plastic bottles or turned into multiflavoured sugary drinks with the dirty effluent dumped back into water sources. It takes up to 600 litres of water to produce just one litre of soda. Most Mexicans don't have access to safe water and yet they're inundated with Coca-Cola bottling plants which extract millions of litres every year. They're then forced to pay European and US corporations for bottled versions of their own water. Former Nestlé Chief Executive Peter Brabeck called water a 'grocery product' that should 'have a market value'. So much for human rights.

And then there's plastic.

Plastic pollution is another twenty-first-century pandemic. Plastic packaging, created by petrochemical giants like Exxon, Total, Aramco and Shell, has become a global industry worth over US$700 billion annually.[14] Global plastics waste has doubled in the past two decades, soaring to 400 million tonnes,

40 per cent of which is packaging. McDonald's churns out over a billion kilos of packaging every year, weighing more than one hundred Eiffel Towers.

The *Break Free from Plastic* 2023 report showed that once again Coca-Cola was by far the world's worst plastic polluter, producing 200,000 single-use plastic bottles every minute.[15] Nestlé come in second followed by Unilever, PepsiCo and Mondelēz International. Such companies repeatedly set (and miss) voluntary targets to reduce virgin plastic use and to increase the recycled content of their products.

Only 9 per cent of plastic waste is recycled and even then, only for a few cycles. Most plastic ends up in landfills or the ocean. Up to 34 billion plastic drink bottles (four for each person on the planet) ended up in the world's oceans in 2018. Plastic producers have known for decades that recycling is not economically or technically feasible. But that's not stopped them from promoting it. As an Exxon employee proclaimed at the American Plastics Council: 'We are committed to the activities [recycling], but not the results'.[16] Imagine this in any other industry –we'll sell you a car, but don't come back to us if it doesn't work.

The first era of colonialism in Africa saw the extraction of value under appalling conditions. Now, it's the dumping of industrial waste: 172 million tonnes of plastic were imported into the African continent between 1990 and 2017, where the average rate of inadequately managed waste is around 74 per cent. Without the hazardous work of waste-pickers, the extent of this pollution would be far greater.[17]

Plastic degrades into microplastics and even smaller nanoplastics (under 1 micrometre across). A 2023 study found nearly 250,000 particles floating in a 1-litre bottle of water, 90 per cent of which were nanoplastics.[18] All these enter our food and water systems and thus our bodies. Most of the world's urban tap water is contaminated. So is a lot of seafood. We don't yet know the implications for our health, though PET (polyethylene terephthalate) has been found to be carcinogenic and bisphenol A, used in food and drink containers, can interfere with hormones, leading to reproductive and developmental problems.[19]

As this happens, Big Food embeds itself in a web of industry groups and 'corporate social-responsibility' initiatives, while lobbying governments to keep the cost of recycling on the consumer/taxpayer. An infamous example is Coca-Cola's 'Keep America Beautiful' campaign with the 'Crying Indian' advert: 'People start pollution, people can stop it' (in which the actor playing the Indigenous man was Italian-American!).

In mid-nineteenth century London, the Industrial Revolution was powered by workers who flooded into the cities from rural areas. Food was transported to the cities to feed the workers. Human excrement from the workers was flushed into the Thames where it piled up on the banks, causing frequent cholera outbreaks which killed thousands. In the heatwave of 1858, Benjamin Disraeli, Tory Chancellor, called it, 'a Stygian pool reeking with ineffable and unbearable horror'.

The capitalist economy wasn't interested in this (literally) downstream effect of its profiteering. It was a 'negative externality' – bloodless economist-speak for the price to be paid for capitalist economic growth. A price to be paid not by the employer, but by those who couldn't afford to insulate themselves from it by living elsewhere. Unintended and hidden consequences that are not reflected in prices paid by consumers or received by producers.

By ignoring externalities, market prices of foods are delinked from the true cost of their production. The more costly production of healthier, more sustainable foods becomes less profitable for farmers and food businesses than the production of unhealthy food that has lower direct costs but much greater externalities.

Food systems are now destroying much more value than they create.

In 2024, the Food Systems Economic Commission estimated the costs that our food systems place on people and the planet at a mind-blowing US$15 trillion per year, equivalent to 12 per cent of GDP in 2020.[20] Much more than food systems contribute to global GDP.

The largest share of this (US$11 trillion) derives from health costs due to negative effects on labour productivity, as a result of diet-related non-communicable diseases, including diabetes, hypertension and cancer. Most of this is associated with the double burden of malnutrition – the lost productivity from 1 billion people living with obesity and up to 757 million people who are undernourished. Most of the rest derives from the type of environmental costs we've just explored.[*]

So, in sum, we have a food system that is accelerating climate change and environmental degradation. Let's look at the reverse direction – the other loop in the vicious cycle.

How the climate crisis amplifies food injustice

The climate crisis generates food crises and malnutrition via global heating, the increased severity and frequency of heatwaves, droughts, flooding, crop failure, reduced quantity and quality of crop yields, higher food prices, increased food-borne and other infectious diseases (such as dengue, malaria, vibriosis and West Nile virus) and civil disorder.[21]

---

[*] US$1 trillion worth of harm derives from the fact our food systems are a source of structural poverty (via the costs of food, and the low incomes of food workers, as seen in Almeria, discussed in Chapter 11).

The state-of-the-art 2023 *Lancet* Countdown on Climate Change and Health report showed that the global land area affected by extreme drought increased from 18 per cent in 1951–60 to 47 per cent in 2013–22.[22] A higher frequency of heatwaves and droughts in 2021 was associated with 127 million more people experiencing moderate or severe food insecurity compared with 1981–2010 (this is expected to rise by another 500 million by 2050). Extreme heat impacts on agriculture workers led to US$863 billion of lost income in 2022.

The biggest contributors to the climate crisis are the ultra-rich.[23] The wealthiest 1 per cent are responsible for double the emissions of the poorest 50 per cent. A billionaire emits a million times more carbon than the average person.[24]

But it is the people who contribute least to crises who will suffer most from their effects. The amount of energy used by an adult in sub-Saharan Africa per year is less than an average American fridge. Hardest hit are the world's 2.5 billion farmers, forest-dependent people, herders and fisher-people. Women bear a disproportionate burden, as they're often responsible for finding safe water and firewood, provisioning and preparing food, including child feeding. It's not just about where you live, but who you are – your race, gender, caste, ethnicity, age.

The climate crisis amplifies food and health inequalities at every level, including internationally. Countries that have historically contributed the least to the climate crisis are being hit hardest by its effects. Global-North countries represent 14 per cent of the world's population, but they emit 92 per cent of the world's carbon dioxide. They have colonised the atmosphere . . . and our future. Global-South countries, on the other hand, are most at risk from the effects. Look at the devastating floods in Pakistan in 2022 – this is a country that contributes less than 1 per cent of greenhouse emissions yet is ranked as the eighth most vulnerable in terms of climate change.

Nil desperandum!

All of this seems overwhelming. In the face of the climate–food nexus, it's so easy to become defeatist. But these impacts and their high costs also reflect the potential pay-off of turning things around. The net benefits of achieving a food system transformation are up to an astonishing US$10 trillion a year (8 per cent of global GDP in 2020). Combined with transitions to low-emission energy, a food system transformation could keep global heating below 1.5°C at the end of this century and meet the 2015 Paris Agreement climate commitment.

10

Pandemic

January 1989, Rome

By the mid-Eighties, HIV/AIDS was accelerating in many countries in Africa. The World Health Organization had sole responsibility, but AIDS was now cutting across boundaries between agency mandates on which the entire UN system had been built, and affecting a lot more than people's health and survival. By the end of the decade, the pandemic looked capable of threatening whole societies and economies.

The UN was not set up to deal with new, cross-cutting problems that didn't fit neatly into sectoral boxes. Malnutrition is one such problem, AIDS is another. And when the two combine, things get really complicated.

In 1989, I spent several months with the UN Food and Agriculture Organization (FAO), trying to get a handle on the implications of the pandemic for food security in Africa. The most productive members of the household – young adults – were most vulnerable to HIV exposure. If they became infected, there was a lag phase of a few years before AIDS (the disease) developed. During this time the young man or woman would get sicker and sicker, and then die. AIDS was incurable and a diagnosis was a death sentence.

We were trying to predict the loss of life due to AIDS and how this would affect different farming systems. We wanted to see if it was possible to predict which system might collapse, which could adapt. No one had done this work before, so we were making it up as we went along. First, we used the WHO's projection model of the spread of HIV to predict the proportion of households losing a productive individual over the next ten years in Rwanda. Then we mapped an individual's chances of dying from AIDS onto the intensity and timing of their labour input into each farming system. Finally, we ranked the main farming systems with regard to their sensitivity to the loss of labour caused by sickness or death from AIDS. Some systems required more labour at certain peak times of the year. Systems that had little slack built in were more at risk of collapse. If this happened, a food crisis, or even a famine, would follow. That was our hypothesis.

Our preliminary findings were so disturbing we went back to run more checks.[1] Major food crops would no longer be viable as they required too much physical work. Families would have to stop growing protein-rich legumes and switch over to less nutritious cassava and sweet potatoes. Coffee cultivation – essential for raising cash – would probably have to stop altogether. Time for fetching water and fuel would be reduced; kids would be pulled from school to help.

And then there was the environmental impact. If families could no longer farm the land, they might just quit and head into the cities, looking for work. This was a big problem for the cities, but also the rural areas. Farmland would return to bush, which could mean the return of the dreaded tsetse fly, bringing sleeping sickness with it.

Any one of these changes would increase the risk of malnutrition. All at once could precipitate famine. The more we looked, the clearer it became – everything was connected. Impacts would be felt economically, demographically, socially, environmentally. The food system was a spider's web: if you severed one link it put more strain on the others. Too much stress, too abrupt a shock, leads to collapse.

November 2001, Mangochi

Twelve years later, I was in the centre of the AIDS pandemic at a workshop in Malawi. Things were far worse than we'd predicted back in 1989. My first wake-up had happened the day before, on the long drive from Lilongwe. We were heading to Mangochi, a tin-shacked town on the inland ocean that is Lake Malawi. The Sun and Sand Resort was more used to catering for African tourists who had come to see the hippos that hung out in its grounds.

We stopped at a roadside shack for lunch. As we spilled out of the jeep I saw row after row of wooden coffins, on both sides of the road, stacked high. Self-taught carpenters had set up along arterial roads – the same roads along which the virus travelled – to meet the new demand. Making a living from death.

In the workshop I mentioned the coffin makers. 'It's bad now,' said a woman from the Ministry of Agriculture. 'When people get sick, their families know they will die, so they don't spend money on medicine for them. They would rather save up the money to give them a good funeral.'

At that time, most of our focus was on mitigating the down-stream impacts on food security – helping people respond *after* HIV had come into a household or community. Historically, African communities had evolved to deal with famine, with a series of sequential steps to dampen down its effects and to survive. But that had all been before AIDS. Now, there was a risk that these survival strategies would collapse as the virus was selectively targeting their foundations. The ability of young adults to migrate and to work was a key part of survival in the past when famines would hit the most vulnerable – the youngest and oldest. But AIDS was decimating the most active group: the twenty to forty-year-olds.* Speculation was rife that the co-existence of drought with a raging pandemic could lead to a 'new variant famine.'[2]

In the project we were running – RENEWAL – we came to realise we needed to work upstream. We needed to get involved in the *prevention* of HIV transmission, not just deal with its downstream consequences. It was a hard sell. Prevention was considered the preserve of behavioural scientists, not food-security folk like us. We scrabbled together some funds, commissioned anthropologists and social scientists in Malawi and Uganda, and scoped other research.

The movement of people was key. Towns closer to big highways and to trading posts were hit hardest by AIDS because these were places where people and goods converged. Sex workers were part of a service market. Although they created rules to ensure their economic and physical survival, this didn't apply to *transactional sex*, whereby desperate young women (including schoolgirls) sold their bodies to raise cash for food and/or medicine to treat sick men in their household. The terrible irony was that many of these sick men had become infected from transactional sex themselves.

The more we looked, the more we uncovered vicious cycles like this.[3] Classic prevention that revolved around education was

---

* Demographers refer to population age pyramids, with a handful of very old people at the top of the pyramid and many more in the youngest age group, at the base of the pyramid. After a decade of the AIDS pandemic, many countries had lost their pyramids. Instead, they had something that looked more like a rotting apple core, as so many young adults in the middle had died.

pointless if these factors were not addressed. The struggle to feed the family was generating huge risks, so of course we needed to be involved in prevention. Food and nutrition were a lot more important than we'd ever imagined.

Through the 2000s, the AIDS pandemic continued to accelerate. Since the first case was reported in 1981, more than 28 million people had died by 2005. In that year alone, AIDS killed nearly 3 million people, and another 4 million became infected. There were 39 million people living with the virus, including 25 million in sub-Saharan Africa, where in some countries one in three adults were infected. The *annual* death toll in Africa alone in the mid-2000s was similar to the *total* global death toll for two years (2020–2021) during the COVID pandemic.

Then things started to turn around, driven by two big advances.

First, a triple cocktail of antiretroviral drugs proved successful in helping people live with HIV indefinitely. From being a death sentence, HIV infection was becoming manageable, like a chronic disease. Second, the price of these drugs plummeted, due largely to the work of an extraordinary movement of activists that had confronted and shamed Big Pharma into slashing the obscene profits they were making.

We were pretty sure that nutrition would remain important for people on these drugs. Nutrition professionals had known for decades about something called the 'malnutrition-infection complex' – that is, any infection is worse if you're malnourished, and infectious disease itself can lead to malnutrition. In 1968, the term 'NAIDS' – Nutritionally Acquired Immune Deficiency Syndrome – had been coined to describe this, thirteen years before AIDS came on the scene.

It was time for us to switch gears.

After four years applying an HIV lens to food policy, we pivoted to applying a food lens to HIV policies and programmes. With Alan Whiteside's group in South Africa, we worked on the links between HIV/AIDS, poverty and vulnerability. Peter Piot, Executive Director of UNAIDS at the time, was also keen to dig into this. As the impacts of the epidemic grew, so did his remit – he'd been called upon to design social safety nets in hard-hit areas.

We showed that, if you are a person living with HIV and you're poor, it will be harder for you to get on a drug regime and stay on it, it will be harder for you to get treatment for co-infections like pneumonia, toxoplasmosis or tuberculosis, which (if you are malnourished) will be more severe, and it will be harder for you to ensure any medical treatment is complemented by a diverse, healthy and reliable diet.

At the household level, poverty will worsen the impacts of other livelihood stresses and shocks, and close down options for responding. At the end of the line, women and children will be hit hardest. We went on to suggest options for safety nets ('social protection') to help families weather the storm.[4]

In 1895, Louis Pasteur said, 'The microbe is nothing, the terrain everything.' When we looked into nutrition as a complement to antiretroviral therapy, we could see that he'd been on to something. The environment was key. We started to see his 'terrain' at many levels. The first level was the nutritional status of the human body itself. Here we asked: How healthy is the individual? Are they well nourished, or not? Beyond the body, we moved up to the household, community, district, country. At each level there are conditions for the spread of disease, or its prevention.

Putting all this together, we could see how important food and nutrition were for every single stage of the HIV timeline, and for every type of intervention.

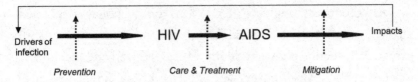

Figure 10.1. HIV timeline with core response strategies.[5]

From left to right, Figure 10.1 shows that:

- Food is vital to *prevent* families putting themselves at risk to access it (sex-for-food was an extreme, but not uncommon, example).
- A healthy diet and a well-nourished body are crucial for *care and treatment*. If you're malnourished when you start treatment, the drugs won't work well, the side effects will be far worse . . . which means you're more likely to stop taking them.
- And finally, on the right side, food or cash transfers to families can help *mitigate* the impacts of AIDS, by providing them with a safety net. In Kenya, we worked with AMPATH (Academic Model Providing Access to Healthcare) – a programme that linked nutritional support with antiretroviral therapy. People living with HIV enrolled in a comprehensive treatment programme that included food, school fees and small business initiatives. It was a big success: participants reclaimed their bodies, their health and their livelihood.*[6]

---

* In 2023, *The Lancet* published 'Food: The tuberculosis vaccine we already have', a paper by Pranay Sinha and Saurabh Mehta (19 Aug 2023, Vol. 402, No. 10402, pp. 588–90) in which they remind us that malnutrition was (and still is) the leading risk factor for TB. Between 1900 and 1944, the death rate from TB dropped by a factor of 4: from 200 per 100,000 to 50. There was no vaccine then. The improvement was due to better living conditions and better diet. The paper reported on the results of a cluster randomised trial in India that highlighted the extraordinary power of nutrition. Simply providing nutritional support to

Food and nutrition was, at last, on the global agenda. The landmark 2006 UN Political Declaration on HIV/AIDS, citing RENEWAL and other work, committed all UN member states:

> to integrate food and nutritional support . . . with the goal that all people at all times, will have access to sufficient, safe, and nutritious food to meet their dietary needs and food preferences for an active and healthy life, as part of a comprehensive response to HIV/AIDS.

January 2020, London

Newsflashes and tweets appeared about a strange new viral outbreak in Wuhan, China. For years we had been told a global pandemic was on the horizon. Not if, but when. But then again, we'd had avian flu, swine flu, MERS, SARS – none of which had crashed the world. Few people paid attention. Months later, some even believed it was completely unforeseen, a 'black swan event' that had come out of nowhere.

Déjà vu. I called up Alan Whiteside. Could earlier lessons from AIDS be applied to the COVID response? AIDS had been like a massive subsidence of land, where things changed slowly but relentlessly. COVID, on the other hand, was an earthquake that had upturned everything very quickly.

With AIDS, we had learned about *upstream* risks: how poverty and hunger exposed people to HIV (including via sex-for-food), how undernutrition weakened the immune system, and how AIDS then led to a whole raft of *downstream* impacts on households and communities.

We saw the same happening with COVID.[7]

---

people with TB could reduce incident tuberculosis by 40 per cent over two years – a huge impact.

On the *upstream*, people who were poor were more likely to be in fragile jobs which could not be done from home or outsourced to Zoom. They couldn't afford to take time off work if they felt sick – if they didn't work, they didn't get paid. The poor were more likely to live in overcrowded contexts and they were more likely to be sedentary and exposed to air pollution that damaged their lungs. All this meant they were at higher risk (than the non-poor) of being exposed and infected by the virus in the first place.

On the *downstream* (post-infection) side, people who were poor were more likely to be malnourished, which meant they were more likely to have severe COVID symptoms, more likely to require hospitalisation, more likely to die.

But this time, it was a different form of malnutrition – obesity – that was raising the risk, according to early NHS intensive-care data. If you were poor, you were more likely to have a diet dominated by junk food, which meant you were:

- more likely to be living with obesity,
- more likely to have an immune system weakened by inflammation,
- more likely to have heart and lung disease,
- less likely to be physically active, and
- less likely to have access to affordable treatment and care.

All of which would put you at a far greater risk of dying from COVID.

Crime and malnourishment

The COVID pandemic was a sudden-onset crisis. Climate change is a slow-burn, albeit linked to shocks like floods and droughts. The single largest cause of illness and death – malnutrition – is also slow-burn. A slow, quiet violence that is unremitting and yet, to many, invisible.[8]

In disasters, we tend to be resilient, resourceful, generous, empathic and brave. Rutger Bregman wrote about this so well in *Humankind: A Hopeful History*.[9] We have the capacity and track record to respond collectively to major sudden-onset crises – the Blitz spirit.

Slow-burn problems – like climate change and malnutrition – however, are the hardest ones for humanity to solve. The drip, drip of attritional damage they cause fails to generate urgency within the public. There's no big explosive cinematic scene to catch our attention.

If you drop a frog into boiling water, it hops straight out. If you drop it into tepid water and heat it to boiling, it will not react until it's too late (not true apparently, but the fable lives on). The COVID pandemic was a sudden shock – the frog jumped out. In contrast, climate and malnutrition crises proceed gradually, month by month. They kill many, many more people than COVID, but they don't instil a sense of urgency. A violence that doesn't look violent. Look at the terminology – the notion of climate '*change*' is a little like referring to an earthquake as a 'land movement'.

The UN Special Rapporteur on the Right to Food, Michael Fakhri, distinguishes four forms of violence that beset our food system:

1. Bodily harm involving the denial of access to food.
2. Discrimination, inequality and social exclusion.
3. Ecological violence including biodiversity loss, water and plastic pollution, greenhouse-gas emissions.
4. Erasure in which ancestral farmland and herding, fishing, foraging conditions are destroyed and food sovereignty violated.[10]

Climate and malnutrition crises are entwined with viral pandemics like COVID and AIDS. The cascade thrives on inequality. Epidemics, like AIDS and COVID, move along the fault lines of society, clustering in places of deprivation and injustice. Not only do they expose inequalities, they *amplify* them. That's why people of colour in the UK were so badly hit by COVID in 2020.

Like AIDS before it, COVID has become a disease that's managed in richer countries, with vaccines and medicines, but continues to disrupt life in poorer countries.[11] Pandemics show that inequality is made by humans. As current UNAIDS Executive Director, Winnie Byanyima, put it: 'Inequalities are a policy choice. They are choices our governments make.'

11

Shackled

Inequalities are growing across the world. We're living at an unusual time in history when extreme wealth and extreme poverty are both increasing. The richest 1 per cent of the world's population have grabbed two-thirds of all new wealth (US$42 trillion) created since 2020 – twice as much as the bottom 99 per cent.[1] In 2022, ninety-five food and energy corporations more than doubled their profits (making US$306 billion and paying out US$257 billion – 84 per cent – of that to shareholders).

In the 1980s, a typical CEO was paid 20 times more than the average worker. By 2016, he or she (usually he) was paid 129 times more. In 2019, the CEO of Taco Bell, Mark King, was paid close to US$4 million in salaries and bonuses – around US$2,000 per hour – whereas a shop-floor worker earned US$14 per hour.[2] We speak of the cost-of-living crunch but we could equally speak of this as a 'cost-of-profit' crisis. Fifty years of neoliberalism, during which time the growth in asset wealth has far outstripped rises in salaries and wages, have generated vast inequalities within and across countries.

Fault lines

Food systems not only encompass inequalities, they generate them, performing poorly on social justice and human rights. The agrifood industry has the world's highest prevalence of forced and child labour.[3]

Upstream, there's unequal access to the means to grow or acquire food – land, water, seed – and to adequate working conditions, pay and terms of trade. Downstream, food environments, as we've just seen, are highly unequal. Globally and locally, the field of play is not remotely level . . . it's tilting precipitously. People's physical and economic access to healthy food, their limited ability to control exposure to advertising and promotion of harmful foods are manifestations of this inequality.

Even in countries where malnutrition has been reduced, progress in the aggregate masks uneven benefits across social groups within the country. A lot of the discourse around setting the 2015 Sustainable Development Goals was on ensuring that 'no one is left behind'. Sounds like progress, but it implies everyone's on the same path, running the same race. This is not true. People are not 'left behind' as if they're lost property, or they're dragging their feet on the road to prosperity. They are actively held back, blocked from realising their agency by structural forces that have generated injustice and exclusion for centuries. Unpowered. Shackled. Inequalities between people are manufactured, intended. This is not passive neglect.

The fault lines that divide people are captured in the PROGRESS+ mnemonic: Place, Race, Occupation, Gender, Religion, Education, Socioeconomic status, Social capital + personal characteristics (age, disability, sexual orientation, etc.). Inequalities intersect across all these axes and their effects compound each other.

It's important to remember that inequality and inequity are linked but different concepts. Inequities are the upstream structural drivers of inequalities. Inequities in power and access cause inequalities in outcomes. If we want to tackle inequalities (in food security, nutritional or health status), we have to get to the roots of inequity. There are three: social injustice, distributional unfairness, and social and political exclusion. To turn these into the positive, we need to pursue 'fair play, fair share and fair say'.

Undocumented

A large swathe of southern Spain is under wraps. Visible from space, the world's largest concentration of greenhouses, covering 32,000 hectares (20 per cent larger than Birmingham), produces 3.5 billion kilos of fruit and veg per year (cucumbers, tomatoes, watermelons, courgettes, etc.).

Almeria's plastic sea is the workplace of a displaced army of undocumented migrant workers who toil away without protection, in 40°C of heat and extreme humidity, surrounded by pesticide-coated crops. Over 120,000 men and women live, work and die here. Most of them come from West Africa, mainly Ghana and Senegal. Every day, a boat brings 30–40 new workers – over 12,000 every year. Others come from within Europe if their host countries crack down on migrants.

Workers sleep in crowded camps, often without electricity and basic sanitation. They may only work a couple of days a week – for just 35 euros per day – but have to stick around for the next opportunity. The work is hazardous. One in three workers suffer from symptoms of pesticide exposure (neurologic disorders, headaches, paraesthesia, tremors), and many suffer from depression. If they can no longer work, they remain trapped in the settlements with nowhere else to go.

And then there's the environmental cost. The greenhouses encroach on protected areas and threaten the region's high biodiversity. In El Ejido, flamingos still visit protected wetlands just metres from the greenhouses. Of the water for irrigation 80 per cent comes from local aquifers which are now polluted to a depth of over 1km due to fertiliser and pesticide leaching. The greenhouses produce 34,000 tonnes of plastic waste every year, most of which is dumped illegally, blocking rivers or ingested by wildlife. A necropsy on a dead sperm whale showed it had died after ingesting 17kg of plastic, most of which was abandoned greenhouse covering.[4]

Much of the harvest ends up on supermarket shelves in the UK. Seasonal farming in the UK also relies on migrant workers who lack health and safety equipment, who live in poor, unsafe accommodation. In the post-Brexit UK, many workers were deceived when signing contracts.

Here are the costs of our cheap year-round fruit and veg that we don't see – paid by people who we don't see, who work in hothouses, way down the food chain. Out of sight, underpaid, unknown.

Ultra-poor, ultra-processed

Poverty has many dimensions – income, energy, food, time, information – all of which intersect and amplify each other. In 2019, the London Child Obesity Task Force published a set of deep-dive case studies of four children from low-income families that highlighted this well. In 2022, UNICEF replicated this approach with three children: Nosipho (age five) from an informal settlement outside Cape Town, South Africa; Meriem (age eleven) from a middle-class neighbourhood in Greater Tunis, Tunisia; and Jon (age seventeen) from a rural municipality in Zamboanga del Norte province in the Philippines.[5] In 2023, similar case studies were done in Sweden.

Reading these stories, I was struck by the common, overlapping challenges. Low-income families across the world all have an extremely hard time accessing healthy foods. There aren't many stores where they're available, and most families cannot afford the time or money for transport to go further afield. Unable to afford bulk purchases, they buy small unit-size food items or just snacks, which are more expensive. Parents work very long hours, for minimal pay, often on zero-hour contracts. They have little time to prepare meals. They're exhausted, often depressed. Kids are looked after by grandparents or older siblings. Living conditions are cramped with few amenities for meal prep and cooking, unreliable and expensive water and electricity. There may not even be a table or enough chairs.

So much easier to throw a plastic ready-meal into a microwave or give the kids spare cash for a burger and Coke at McDonald's or Burger King. The ultra-poor live on ultra-processed foods which make them ill and poorer and thus . . . more dependent on cheap ultra-processed foods.

Companies capitalise on all this – exposure to unhealthy ads on the streets, internet, social media, TV is wraparound. Social norms and parents' own relationship with food and drink reinforce the default to junk.

Other drivers of poor health interact with, and compound,

poor eating. Obesogenic environments have few accessible sports facilities, clubs or parks. They are often congested with traffic gridlock, pollution, noise; high-rise buildings with few functioning lifts; neighbourhoods that are poorly lit and not safe. Stressful places to live – and we've seen what stress can do.

Food apartheid

More than 370 million self-identified Indigenous and tribal peoples live in some ninety countries, representing as many as 5,000 diverse cultures.[6] Only 5 per cent of the world's population, they account for 15 per cent of the global poor.

Across the world, there are big differences between ethnic groups in food, nutrition and health outcomes. In Guatemala, two-thirds of Indigenous children under five are stunted compared to one-third of non-Indigenous children.[7] Indigenous peoples are twice as likely to experience obesity than non-Indigenous individuals in Canada, with a much higher prevalence of diabetes and cardiovascular diseases.[8] Life expectancy of Indigenous peoples is more than five years lower than the non-Indigenous population in the USA.[9]

Recognised by the World Health Organization as a social determinant of health, colonialism has disrupted the food systems of Indigenous peoples by forcing them to leave their ancestral lands for barren reservations, or by extracting rents and taxes from them to stay, or by stealing it and hiring them back to work it, at minimal wage.

In rural Australia, older Indigenous adults have a five to seven times higher risk of experiencing food insecurity compared to their non-Indigenous counterparts.[10] In Canada, First Nations, Métis and Inuit people have had to change their traditional diet and ration food.[11]

Inequalities are manifest in higher rates of obesity and under-nutrition. In the USA, the highest proportion of obesity is seen among Black and Hispanic adults who live, on average, six years less than white adults.[12] In England, the highest prevalence of overweight (71 per cent compared to the 64 per cent national average) and obesity (34 per cent compared to 26 per cent) is found among adults who identified as Black. Thirty-two per cent of Black/African/Caribbean ethnic households experience food insecurity – compared to 13 per cent among white households.[13]

Food Fighter: Karen Washington

Structural racism means that ethnic minority groups are much more likely to live in junk-food swamps and healthy-food deserts. Food justice activist Karen Washington however has a different term:

> It's food apartheid. 'Food desert' makes us think of an empty, desolate place. It sugarcoats the issue. But there is so much life and vibrancy and potential. Calling it what it is forces you to look at the root causes.[14]

When she worked as a physical therapist in the 1980s, most of her patients, predominantly people of colour, had diabetes, obesity and hypertension. Why, she thought, does no one talk of prevention? Why are the prescribed solutions always medication and surgery? On every block in her neighbourhood she saw drugstores next to fast-food outlets.

They go hand in hand ... if you do prevention, someone is going to lose money. If you give people access to really good food and a living-wage job, someone is going to lose money. As long as people are poor and as long as people are sick, there are jobs to be made. Follow the money.

Washington then moved to the Bronx, in New York, where she transformed numerous empty lots into community gardens to grow fresh, healthy food before launching a farmers' market. In 2009, she co-founded Black Urban Growers which continues to spearhead the struggle for food justice.

Patriarchy

Most workers in the food sector and most smallholder farmers are women. Women produce more food than men, yet they have far less power and agency than their male counterparts.[15] They have fewer assets, lower wages and less access to land, information, credit and public services than men.

In the Laknavaram forest, when the heat ramped up in May and bore wells ran dry, I remember seeing lines of tribal women leave at dawn to find water. This was also the time to stock up on firewood, while the forest was accessible and the wood was dry. Up to fifteen miles a day, they'd trek, half of which was done with huge bundles of timber balanced on cloth pads on their heads. I would see Koya women, legs buckling under loads that weighed more than they did. Once the monsoon came in June they'd switch to rice transplanting. By mid-July, the nursery (*naru*) beds brimmed with electric-green fledgling paddy. This was the beginning of a two-week window when every one of these saplings

– tens of thousands of them – had to be transplanted by hand into the main (*natu*) field. The *natu* army of women worked throughout the day, bent double, in scorching heat and sapping humidity.

Forty years later, I read an article in *The New York Times* about sugar-cane cutting in the neighbouring state, Maharashtra.[16] In Beed, an impoverished district that's home to 82,000 sugar-cane workers, girls and young women – some of whom have been pushed into illegal child marriages – cut cane all day in forced labour for sugar mills run by companies who supply Coca-Cola and PepsiCo. Up to one in three of them have had hysterectomies in order to keep working to pay off advances made by their employers (if they can't work, they have to pay a fee). PepsiCo said the investigative report was 'deeply concerning' and they would launch an inquiry. Coca-Cola declined to comment.

As well as being the main farmers in the world, women are the main home workers and caregivers, provisioning and preparing food, but the first to skip meals when times are bad. In South Asia men consume more nutrient-rich, animal-source foods than women.[17] Although women need about 25 per cent less energy per day than men, they require the same amount of nutrients, which means they need to eat more nutritious foods than men to fulfil their needs. They need more iron but rarely get enough, which is why anaemia rates are so much higher among women than men.

Women are responsible for conservation of the land to protect against biodiversity loss, when men migrate to find work in cities. Women are usually more knowledgeable about traditional crop varieties and practices that can improve health and environmental outcomes. They disproportionately bear the effects of shocks and crises including climate change, disease outbreaks, droughts.

During the AIDS epidemic, in southern Africa in the 2000s, despite chronic hunger, illness and death from the virus, the hypothesised 'new variant famine' did not actually happen. The main reason for this lay in the extraordinary resilience of millions of women. *The New York Times*, excited by the dramatic hypothesis, was less interested in the actual outcome.

Overexposed

Disease causes inflammation which is the body's way of mobilising resources to heal injured tissue. In a balanced system, once the damage has been repaired, inflammation subsides. But if the damage returns over and over again, the inflammatory response goes into overdrive and starts to create damage itself. In their book, *Inflamed*, Rupa Marya and Raj Patel use the concept of an 'exposome' – the sum of a lifetime's exposure to structural drivers of ill-health – to show why some people are more prone to chronic inflammation and illness than others.[18]

The ultimate source of damage is not the pathogen that infects you. The root cause can only be found in deeper systems that make you more likely to be exposed (to the pathogen) and, if exposed, more likely to fall sick or die as a result. It's Pasteur's terrain again. Structural racism, patriarchy, violence, economic deprivation, pollution, contaminated water and poor diet all combine to generate chronic inflammation in an attritional cycle of human erosion.

The tyranny of merit

Six decades ago, Martin Luther King Jr. said: 'It is obvious that if a man is entering the starting line in a race 300 years after another man, the first would have to perform some impossible feat in order to catch up with his fellow runner.'

Treating people with different needs in the same way is not

fair. Equality is not equity. We would not give wheat bread to someone with coeliac disease. Even if everyone has the same opportunity to apply for a job, it's not a fair competition if they cannot avail themselves of the opportunity. Some applicants might have had their brain development stunted by childhood malnutrition, or been forced, by poverty, to leave school early.

Equality of opportunity means nothing unless and until every member of society has the minimum necessary capabilities *to make use of the opportunity*; for example, guaranteed minimum income, access to food, education, health care.

In *The Tyranny of Merit*, philosopher Michael Sandel challenges the meritocratic ethic in which you control your destiny by working hard.[19] Encouraging people to think of themselves as free agents – responsible for their fate, not as victims of forces beyond their control – sounds empowering. But it has a dark side. The more we view ourselves as self-made, the less likely we are to take care of those who are less fortunate than ourselves. Meritocracy and community don't go well together. We have already seen how myopic and unfair the notion of individual responsibility is in the context of obesogenic food environments.

Under conditions of rampant inequality, reiterating the message that we are responsible for our fate and deserve what we get, erodes solidarity and demoralises and stigmatises those who are shackled. And yet, political rhetoric and public attitudes continue to adhere to the notion that economic rewards align with merit, that we get what we deserve.

When it comes to food, nutrition and health, the relevant equality is the equality of outcome of an individual's *parents* – the generation before – achieved through income redistribution, guarantee of access to quality basic services and regulation of markets. So long as there are entrenched structural inequalities, unchanged over generations, 'levelling-up' remains a hollow promise peddled by politicians who have no intention of changing the status quo.

12

Food Barons, Russian Dolls and Trojan Horses

In most segments of the agrifood system today, just a handful of corporate players dominate markets. They operate at all levels (local, national, regional, global) and have tremendous economic power – more than many national governments.[1] This imbalance in power threatens the governance of food systems which, in turn, jeopardises their purpose. A system that was intended to support and sustain a healthy population becomes one that prioritises profit for a few monster companies who span the globe. The more that power is concentrated in Big Food, the less likely we are to have a diverse supply of affordable, accessible, healthy foods.

Never before have we seen such a hyper-concentration of power, at all points from farm to fork. The global food system is following the same path as the global finance system at the turn of the century, and we all remember how that story ended. Companies have become gargantuan and their links more rigid.[2]

Upstream, two-thirds of all the agricultural land in the world is controlled by 1 per cent of its farmers. Five companies – ADM, Bunge, Cargill, Cofco and Louis Dreyfus – control 70–90 per cent of the global grain trade.[3] A quarter of a century ago, a Cargill brochure included the brag: 'We are the flour in your bread, the wheat in your noodles, the salt on your fries . . . the corn in your tortillas, the chocolate in your dessert, the sweetener in your soft drink . . . the oil in your salad dressing and the beef, pork or chicken you eat for dinner.'[4]

Another four companies – ChemChina, Corteva, Bayer and BASF – control 66 per cent of the world's agricultural chemicals market, while a similar cluster (with BASF replaced by LimaGrain) owns 53 per cent of the global seed market.[5]

On the downstream side, three-quarters of global food retail is controlled by five companies (Nestlé, Coca-Cola, PepsiCo, General Mills, Unilever), with combined annual profits of over US$100 billion. These behemoths *each* have revenues larger than half the countries in the world.[6] In the thirty years between 1989 and 2019, UPF manufacturers doubled their sales to US$1.1 trillion, driven by rocketing growth in low and middle-income countries.[7] That's US$3 billion *per day*.

A recent study of US-listed food and agricultural corporations found that UPF manufacturers and food services (including fast-food outlets) distributed 50 per cent and 13 per cent respectively of all shareholder capital (US$2.9 trillion) in the six decades between 1962 and 2021.[8] Fake foods, cornered markets, big profits.

Look at Nestlé. With over 2,000 brands, its annual sales are over US$100 billion – similar to the gross national products of Sri Lanka or Kenya. The infant formula marketing industry alone is worth US$55 billion.[9] Some supermarkets are now bigger than countries: Walmart, which feeds one in five American shoppers, is the tenth largest economic entity in the world with higher revenues than the governments of Australia or Spain.[10] In 2017, Global Justice Now found that 69 of the world's top 100 economic entities are corporations.

Giant corporations are like Russian nesting dolls. Mondelēz owns Cadbury, Oreo, Milka, Bournvita and other companies. Each one of these in turn contains multiple brands. Nestlé owns

Cheerios, Maggi, Milo, Nescafé, Perrier and KitKat. There are over 300 versions of the sugar-packed chocolate bar now, and Nestlé recently released KitKat Cereal, so you can start the morning with them. In the UK, the top five supermarkets (Tesco, Sainsbury's, Asda, Aldi, Morrisons) hold 75 per cent retail market share; the top ten, 95 per cent.[11]

Big Food corporations may be voracious consumers of smaller companies, but they themselves are being bought. Hedge-fund and asset-management monoliths, like BlackRock and Vanguard, are buying up large slices of these food companies and using their power to keep the focus on short-term profit, regardless of the costs to people and planet.*[12] 'Shareholder primacy' is all they are interested in. Windfall profits are followed by share buybacks (when a corporations buys back its own shares), so that profits are transferred to shareholders, rather than being invested in something useful, like research into ways to improve equitable access to nutritious foods.[13] The food system has become financialised.[14]

Corporate capture is dangerous for people and planet. We have a right to food, but we really only have a legally enforceable right to consume what we can grow or buy, and we can only buy what we can afford out of what's available and accessible to us (as we saw in Chapter 8). Commercial forces limit our freedom of choice a lot more than we think.

---

* The combined share ownership of BlackRock, Vanguard and State Street amounts to one-fifth of all existing shares in Yum! Brands (which owns KFC, Taco Bell, Pizza Hut, among other companies), McDonald's, Mondelēz and Coca-Cola. A fascinating recent analysis has revealed how four asset management firms (BlackRock, Vanguard, State Street and Capital Group) voted overwhelmingly against public health and other ESG-related (environment, social, governance) proposals between 2012 and 2022, while supporting proposals to increase shareholder payouts, political donations and lobbying expenditure (Wood et al. 2023, see note 12).

Half of all the calories we consume come from rice, wheat and maize. Just three crops out of a total of 6,000 plant species that humans have eaten over time. Another quarter comes from potato, barley, palm oil, soy and sugar.[15]

Diets have become homogenised and less diverse across the globe. A Big Mac can be bought anywhere now. The Global Standard Diet creates the Global Standard Farm which drives the Global Standard Diet – one more positive feedback loop for Big Food, one more vicious cycle for the rest of us.[16]

In its May 2023 report *Who's Tipping the Scales?* the International Panel of Experts on Sustainable Food Systems linked the growing influence of the Big Food cartel to poor enforcement of antitrust policies and technological changes, which have enabled rival companies to be swallowed up.[17] The expansion and entrenchment of power, accelerated by recent mega-mergers (including Kraft and Heinz in 2015 combining thirteen brands valued at more than US$500 million each), has nothing to do with public health. It's an oligopolistic power grab designed to ramp up profits by stifling competition. Most mergers and acquisitions in the food system this century have occurred between UPF manufacturers.[18]

Increasing the 'share of stomach' that's colonised by a corporation increases the market power it holds. The bigger the company, the more it can spend on research and development (R&D), a lot of which is 'defensive R&D' aimed at locking the system in its status quo and preventing innovation from other companies reaching the market – a kind of 'anti-innovation'. This means a race to the bottom to develop ever more profitable and inevitably ultra-processed foods, so the company can spend more on advertising. Nestlé spent around US$18.5 billion on marketing in 2022, more than the health budgets of most low- and middle-income countries, and *five* times the operating budget of the World Health Organization.[19, 20]

Power lines

Power is multipurpose and tradable. The bigger the company, the greater its ability to exploit the benefits of globalisation, trade liberalisation and digitalisation, the more clout it has in patent protection, the higher the licensing fees it can charge in intellectual property rights negotiations, the lower the prices it needs to pay its suppliers and the higher the prices it can charge to consumers. Average global mark-ups – the prices companies charge for goods over what it costs to produce them – virtually tripled from 21 per cent (above costs) in 1980 to 61 per cent in 2019.[21] The extra 40 per cent that you now pay is effectively a private tax levied by Big Food. This is what 'greedflation' looks like.[22]

To understand how our food systems have become so inequitable, we need to unpack power. Power exists in many forms and is used for many purposes to gain and lock in advantage. The types of power held by individuals and organisations and its balance within the food system determines who wins and who loses.

Unlike health and wealth, power is relational. If I have more power in any negotiation with you, then you have less. In food systems, if power is concentrated in one group of organisations (transnational corporations) then there's less in others (everyone else, including governments).

Power is also a shapeshifter, with several variants:

- Instrumental power of an actor (individual or organisation) over (or with) other actors, including Government, industry, civil society, local communities. This is the ability to make or influence decisions and actions.
- Structural power of societal systems (like neoliberalism) and institutions (e.g. national governments, food industry.) This

shapes the environments in which people interact – the 'choice architecture'.[23]

- Discursive or epistemic power: the power of ideas and stories that shapes norms and values and thus influence processes and opinions.*

In the arena of food systems, we can start to see how power operates. All three forms – structural, instrumental and discursive power – are used at different times, and all three interact. The ultra-processed food industry uses its economic and financial power to leverage political power in order to extend its financial power in an inexorable cycle of profit maximisation. The arena for these games is Planet Earth – anywhere and everywhere – but especially in under-regulated markets in the Global South.

The bigger that Big Food becomes, the harder it is for governments to regulate it. But it's not just passive resistance. The ultra-processed food industry actively seeks to influence public health, food and nutrition policy through a wide palette of tricks and tactics, as we'll see shortly. 'Influence' is the polite word, but it's really interference through infiltration.

Power is key for accountability. We need to understand who holds the power to make a difference and who is holding them to account for their actions or inaction. The three main actors (governments, food companies and civil society) all have roles to play, as do media, investors and international organisations. Industry holds commercial and financial power, some of which it seeks to translate into political power (Chapter 13).

---

* And these different types of power have differing degrees of visibility. Some are visible (in public spaces or formal arenas: e.g. parliaments, civil society meetings), some are hidden (behind-the-scenes power: lobbyists, old-boys networks) and some are invisible (ideologies, norms, beliefs, values).

Governments hold political power, which should trump all others, but the problem is they seldom use it to improve food systems (Chapter 14).

Behind the big tent

The private sector encompasses organisations that engage in profit-seeking activities and have a majority private ownership. As well as transnational companies, there are smaller enterprises, co-operatives, individual entrepreneurs, market vendors and small-holder farmers, who operate in both formal and informal sectors.

'Private sector' is not a helpful term for us here: it's way too broad. We need to distinguish small- and medium-sized enter-prises that could collaborate in the social change process from the giants that derive their power from peddling junk food.

One way governance has become jeopardised is through the development of public–private partnerships – between a cor-poration or business association and a Government or other public sector body. Many are riddled with conflicts of interest, which arise when there is an incompatibility between a private interest and a public duty, when one's professional judgement may be unduly influenced by a personal interest, such as financial gain. For-profit corporations have a conflict of interest when they engage in public governance.

'Multistakeholderism' is the latest vogue, a form of public–private partnership popularised by the World Economic Forum (as showcased in its Davos jamborees), in which the door is flung wide open for *any* organisation to participate. The 'big tent' sounds democratic but it's really an illusion, a mirage, one more step towards the privatisation of global governance. The confla-tion of interests or 'stakes' with rights and duties is deliberate. Multistakeholderism is a passport to corporate capture, a 'blue-washing' as predatory companies get to hang out with the UN.

Prominent public–private partnerships – like the Scaling up
Nutrition (SUN) Movement, the Global Alliance for Improved
Nutrition (GAIN), the Alliance for a Green Revolution in Africa
(AGRA) – open up inside tracks for corporations to access deci-
sion-making processes.

The UN Food
Systems Summit (UNFSS)

In 2021 the UNFSS emerged from a strategic partnership
between the United Nations and the World Economic
Forum. From the start it was structured as a giant multi-
stakeholder initiative, led by the director of AGRA. The
goal was nothing less than the *transformation* of the global
food system.

From the outset, the summit was attacked as being
co-opted by big business. The UN was the nominal host,
but it wasn't running the show. So much about the summit
was shady: no one knew how workstream leaders were
chosen, or how they operated. Major conflicts of interest
and power asymmetries were simply ignored and human
rights, the very basis of the foundational UN Charter, were
nowhere to be seen.

And then, as criticism grew, overnight the conference
morphed into 'The People's Summit' with the mantra
'Everyone is welcome at the table' repeated in every update.
The big tent was back. Power hadn't changed a bit and
decision-making was still a one-way street.

In response, three UN human rights commissioners
asked: 'What if the table is already set, the seating plan

non-negotiable, the menu highly limited? What is *on* the table is as important as who is around it.'[24] Many non-governmental and Indigenous peoples' organisations boycotted the summit. La Via Campesina organised a countermobilisation.

The Private Sector Guiding Group of the summit was led by the World Business Council for Sustainable Development (WBCSD), a business association whose members included tobacco giant Philip Morris and many Big Food multi-nationals. Two of the latter, Nestlé and PepsiCo, were invited to speak at several sessions. For them, it wasn't about what they said – it was the simple fact they were there, at the global policy table. Summit leaders adopted the standard industry approach of meeting criticism and questions with silence or aggressive *ad hominem* attacks. If you questioned why PepsiCo and Nestlé had been included as speakers, as I did, you were blocked on social media by summit leaders.

One cliché kicked around to justify this corporate infil-tration was, 'the private sector may be part of the problem, but it can also be part of the solution'. Whenever anyone raised legitimate questions about conflicts of interest, the response would be: 'Oh, we'll be asking very tough questions, urging them to improve, don't worry'. It was a charade. The idea that food companies somehow did not actually *know* what to do to reduce the harm of their products and they needed to sit down with a bunch of nutritionists in a policy-making forum to gain this knowledge, was a joke.

I hadn't seen anything like it since I'd joined the UN in 1989. The UN, the world's premier international deci-sion-making body, which derives its legitimacy from governments across the world, was providing the ultimate high-level platform to malnutrition-generating companies where the shape of future food systems was being discussed, and where big policy decisions with long-term consequences were to be made. The fox was having a great time hanging out in the henhouse . . . this time with room service (another analogy used was of Dracula being invited to run the community blood bank).

Similar things were happening at the annual UN COP climate conferences that were rammed with greenwashing fossil-fuel reps. As Greta Thunberg put it at COP27: 'If you want to address malaria, don't invite the mosquitoes.'

The elephant skulking quietly in the corner at most multistakeholder events is *power*. The most powerful are always there, in some shape or form, and the last thing they will talk about is power. That was why the UNFSS was blind to it and why it blocked discussions of it. If the UN had been true to its founding principles and focused on human rights – the right to adequate food, health and nutrition – the summit would have focused on power imbalances and food injustice. This is what should be on the table in any discussion of future food systems. Otherwise, transformation is just a word, a hollow promise.

13

The Dark Arts

*Doubt is our product since it is the best means of competing
with the 'body of fact' that exists in the mind of the general
public. It is also the means of establishing a controversy.*

British American Tobacco, 1969

In December 1953, the CEOs of the top five tobacco companies
came together at the Plaza Hotel in New York City. They couldn't
stand each other, but something had to be done in the face of
mounting evidence of the damage caused by smoking. They'd also
invited the president of the leading US public relations firm, John
W. Hill.

After much discussion, a consensus emerged through the blue
haze. They knew they could no longer ignore the science, so they
figured the best move now was to *secure* it. To do this, they
mapped out a strategy to identify sceptical scientists, support
their work and amplify their views. Hill formed the Tobacco
Industry Research Committee (TIRC). No one was interested
in answering research questions; the goal was to control the
science. So long as doubt and controversy prevailed, the industry
could fight off regulation and litigation. Scientific uncertainty
facilitated the attribution of risks to the smoker, not the cigarette.

Hill then realised he needed a second unit, separate from the

TIRC, to act as a trade association and lobby for Big Tobacco. Within a few years, the imaginatively titled 'Tobacco Institute' became the most powerful political lobby in Washington DC. Big Tobacco effectively invented the modern conflicts of interest that now play out across the interface between people and business in food, nutrition and public health.[1] The UPF industry has adopted and adapted the tobacco industry playbook and developed new tricks of its own.[2, 3]

In 2020, I spoke at a UNICEF–WHO seminar on industry interference in nutrition policymaking.[4] For some months, I'd been researching the array of tactics used by industry to escape regulation. Not only had Big Food figured out how to addict us to fake food and drink, it had mastered the dark arts of obstruction when confronted by anyone who stepped in its way.

Here are the top tactics I summarised – the five Deadly Ds of the Dark Arts:

1. Dispute and doubt

Like the tobacco cabal before it, Big Food seeks to change the narrative, to sow doubt and uncertainty.[5] This is done by funding research, publishing it, or suppressing findings that highlight UPF harms, as well as disseminating cherry-picked industry data to media and directly to policymakers.

Big Food disputes or casts doubt on the burgeoning evidence of the multiple harms caused by its products. Even when the evidence is overwhelming, well beyond the threshold at which public health action would normally be taken, the industry will continue to insist it's not enough, claiming 'more research is needed' and remedial action is not warranted.[6]

When cornered, Big Food denies culpability and blames the individual. This 'overeating, underexercising consumer' line – allied with the 'nanny state' attack that we'll explore later – is the playbook's go-to defence move.

In addition to the panoply of harms described earlier, many studies have challenged industry statements about its products. But the industry continues to fight back. On 5 March 2023, *The Washington Post* reported that breakfast cereal companies were challenging the Food and Drug Administration definition of a 'healthy' food, citing its First Amendment right to exercise 'corporate free speech'.* Again, the get-out-of-jail card was in play: health is about lifestyle choices around exercise, they argue, not food. Fighting their corner was the Washington Legal Foundation, the same group that challenged Government rules about another dangerous, addictive product (OxyContin) on behalf of Purdue Pharma, owned by the Sackler family.[7]

More recently, large corporations have targeted the anti-diet movement – a social media juggernaut that initially aimed to combat weight stigma. In April 2024, an investigation by *The Washington Post* and *The Examination* uncovered a systematic multipronged campaign by General Mills, who own Cocoa Puffs and Lucky Charms among other brands.[8] The company was showering product handouts on registered dietitians who promoted its cereals online (using hashtags like #DerailTheShame, #NoBadFoods, #FoodFreedom, #DitchTheDiet). An analysis of more than 6,000 social media posts by sixty-eight registered dietitians revealed that 40 per cent of these influencers (with a combined reach of more than 9 million followers), repeatedly used anti-diet language. Most of them were paid by companies

---

* In 2010, the US Supreme Court decided that corporations were persons under law which, as well as free speech rights, opened the door to unlimited corporate donations to political campaigns. Activists have since proposed a 28th Amendment to the US Constitution to establish that corporations are not *de jure* persons and do not have the political or legal rights of human beings (Freudenberg, N. *At What Cost? Modern Capitalism and the Future of Health.* Oxford University Press, 2021).

to promote their products. The Democrat senator Richard Blumenthal said: 'It's reprehensible for the food industry to prey on the vulnerabilities of people'.

Caveat lector

As well as challenging science and evidence, the industry sows division by denigrating researchers who investigate nutrition and health outcomes associated with UPF consumption. Derogatory labels (non-experts, nanny-state lovers, food fascists) are scattered about. In parallel, the industry funds biddable scientists to do pseudoscientific studies as red herrings (e.g. physical inactivity as the main driver of obesity) or write essays for glossy industry reports. I have declined thousands of dollars on two occasions to contribute to annual reports.

Conflicts of interest are a big deal for researchers in food, nutrition and health. Multiple studies and reviews have shown the unequivocal effects of corporate influence on research.[9] Published articles sponsored by the food and beverage industry are four to eight times more likely to have conclusions favourable to the financial interests of the sponsoring companies.[10]

There are several ways in which research can be skewed. Agendas can be steered away from research questions that are most relevant for public health, towards products and activities that can be commercialised. The way questions are stated, the methods chosen, the analytical frameworks employed, the way results are interpreted and reported, conclusions arrived at . . . any one of these steps might be framed in ways that support industry interests, or at least don't threaten them.

In a brilliant and amusing short article in the Christmas 2015 edition of the *British Medical Journal*, bioethics professor Daniel Goldberg laid out the 'flaccid justifications' that scientists provide to rationalise their deep relationships with industry. The 'COI

Bingo chart' includes twenty-five reasons (five rows of five squares) – everything from 'it's just a pen' to 'sponsorship is required to bring in the top experts'. My favourite is 'How dare you.'[11]

Trust has been severely eroded. Many public health nutrition researchers now start to review new journal articles at the end, where author disclosures are made. In 2018, Mélissa Mialon investigated the affiliations of authors of papers that criticised the NOVA classification of foods. She found that the authors of thirty-three of the thirty-eight papers were affiliated with the food industry. Most papers weren't even peer-reviewed. This isn't science, it's public relations.

It's not hard to find examples of industry recruitment strategy. Several years ago, Nestlé South Africa commissioned a consultancy group to map all the key players in nutrition in the country. One page showed a 2 × 2 grid with four quadrants. The vertical axis was 'Peer Credibility', the horizontal was 'Disposition to Nestlé'. Individuals who were judged to be in the bottom left quadrant (low credibility, low disposition) were ignored . . . not a threat, not worth bothering with. The target for Nestlé was to get scientists into the upper-right box (high peer credibility/high company disposition). If they were judged to be there already, the strategy was 'retain and reward'. The strategy for individuals in the other two quadrants was to increase their credibility and/or company disposition in order to shunt them into the top-right box. It was a systematic approach to winning hearts and minds using power and cash.[12]

Another approach for big name critics is 'seduce and silence'. This was tried out with Chris van Tulleken recently. In an Afterword to the 2024 paperback edition of *Ultra-Processed People* he described being offered £20,000 to give a talk by a transnational food company. He thought about it and decided he could donate the money to a charity so he asked to see the agreement. When he read it, the penny dropped. Signing it would have banned him from disparaging the company, its customers, its products or services 'throughout the universe in perpetuity'. It was the mother of all gag clauses. He turned it down.

The big issue for food and nutrition research (or any other discipline) is not the integrity of one individual researcher but whether industry funding confers a *significant and systematic* bias. The answer to this question is unequivocal – the bias is systematic and it's very large. Conflict of interest is not good for the integrity of the research community and its ability to engender trust, and it's not good for the public whose health will be affected by governmental failure to act.

It's also not something that can be 'managed'. A disclosure of a conflict (such as those at the back of journal papers) doesn't nullify it. It's still there afterwards. The best approach is to avoid them altogether.

Food Fighters: Caroline Walker and Geoffrey Cannon

In October 2023, I called Geoffrey Cannon at his home in São Paolo. I first met Geoffrey in the late 1980s at the WHO in Geneva, where he shared some eye-popping stories of corporate shenanigans. He had become disenchanted with Britain and moved to Brazil as the new millennium dawned. In São Paolo, he worked with Carlos Monteiro to develop the NOVA system. Prior to the call he sent me a bunch of press clippings from *The Times* and *Sunday Times* for whom he'd worked as a lead journalist in the early 1980s. Headlines from 1983–84 included, *The Cover Up that Kills* and *Censored – a Diet for Life or Death*.

His recall was extraordinary. This is the story that led to these headlines.

In July 1979, the new Government set up the National Advisory Committee on Nutrition Education (NACNE) to provide 'simple and accurate information on nutrition'. An expert group was convened in January 1981 to synthesise evidence and make recommendations. Chaired by Sir Philip James, it included leading Government scientists and representatives. It also included representatives of the British Nutrition Foundation (BNF), a body funded by the food industry. The first draft of the report was prepared in April 1981. Then it disappeared.

Two years later, Cannon was about to attend the BNF annual conference in London with the theme, 'Implementing Dietary Guidelines'. On the eve of the conference, he received a copy of the draft that had never seen the light of day. A friend of a friend of a friend had mailed it over to him.

Cannon was stunned by the report. Not only had it comprehensively laid out the evidence linking obesity and heart disease with the rapidly changing British diet, but it also put forward quantified targets, including the reduction of fats (by 25 per cent), sugars (by 50 per cent) and salt (by 50 per cent), with corresponding increases in fruit and vegetables. It also made a strong recommendation for the Government to step in to make it happen. This was, he realised, the first integrated, progressive statement on nutrition and public health since the Second World War.

So why, two years after it had been finalised, hadn't it been published? He was determined to find out. At the conference the next day he waited until the final session before asking why no reference had been made to the

NACNE report? And why had it never been published? The chair of the conference (the BNF Director General) looked surprised. The report was really not relevant, he blustered . . . and no, it would not be published. In Cannon's words: 'he was obviously not expecting the question . . . he was incoherent . . . the wheels were falling off'.

A young public health nutritionist, Caroline Walker (who had been the committee's secretary two years earlier), stood up to say the BNF was not fit for purpose.

The next day, Cannon went to see the chief editor of *The Sunday Times*. 'What if I were to tell you,' he said, 'that a report originally commissioned by government has concluded that the food we typically eat in Britain is a major cause of killer diseases, and that this report is being suppressed by government because of its implications?'

'You've got the lead story,' was the response.

What happened then was, in Cannon's words, 'seismic.' Hundreds of follow-up stories appeared in the summer of 1983 in the broadcast and print media. Nutrition was flavour of the month. The veil had dropped, light was coming in. The Government then published the full report on 10 October 1983. Over the next two years UK television, radio and print media carried 'hundreds, maybe thousands of stories'.

The media and the public were fascinated by the report's suppression by Government following aggressive lobbying by a food industry front group. Speculation was rife that the decision had come from the very top. Before politics, Margaret Thatcher had worked as a food chemist at the cake maker, J Lyons & Co. where she had figured out how to increase profits by aerating ice cream using emulsifiers and air. Could she have authorised the block?

Caroline Walker and Geoffrey Cannon wrote *The Food Scandal,* which became a number one bestseller in 1984 and led to a TV documentary. After Walker died in 1988, in her late thirties, the Caroline Walker Trust was set up in her memory. It continues to campaign on diet, health and equality.

More than four decades after the NACNE fiasco (see textbox), scientific academies and advisory committees are still riddled with conflicts of interest. In the USA in 2022, an investigation revealed that the US Academy of Nutrition and Dietetics (AND) was investing in the stocks of Nestlé and PepsiCo, who were also funding it – a novel, circular form of conflicted interest by an agency supposed to be working to reduce the harms caused, in large part, by its own funders.[13] AND was also investing in Abbott, a company that has often violated the 1981 International Code on the Marketing of Breast-milk Substitutes established by the World Health Organization.[14]

A US Right to Know investigation in late 2023 revealed that nine out of the twenty members of the US Dietary Guidelines Advisory Committee (DGAC) were found to have conflicts of interest with food, pharma or industry groups.[15] An additional four members had possible conflicts of interest and Abbott, Novo Nordisk, the National Dairy Council, Eli Lilly and Weight Watchers International had ties to two or more DGAC members.

In the UK in 2023, Erik Millstone and Tim Lang – food policy experts with ninety years of experience between them – investigated conflicts of interest in nine food regulatory institutions. They discovered that every committee had several members who were paid by the food industry. The most 'conflicted' was the Scientific Advisory Committee on Nutrition (SACN) with nine of fifteen members funded by the ultra-processed food industry (likely an underestimate as declarations are voluntary and several are ambiguous).

In 2023, after the publication of Chris van Tulleken's *Ultra-Processed People* and Henry Dimbleby's *Ravenous*, the industry went into face-saving overdrive. Media coverage of UPFs had never been so high. In July 2023, the SACN released a statement which concluded: 'The observed associations between higher consumption of (ultra-) processed foods and adverse health outcomes are concerning, however . . . the evidence to date needs to be treated with caution.'

In a blog, shortly afterwards, Rob Percival, Head of Food Policy at the Soil Association, questioned why the committee had not referred to the way in which UPFs have displaced recommended foods and dietary practices.[16] Three-quarters of the calories in the diets of many children are now ultra-processed. Why didn't SACN address this displacement effect?

Percival then looked into the committee members. Of the sixteen members, most receive/d funding from the ultra-processed food industry and/or are members of organisations like the British Nutrition Foundation (BNF), who are funded by the ultra-processed food industry.

The BNF had earlier stated its position on UPFs (April 2023) that: 'due to the lack of agreed definition, the need for better understanding of mechanisms involved and concern about its usefulness as a tool to identify healthier products, UPF does not warrant inclusion within policy.'

2. Distort and deceive

Let's look at the second tactic. Big Food distorts the discourse on food and nutrition via carefully cultivated media connections and powerful lobby groups. Obesity is reframed (without evidence) as being a problem of individual responsibility, poor choice and/or physical inactivity (the 'lazy, ignorant consumer' again).

In 2009, Georgia Governor Sonny Perdue proclaimed May as

'Exercise is Medicine Month . . . supported by Coca-Cola'. In 2015, Coca-Cola set up the Global Energy Balance Network that promoted the joint lies that obesity was nothing to do with sugary drinks and that exercise was all that was needed to lose weight. And in 2021, Coke funded the Latin American Nutrition and Health Study, which published results showing that inactivity was driving obesity. The authors of the paper claimed no conflict of interest.

Straw men are created to distort debates. Public health professionals are accused of being against the entire private sector, not just junk-food companies. Another ruse is to accuse critics of ultra-processed foods of being against *all* forms of food processing. This one never goes away. In another paper, industry-funded scientists stated: 'The NOVA classification system, which advocates the complete removal of all UPFs'. Distortions like this are picked up and repeated in other papers.

Language is used to obscure and deceive. Classic nutritional advice over the years has included phrases like 'eat a balanced diet as part of a healthy lifestyle'. Marketing departments will steal these words and slap them on products that could never be part of a healthy diet. 'Lifestyle' is a great marketing word as it keeps the spotlight on the consumer, not the product. Libertarian think tanks (*sic*) like the Institute for Economic Affairs have 'lifestyle economists' (without economics degrees) who relentlessly denigrate the nanny state, while 'lifestyle medicine' gurus flood social media with their nutritional advice. 'Nutritious', 'natural', 'goodness' are all words that companies are free to use, unhindered by definition or regulation.

And then there's lobbying
The International Standards for Lobbying Regulation defines lobbying as 'any direct or indirect communication with a public official that is made, managed, or directed with the purpose of

influencing public decision-making'.[17] At worst, lobbying involves a form of legal distortion in which a company (or group of companies) funds lobby groups to cherry-pick data and arguments to convince policymakers and politicians to act in the company's interests. Analysis has shown that countries with a greater degree of corporate permeation are less likely to implement evidence-based health policies endorsed by the WHO.[18]

The Food Research Collaboration of London's City University examined publicly available data on meetings held by relevant ministers, civil servants and political special advisers, between July 2020 and July 2021 – a period that encompassed the launch of the UK Government's strategy to tackle obesity.* The research found significant differences between the ambition of the policy and the reality on the ground. Interactions between corporate reps and ministers vastly outnumbered those with charities and NGOs. Businesses were able to successfully put pressure on the Government to apply only light-touch regulation by exploiting loopholes that allowed for continued advertising of high-fat/salt/sugar (HFSS) products. Or just to delay it indefinitely. The Government's originally stated goal to make healthy options the easier choice for consumers was completely undermined.

It's no surprise that the richest companies have the most skilled and most powerful lobbyists, and they spend a lot on lobbying. Analysis by the Union of Concerned Scientists shows that between 2019 and 2023, giant agribusiness companies and industry associations spent well over half a billion dollars lobbying

---

* British lobbying disclosure is woefully inadequate. The online register of meetings on the Government website only reveals interactions between businesses, charities and NGOs and the very highest levels of political power. No detail is provided on who is lobbying whom, for what purpose and with what outcome. Lobbying of lower-ranking officials (who advise their superiors) is hidden, with no public record of meetings, issues discussed or the amount of money spent.

US Congress to influence food and agriculture legislation.[19] Food policy is becoming 'pay-to-play'. Another 2024 study of lobbying in the USA used the OpenSecrets database to reveal how, between 1998 and 2020, UPF manufacturers spent US$1.15 billion on lobbying, much more than any other industry – the second highest was gambling (US$817 million), followed by tobacco (US$755 million) and alcohol (US$541 million).[20]

The financial clout of pro-industry lobbying on top of advertising spend dwarfs the budget of the World Health Organization and other agencies responsible for mopping up the damage the industry causes.

The World Health Organization itself is targeted. In 2003, the Sugar Association ('the scientific voice of the US sugar industry') lobbied the US Government to withdraw its funding to the WHO, because the organisation had the temerity to cite numerous scientific papers in its draft Global Strategy on Diet, Physical Activity and Health, which provided evidence of the links between sugar consumption and non-communicable disease.[21] The strategy had simply made the tame recommendation to restrict added sugar intake to 10 per cent of daily energy consumption and to create a safe nutrition environment for children in schools. The Sugar Association wrote to the then-US Minister of Health, Tommy Thompson, asking him to withdraw US funding to the WHO unless this recommendation was removed. He did so. A 28-page, single-spaced report was sent to the WHO in which the science of the harms of sugar was attacked, along with the standard three-pronged pushback: individuals need to take responsibility for what they eat, they need to become more physically active, and 'there's no such thing as a harmful food, only harmful diets'. Thompson's assistant was sent to Geneva to hand-deliver the report and put pressure on other countries to block the strategy.

*

On 2 January 2023, Calley Means tweeted a thread in which he described how, early in his career, he had consulted for Coca-Cola to ensure sugar taxes failed and that soda (fizzy drinks) was included in the Supplemental Nutrition Assistance Program (SNAP) for low-income households.[22]

The first step for Coca-Cola was to pay the National Association for the Advancement of Colored People (NAACP) and other civil rights groups to call opponents of the move racist. Millions of dollars were paid directly (and via front groups like the American Beverage Association) to the NAACP and the Hispanic Federation. This picked up in 2011 when the Farm Bill and new soda taxes were under consideration. It was a big success – the message was carried in thousands of articles between 2011 and 2013. Means watched as the Food and Drug Administration funnelled money to university professors and think tanks on the left and right to create studies showing soda taxes hurt the poor and drinking soda does not cause obesity.

After racial tensions flared, soda spending was kept in SNAP funding, and many of the taxes were defeated. A disaster for low-income communities which were inundated with cheap, sugary drinks, now subsidised by the Government.

The same game is played on a global scale. A chilling example occurred in 2018 when the Ecuador delegation brought forward a resolution at the World Health Assembly in Geneva to address conflicts of interest in nutrition programming. Not only did the US delegation oppose the resolution, it threatened to retract US military support to Ecuador if the delegation continued to pursue it. The most powerful delegation, swimming in conflict of interest, was blocking any move to challenge its modus operandi.

Even when the then-US President Donald Trump threatened to pull all funding from the WHO two years later, he was challenged by the US food industry. This sounds odd until you realise the motive – the industry was worried that losing its US Government friends in Geneva would reduce its ability to challenge any new health resolution that would hit its bottom line. Profit first, as ever.

Another country that actively opposes WHO dietary guidelines is Italy – a stance they like to portray as defending the Mediterranean diet, but which is really about the political power of the confectionery giant Ferrero and other junk-food manufacturers in Italy. The Italian delegation to the WHO routinely includes senior advisers to Ferrero.

Revolving door

Lobby power is fuelled by the 'revolving door' among Government, international agencies and industry. CEOs know politicians' time in power is limited, and they're happy to dangle the carrot of a huge salary on the other side . . . so long as they back off with any plans for regulation. It's all about nods and winks – you scratch my back, I'll scratch yours – between public and private sectors.

The most famous revolving door in the world of public health nutrition led to the 'coca-colonization' of Mexico, over two decades ago.[23,24] Ex-President Vicente Fox was employed by Coca-Cola for fourteen years before becoming a politician. In 1999, he created Amigos de Fox, a civil society organisation to support his political campaign, with a large start-up donation from Coca-Cola. Nearly half of all Coca-Cola destined for Latin America was consumed in Mexico then, the largest (per head) of any country in the world.

After becoming President in 2000, Fox employed his Coke employee Cristóbal Jaime Jaquez as Director of the National Water Commission. Jaquez wasted no time in tripling water concessions granted to Coca-Cola and Nestlé. Fox also invited Fernando Elizondo Barragán – the grandson of the largest Coca-Cola bottling plant founder in Latin America – to be the Secretary of Energy. After Fox, Ernesto Zedillo (President from 1994 to 2000) joined Coca-Cola as an adviser.

By the time Fox's six-year term ended in 2006, Mexico had the highest sugary-drink consumption in the world alongside a soaring obesity rate. One in six people were living with diabetes due to *comida chatarra* (junk food). Most were unaware they were sick, until they went blind or needed a limb amputated. Even then they didn't link it to high blood sugar. More than 40,000 deaths per year in Mexico in the early 2010s were attributed to the consumption of sugary beverages – one every thirteen minutes of the day and night.

The door spins both ways, from corporations into Government, from Government into corporations.* The OpenSecrets website has a revolving-door database with information on the previous Government employment of US lobbyists. Two-thirds of lobbyists were former Government employees.[25] Poachers can turn gamekeepers and some then decide to go back to poaching. Each time they go to the other side, they bring new inside knowledge with them.

3. Distract and deflect
Here's the third tactic. Big Food distracts public (and governmental) attention through 'corporate social responsibility' (CSR) campaigns and projects, funding a few good causes, here and

---

* Derek Yach, a former WHO executive director for non-communicable disease was recruited by PepsiCo as Senior Vice President in 2007. Janet Voûte joined Nestlé as Global Head of Public Affairs after leading the development of WHO's non-communicable disease network.

there. CSR is the small-scale 'good' which seeks to distract attention from the large-scale 'bad' (the core business of selling unhealthy products). The left hand of CSR that's waving at you, trying to divert your attention from the much larger right hand of a company's core business. This is how large corporations seek to create and build a social licence to operate.[26]

High-profile boutique projects and the media froth they generate are performative gestures designed to confer legitimacy on core business practices that run in a very different direction. The journalist and thorn in the flesh of plutocrats, Anand Giridharadas, refers to them as 'dangerous side salads', reflecting the way fast-food restaurants bang on about their salads while continuing to serve heart-attack burgers.[27] CSR is ultimately a tax-deductible public relations exercise aimed at laundering reputations and burnishing corporate haloes.

'Youthwashing' and child-targeted CSR is a particularly aggressive and insidious form of marketing as the industry seeks to build brand loyalty at a very young age, reshaping social norms, eroding cultural diets to create dangerous lifelong eating preferences which may become addictions.

The new kid on the block is 'nutri-washing' where companies that cause overnutrition pledge to reduce undernutrition. Companies whose products and marketing practices shape obesogenic food environments gain kudos by pledging to fight hunger while continuing to drive obesity. PepsiCo was by far the biggest donor to the Zero Hunger Pledge (set up by the Global Alliance for Improved Nutrition – GAIN), which emerged from the 2021 UN Food Systems Summit. José Graziano da Silva – former FAO Director General and architect of the pioneering *Fome Zero* anti-hunger scheme – tweeted his concern about sugary drinks companies being involved. In recent years, PepsiCo, Unilever, Mars, Yum! Brands and Kentucky Fried Chicken have all secured partnerships with the UN's lead agency on hunger, the World Food Programme.[28]

Crises are opportunities. The COVID pandemic brought rich rewards in corporate virtue-signalling. In 2020, the NCD Alliance compiled multiple examples, highlighting: 'the sheer scale and global reach of corporate responses to the COVID pandemic across unhealthy commodity industries . . . the volume of initiatives, activities and donations . . .' Obesity was a major predictor of premature death during the pandemic. As patients struggled to breathe in intensive care, Krispy Kreme reps were handing out free doughnuts in hospital receptions.

It's everywhere . . . including, I belatedly came to realise, in my own organisation, the International Food Policy Research Institute (IFPRI). In 2016, a decision was made to accept funds from McDonald's to support research in Ethiopia to improve the production of sesame seeds for burger buns. Our department – the poverty, food and nutrition division – learned of this *after* the event. My colleague (whose project was receiving the funds) didn't think it was such a big deal. He told me the project would benefit impoverished farmers in Ethiopia. I argued that missed the point and we should not accept funds from companies whose products and practices generate malnutrition. It doesn't matter that this particular project may have benefited a few poor farmers, we need to look at the bigger picture of what the company is doing on the global stage. Companies like McDonald's have well-resourced CSR units and foundations whose job is to 'do good', but most importantly, *to be seen to be doing good*. By taking their money, we provide them with a reputational boost and we disincentivise reform of their harmful core business practices.

We had a frank, collegial discussion, but it was too late. IFPRI was yet another bestower of kudos and acceptability to a junk-food multinational. We had guidelines that banned our involvement with 'no-go' companies linked with tobacco, fossil fuels, child labour, arms, alcohol, gambling, but there was nothing about junk food. In 2018, we updated them.

But then in 2024, three years after I'd left IFPRI, I read about the appointment of a new Chair of the CGIAR System Board (the mother network in which IFPRI sits). The fact that she was (and still is, at the time of writing) a Nestlé board member apparently hadn't interfered with her appointment. After years of struggle by senior nutrition staff to challenge Nestlé's predatory behaviour around the world to protect mothers and children, this was bewildering. I wrote to her to ask about the CGIAR's policy on conflict of interest. She didn't respond, so I wrote again. Silence. Then I found the policy online: the responsibility for addressing conflicts of interest in board members lies with one person . . . the Chair![29]

Just leave it to us

Another distraction comes in the form of self-regulation. Big Food deters and delays Government regulation (ingredient bans, sugar taxes, etc.) by promising to regulate itself by reformulating its products to reduce fat, salt, sugar. This is a scam within a scam. Voluntary self-regulation does not work – it never has, never will.[30] Comprehensive analyses in the USA, Australia, Canada, China, New Zealand and Spain all show the same results – zilch. Nothing changes. That's because voluntary regulation is not intended to work. The goal is not to improve the nutritional quality of food products, it is to delay and deter Government from mandating change, which is exactly what happened in the UK when the Tories launched the Public Health Responsibility Deal back in 2011. The poster boy of regulatory failure, a deal that was great for the industry but no one else.

Sometimes, a company will pledge to reduce the calorie-density of its food by a certain percentage. But 10 per cent less junk is still junk. Reducing calorie-density or size of food portions while ignoring quality is like trying to prevent deaths from shark attacks by filing their teeth.

We now know the issue is not just the balance of nutrients in foods (salt, sugar, fat), it's also the degree of processing a product has undergone. The question then is whether it is even possible to reformulate a UPF to make it healthier. Replacing sugars with artificial sweeteners, for example, is not a strategy that leads to a greater share of unprocessed food in the diet.

Even if it was possible, we would need to consider the scale, scope and speed of *re*formulation against the scale, scope and speed of formulation. Investing in the reformulation of snack foods while simultaneously disavowing the systemic dynamics of formulation is 'leanwishing'.[31] Any reformulation that does happen is always dwarfed (in pace and scale) by formulation. It's a big game.

Sometimes you have to catch yourself. A Food and Drink Federation spokesperson was recently quoted as saying: 'We are continuing to invest a great deal in the science and innovation required to remove calories, salt, sugar and fat and to add fibre, fruit and vegetables to popular, everyday products.'[32] I had to read that twice. Foods broken down through multi-step industrial processes and turned into products which are then turned into different products. Where did the food go?

If a Government does stay the course and forces through legislation, companies hire lawyers to threaten lawsuits. The four common arguments in the legal toolbox are that the law is discriminatory, that the Government does not have the mandate, that marketing restrictions impinge on the commercial right to trade, and/or that the restriction is too severe.[33]

Legal threats are also intended to buy them time for other tactics to bear fruit. In the UK, for example, a court ruled in

2022 that Kellogg's would not be exempt from a ban on promoting sugary cereals in supermarket special offers. Kellogg's had taken the Government to court arguing the rules did not take into account the nutritional value of added milk. They failed but they'd bought time. The notion of 'trust but verify' does not work. We have to focus on the walk, not the talk – actions, not words. It should be reversed: 'verify then trust'.

4. Disguise

The dark art of camouflage. The industry disguises itself by hiding within 'non-profit' front organisations that tend to have names that include the word 'global' or 'sustainable' or 'development'. Again, they've learned from the tobacco industry who pioneered this subterfuge. Examples include the US$450 million provided by cigarette manufacturers to the Council for Tobacco Research, which led to more than 7,000 sympathetic scientific papers.[34]

Companies make use of public relations firms – the obvious move – but they can also join forces and set up a 'trade association' that acts on behalf of the entire industry so that no single brand appears to be responsible. These front groups are the attack dogs. Corporations pay their member fees and hide behind the scenes to avoid reputational damage.

This Trojan-Horse tactic helps Big Food to get to the policy table and into conferences, by proxy. Once there — whether in plenary discussions, corridor meetings or their cocktail parties – they get to make friends and influence people. The World Business Council for Sustainable Development who chaired the private sector group at the UN Food Systems Summit in 2021 is a prime example.

Another Trojan Horse is the International Life Sciences Institute (ILSI), which defines its mission 'to generate and advance emerging science and groundbreaking research to ensure foods are safe, nutritious and sustainable'. ILSI has used most of the tactics described above on behalf of the industry since it was founded by a former Coca-Cola Chief Executive in the late 1970s.[35] ILSI influenced the US Dietary Guidelines for Americans 2020–2025 to rule out any further reductions in sugar consumption, despite a wealth of robust scientific evidence highlighting the damage caused by Big Soda and their products. When exposed as a front group, ILSI's Research Foundation changed its name to the Agriculture & Food Systems Institute.[36]

There is a whole network of camouflaged lobbying in the world of infant feeding. The International Special Dietary Foods Industries, through its twenty member associations across the world, lobby specifically to support the marketing of commercial milk formula foods which places them in direct opposition to the WHO. Some of their members sound like professional bodies – like the Infant and Pediatric Nutrition Association of the Philippines. But they're not interested in paediatric nutrition, they're only interested in selling baby food.

Big Formula hides behind a network of trade associations and front groups that it sets up and controls to lobby against implementation of the Code, and other breastfeeding protection measures, nationally and internationally.

Delay is a core goal. When the South African Government passed national legislation to turn the Code into law in 2012, formula manufacturers joined forces to form a new lobby group, the Infant Feeding Association, which demanded amendments to the regulations. It took nine years for the law to come into force.

A groundbreaking new study from Australia has exhaustively scoped the connections between Big Food corporations and various interest groups. Scott Slater and colleagues identified 268 interest groups affiliated with the industry. The largest corporations had the most links. Nestlé was a member of 171 of them, Coca-Cola 147, Unilever 142 and PepsiCo 138. Most interest groups are headquartered where public power is concentrated: one-third in Washington DC and Brussels, and the rest in the capital cities of major UPF markets. Tens of millions of dollars are paid in member fees to this influence network by these corporations to protect against risks to profiteering.[37]

Finally, there's 'astroturfing', another disguise in which transnational companies employ grassroots organisations to convey their messages and generate a false picture of support for their products. Many use stolen or stock photos, fake bios with tags to real accounts. As with product advertising, language is co-opted to generate a false impression, using buzzwords like 'sustainable', 'transformational'. Tokenism is rife, especially when it comes to youth.

5. Dodge

The playbook described here is designed to help Big Food avoid regulation, which often means avoiding tax. There are taxes on products (like sugary drinks) and then there's corporation tax which opens up a whole new field of battle. The bigger the company, the greater its taxable revenue, the more powerful it is, with more options to duck, dodge or delay tax. Some tax-dodging is legal (avoidance), some is not (evasion).

The *Lancet* Series on Commercial Determinants of Health in 2023 included a novel analysis that showed as share of profits (to initial capital) increased, the effective tax rate paid by corporations declined. Profits are privatised, as we've seen, while harms are paid by the public (malnutrition and ill-health) and the planet (carbon and plastic). Most profits of transnationals end up in high-income countries while most harms are paid by citizens of low-income countries.

In March 2022, the UK-based War on Want brought out an in-depth investigative report 'Secrets and Fries', which described how McDonald's had been driving billions in global profits through the City of London, but not stopping to pay its share of UK tax.[38] Using a circular paper transaction, the company had shielded its UK-generated income from at least £295 million in tax. This happened during the COVID pandemic as McDonald's availed itself of £872 million in UK Government tax breaks and support, including £229 million from the Coronavirus Job Retention Scheme, and £143 million from the crass and deadly 'Eat Out to Help Out' scheme. In the same year, as sales soared, nearly £3 billion was paid out as dividends to shareholders.

Like other mega-transnationals, McDonald's profit-shifts by using a franchise business model. It no longer sells burgers, it sells the *ideas* behind the burgers – the branding and intellectual property rights. Legally separate subsidiary companies are set up to charge franchises for using the McDonald's packaging, branding, logos, and so on. Income from such deals counts as 'expenses' for the franchisee and national McDonald's subsidiaries, which means there's less tax to pay in the country where the actual burger is sold. Before Brexit, McDonald's used Luxembourg as a tax haven. An EU investigation found their arrangement to be unfair, but not illegal (avoidance, not evasion). But McDonald's clearly felt that too much sunlight was getting in. A year later, they moved to London to escape EU jurisdiction and benefit from the UK's low rate of corporation tax. Meanwhile, employees in McDonald's earned, on average, £8 per hour. 'McJob' is included in the *Oxford English Dictionary* as 'a low-paid job with few prospects'.

Transnationals can easily move operations from one jurisdiction to another to dodge taxes and State regulation. Profitable operations are shifted to tax havens. Organisations like Global Witness publish regular exposés of more blatant forms of corporate malpractice. The painful paradox is that the more a government needs foreign investment, the worse the deal it's likely to get.

There are some bizarre stories too, including the beautiful irony of a Big Food corporation going to court to assert publicly and expensively that their product is fake, in order to avoid paying VAT. In 2009, after a long court case between Procter & Gamble and HM Revenue and Customs, it was decided that Pringles are crisps after all. P&G were forced to pay over £100 million in backdated tax.

In Seattle, Coca-Cola and PepsiCo pushed for a Washington-statewide ban on food and beverage taxes, feigning altruistic concern about taxes on groceries when their real intent was to block taxes on their products.

Tax avoidance is just normal behaviour for a company that seeks to maximise profit at minimum cost to itself.

14

Do-Nothing Politics

Sugar, rum, and tobacco are commodities which are nowhere necessaries of life, which are become objects of almost universal consumption, and which are therefore extremely proper subjects of taxation.

Adam Smith, *Wealth of Nations*, 1776

Malnutrition of all types (undernutrition, hunger, micronutrient deficiency, obesity) is inherently political in its origins and its resolution. Ultimately, the Government is the largest body in the country with power, duty and responsibility to act at scale, on our behalf.

Governments need to act because malnutrition represents what economists call a market failure, a negative externality – and what the rest of us call an injustice. A large-scale harm perpetrated by forces which the Government is supposed to control. Though governments are the only organisations with the power to set the guard rails and rules (laws, regulations, policies) within which food systems operate, the problem is they rarely use it.

The UK Institute for Government's April 2023 report into Britain's obesity crisis started with the 2021 statement by Dolly Theis and Martin White: 'Since 1992, there have been 14 strategies, 689 policies and 10 targets, and at least 14 key institutions and agencies variously created and abolished.' Three decades in which obesity rocketed.

Market failure is usually met with political failure. Governments are beset by policy inertia, and they choose not to act. Inaction though is a political choice. Politicians need to be held accountable for failing to act – just as they would if they chose to act.

Why must governments act? There are several reasons:

1. Malnutrition is multicausal in nature. It requires a 'whole-of-government' response. There is no Ministry of Nutrition. Many sectors, including health, agriculture, social welfare and education, need directives (policy) or incentives from Government to promote nutrition, given that it's not their core business. Sometimes acting multisectorally requires sectors to apply a nutrition lens to their own programmes; sometimes it means sectors must be brought together to implement joint or integrated programmes. This is hard because sectors have different objectives, and competition (for limited financing) is the default, not collaboration.

2. Economic growth won't fix it. Nor will technology. We have strong evidence that a core package of ten nutrition interventions —if scaled up to 90 per cent coverage in the countries with the highest burden of child stunting—will avert only *one fifth* of the burden of stunting in those countries.[1] To tackle undernutrition globally and successfully, solutions need to come from elsewhere.

3. Corporate capture. Our food system is dysfunctional because the power of corporations is not being balanced by the power of Government. Malnutrition is (in part, as we've seen) caused by the products and practices of transnational food corporations which need to be regulated. This is the

Government's job. Companies won't rein themselves in – voluntary regulation does not work.

4. Many of the biggest companies are tax dodgers. Tax avoidance and evasion are as much about political failure to design, enact and enforce tax legislation as it is about industry malpractice.

5. Malnutrition meets all the criteria for being a 'public' problem – it's widespread in the population, caused by structural factors outside individual control and it affects public goods, like health care, that are managed by the State.[2]

Company CEOs face a double-bind: a fiduciary responsibility to grow market share on the one hand, and a social responsibility to decrease consumption of unhealthy products on the other. These two don't go together. If we apply a marketing and behavioural economic frame to this public health challenge, we arrive at the 'tragedy of the commons.'

In his seminal 1968 paper, the American ecologist Garrett Hardin argued that people will do things that are against the common good if they think it will help them get ahead, and if they think they can get away with it. We are hardwired to be selfish consumers not good environmentalists. Focused on tomorrow, not next year . . . never mind the next generation.

A food swamp where town centres are inundated with fast-food joints is an example of the 'tragedy of the commons', as is the excessively high percentage of ultra-processed foods in company portfolios.

Another problem is 'stimulated exploitation' wherein one company sees another company cornering the market in quasi-addictive UPFs and is impelled to innovate to capture a higher share; a race to the bottom in which public health suffers. Diversification is an insurance strategy even for corporations. If a benevolent CEO decided to focus on health not profit, their company would lose market share, see profits reduced and lose shareholders.

We should not therefore assign moral agency and responsibility to the food industry so long as the Government has failed to set the rules – to define what's permissible and what isn't – to regulate industry to protect the commons for future generations.

Why do governments resist? Again, there are several reasons:

1. Malnutrition, including child stunting and many micronutrient deficiencies ('hidden hunger'), often goes unnoticed where it's most prevalent.[3] It's become normalised. When I worked in India in the 1980s, so many kids were growth-stunted that everyone – from parents to policymakers – perceived them to be normal.* Statistically, they were normal, but their failure to grow had sown a bad seed of future ill-health. This normalisation is happening now with obesity. Such a lack of visibility results in little community voice or bottom-up pressure for change.

2. It takes time. Just as becoming malnourished is a slow violence, the benefits of becoming well-nourished only accrue fully in the long term, including for the next generation. Way beyond the mayfly lives of politicians in office. Quick wins are rare, which is why politicians often look for other causes to support. Immunisation, for example, is far easier; results are quick, visible and directly attributable to a politician's decision to act.

3. Flying blind. There is a pervasive lack of timely, actionable

---

* Over the course of two years living and working in a village in central India, I gradually became undernourished (dropping from 73kg to 57kg) without realising. It was only when I got back to the UK that I saw it.

data on levels and types of malnutrition in many countries which leads policymakers to be less accountable to citizens. Governments don't respond – if it's not measured, it's not done. It's also unclear how much governments spend on nutrition (within sectoral budgets) or on what, further reducing transparency and accountability. With limited pressure to act, and with limited data to hold them to account, politicians stay in their comfort zone of 'business as usual', sit on their hands and do nothing.

4. Free markets or free people? Many politicians still believe in the power of market-based and educational solutions to address malnutrition – a convenient fallacy. They are spooked into inaction by powerful lobbying. A 2023 study found 'the strategies adopted by the companies that produce these products constitute the main barrier to these policies in all the studied countries'. Politicians are intimidated by media controversy so they choose to invest their limited, time-bound political capital on other issues. They may see the revolving door on the horizon. This all amounts to 'regulatory chill' – a default to inaction that persists, year after year, Government after Government, despite worsening trends and despite the usual parade of public pledges to act. Both industry and governments are good at the 'talk', but not the 'walk'. All this is reinforced by the anti-nanny-state argument for doing nothing, supported by governments and Big Food alike.

5. Fear of the electorate. There's a view that the challenge is too big, too widespread and that a pledge to make it harder to buy cheap junk food – even if it leads to better diets becoming more affordable – is just too hard to sell. In the run-up to the UK general election in 2024, Labour seemed scared of losing votes in deprived so-called 'Red Wall areas',

where most poor households depend on cheap, calorie-dense, nutrient-poor food. The Tory party meanwhile just stuck to their 'nanny-state' mantra.

6. Blurred lines. Governance may be polluted by multi-stakeholder initiatives that blur the lines between the roles and responsibilities of rights-holders (citizens), duty-bearers (i.e., governments who are the upholders of those rights) and those acting on behalf of corporate agendas. They duck accountability, both legally and financially, when their practices cause harm to others. This enables corporate impunity for operations and practices and no recourse for those who have been harmed, even in cases of human rights abuses.[4]

The reality is, the public really *wants* the Government to act. A series of 'deliberative dialogues' for the 2021 National Food Strategy showed strong public support in the UK for governmental restrictions on the advertising and promotion of junk food.[5] A Health Foundation study found fewer than one in five people think the Government is working effectively to improve diets, a 2020 study by the Obesity Health Alliance found three-quarters of the public support Government action to address obesity, and a 2023 study by the Food, Farming and Countryside Commission uncovered similar levels of support for policies to improve the healthiness of food from every population segment, generation and political affiliation.[6]

Inside the black box

By 2012, we knew a lot about the causes of undernutrition: what they were, where they were, how to measure them, how to respond (with our toolbox of direct nutrition interventions). But we also knew these responses could be overwhelmed by wider, deeper causes of poverty and inequality. These structural constraints had always been confined to a 'black box' – a kind of no-go zone for nutrition researchers and advocates.

Conventional wisdom had it that we could never understand the dynamics within the box, and we could certainly never influence them. The 'political economy of nutrition' – the competing interests, incentives and ideologies of multiple actors who influence the state of nutrition – was viewed as an insurmountable problem. Many felt that nutrition professionals should stay in their corner, and not overreach themselves. To me, this was professional neglect and a big untapped opportunity.

In 2012, I was asked to lead the final paper for the *Lancet* Maternal and Child Nutrition Series on the politics of reducing malnutrition. With a great team, we had a chance to address the question: What's needed for political commitment to be generated and to be translated into action on the ground?

We knew the political environment was a key factor. In 1999, nearly a century after Louis Pasteur had described the stability of the body's *milieu intérieur* as 'the condition for a free and independent life', Nobel laureate Amartya Sen wrote *Development as Freedom*. Shortly after that, Mahbub ul Haq launched the first UN Human Development Report, building on Sen's work. An 'enabling environment' for them was one that preserved the future capability to act, that kept an individual's set of life choices open. Human development was all about expanding the richness of human life, not the richness of the economy – impressive, coming from two of the world's leading economists!

In our paper, we defined an enabling environment for nutrition as the 'wider political and policy processes which build and sustain momentum for the effective implementation of actions that prevent or reduce (mal)nutrition.' We dug into the literature on politics and policy, interviewed scores of people in many of the hardest-hit countries, and ran a week-long online consultation with seventy-five policymakers, civil society leaders and leading academics in six countries: Bangladesh, Nepal, Indonesia (in Asia), and Nigeria, Ethiopia and Kenya (Africa). This led us to three domains:

1. political commitment, effective governance and sound policy
2. knowledge, data and evidence and its framing and communication, and
3. leadership, capacity, and financing.

We could see that political will is, in reality, political *choice*. A politician chooses to do something about nutrition, or not. He or she needs to be held accountable for that decision – and for the right choice to be made, the case for addressing malnutrition has to be made.

But then, political commitment to act isn't enough. Politicians love to make pledges at conferences, but we need to look at the realities. We broke political change down into four stages:

1. political attention (stated intent; e.g. a president's speech);
2. political commitment (intent reflected in policy);
3. institutional commitment (changes in procedures and actions); and finally,
4. financial commitment (new actions budgeted).

Because it's a choice, political will needs to be fought for and built proactively – it doesn't fall from the sky.

Politicians follow trends and social mores, they don't drive them. They support policies they think will be popular and lead to votes. It is citizens, social movements, media and the food industry that drive decisions on policies. Policy is shaped by whoever prevails in framing problems and their solutions. The narratives, stories and language picked up by the media and the public percolates through to policymaking. As James Grant, the former Executive Director of UNICEF, said:

> Each of the great social achievements of recent decades has come about not because of government proclamations, but because people organized, made demands, and made it good politics for governments to respond. It is the political will of the people that makes and sustains the political will of governments.

Nanny nonsense

The term 'nanny state' was devised by the British ruling class who were reared by nannies, the latest poster boy being ex-Tory MP, Jacob Rees-Mogg. The term, which manages to encapsulate both libertarianism and misogyny, was actually first heard in Parliament in 1965 when another Conservative MP objected to a 70mph speed limit on roads.

It's still a Tory trump card. In October 2020, MP Brendan Clarke-Smith wheeled it out when he objected to Marcus Rashford's campaign to extend free school meals during the pandemic, asking the Commons: 'Where is the slick PR campaign encouraging absent parents to take some responsibility for their children? I do not believe in nationalising children.' In response, Kate Green of Labour pointed out it was the Government's responsibility: 'Children don't stop being hungry just because the school bell rings for the end of term'. Tories voted against the extension.

The demonisation of the nanny state is predicated on a mystical appeal to freedom of choice and personal responsibility. The food industry weaponises this notion of individual liberty to protect its profit margins. In the USA, the industry invokes First Amendment protections, especially when the Government attempts to regulate the sale of junk food and soda to kids in school (the ultimate consumer because they will be around the longest).

The 'nanny state' is a hollow cliché that can be easily reframed positively by pointing out all the benefits caused by regulations and standards that we all take for granted. Seat belts and air bags in cars, bans on smoking and on the sale of alcohol and cigarettes to kids, ozone-damaging aerosols, asbestos in buildings, light-bulb specifications, lead in petrol, speed restrictions on roads, motorcyclist crash helmets, shatterproof glass in showers, smoke alarms, quality standards for condoms, controls on air pollution, on sewage and sanitation, abattoir standards, gun-ownership laws, water fluoridation, lockdowns during pandemics – all examples of proactive measures taken by the State to protect public health and wellbeing. Junk food kills more than any of these.

There is a social and political responsibility to regulate widespread environmental harms. This does not mean that individual responsibility is not important – there's a lot we can do, as we'll explore shortly. But it does mean that governments need to act to protect the public when faced with such harms. The libertarian 'nanny state' excuse for inaction ultimately represents an abrogation of responsibility, a political failure to act to protect the public.

Right now it is the food industry that is guilty of nannying, by insisting on 'protecting' the public from Government policies that are designed for our benefit. A nightmare nanny. The hypocrisy of the agrifood industry's stance becomes even more ludicrous when viewed against the US$800 billion of Government subsidies it happily pockets every year. If it fails to rein in industry,

Government is failing in its duty to defend the liberty of citizens to be healthy and free from illness and malnutrition.

The architects of 'nudge' economics, Thaler and Sunstein, point out that the 'choice architecture' is already in place.[7] It's called taxation. It just needs to be managed for the benefit of people, not profit. The Government's role here is to use regulation (including tax) to ensure the 'greatest happiness of the greatest number'.[8]

Rebel Tory William Hague wrote in *The Times* about the need to treat junk food like tobacco. In 1999, Tony Blair's New Labour banned tobacco advertising. Until that time, when clear evidence had accumulated that smoking was harmful and addictive, smoking was viewed as a personal choice. For years, governments had failed to change habits with expensive educational campaigns. After the ban, smoking rates fell off a cliff. The main freedom to be defended, Hague concluded, is the freedom to be healthy.

Over a decade later, a light is flashing at the end of the tunnel. We may be about to witness the slow death of the 'nanny state' argument. Explosive new research suggests it may not even be necessary to *eat* junk food for addiction pathways in the brain to start to fire up. All that's needed is to live in a junk-food swamp.[9] The sight and smell of junk food in such a highly polluted environment is similar to passive smoking. If this body of evidence is consolidated and communicated, it will kill the personal responsibility narrative. Or rather, it *should* kill it – there will be big pushback, just as there was by the tobacco industry. It may take time . . . let's see . . .

The precautionary principle, enshrined in international treaties and national legislation in many countries, states that: 'if a product, an action or a policy has a suspected risk of causing harm to the public or to the environment, protective action should be supported before there is complete scientific proof of a risk'.

Governments need to activate this principle regarding ultra-processed foods.[10] This does not, of course, change the need to continue to research the mechanisms behind the harms associated with them, whether they relate to energy density, hyper-palatability, the effects of certain additives, or whatever else.

But it would mean that governments ditch the do-nothing politics, step up and act. For a sitting Government to be sitting on its hands on this is unethical. A range of public action can be taken now to begin to turn the tide and shift the balance towards healthier diets for all. Let's dig into this now. Time to act.

IV

TRANSFORMATION

The global food system that we have now is not broken. It's working the way it was designed, over fifty years ago, to mass-produce cheap calories. The problem is the world is not the same as it was back then. It's a system from a different time. We don't need to fix it, we need to change it. To transform it into one where the health of people and planet is prioritised above the relentless drive for profit. It's too late for incremental change, yet more tweaking at the margins – we need a radical overhaul.

The good news is we can do it. We know what's been happening and why. And we now know what to do about it. After decades of food and nutrition policy, practice and research, we have a library of experience and insights from all over the world. We know what works to protect people's right to nutritious food. We need to amplify and harness the growing social and political will and use it to propel us forward. In the face of a food system controlled by powerful transnationals making mega-profits from unhealthy food, we must insist our governments show vision and leadership. And we must get organised.

This fourth and final part of the book plots our way to this new era. We walk through the different roles and responsibilities of governments, municipalities, civil society, international agencies, citizens, researchers, media and company CEOs in this transformation, concluding with a manifesto for the future.

15

Regulate

Better put a strong fence 'round the top of the cliff, than an ambulance down in the valley.

Joseph Malins, 1895

Today's dietary patterns have formed over a period of at least 70 years. We will need long-term political commitments to reverse them.

UK National Food Strategy, 2021

At national, state and municipal levels, governments have the powers to set and enforce the rules (policies, regulations, laws) within which food systems operate. They have the power to stand up to transnationals who put profit ahead of people, the power to use various policy levers to rebalance diets away from unhealthy UPFs towards a diverse range of fresh and minimally processed whole foods. Dangling a few carrots as incentives to Big Food to produce nutrient-rich, healthy foods will never be enough.

Governments can use tax, laws on marketing, labelling, advertising and ingredients, and other policies to reduce the toxic elements of company portfolios and the way they're foisted upon us. They can provide social and economic safety nets for vulnerable populations and strengthen health systems to protect growing children and provide essential care and treatment for all who need it.

With an array of tools at their disposal, governments influence both the structure and operations of the food system. Every step in the chain in which food is produced, processed, packaged, distributed, labelled, priced, consumed or wasted represents an option to intervene. This is not about individual products or the individual consumer – those boring questions about whether this or that food is good for you, or not. This is about systems and environments.

Governments have a duty to prioritise the freedom and health of those who elect them, to act in the public interest and be held accountable for just that. Addressing the power imbalances that beset our food system is a *sine qua non* for reducing inequalities and preventing malnutrition and ill-health.

Not only is this essential, we now know it's feasible. As knowledge of the double burden of malnutrition has grown, so has evidence and experience with strategies to address the shared drivers of all forms of malnutrition simultaneously – so-called 'double-duty actions'.

The two most important double-duty actions are infant and young child feeding and action to ensure access to an affordable healthy diet for all citizens.[1] The former tends to be delivered through the health system, the latter via the food system. In this chapter, we will look at global experiences with both food and non-food policies and interventions that target all forms of malnutrition. We can divide the set of Government actions to improve food systems and food environments into three I's:

1. *Institutions*: governments have budgets to procure healthy foods (and limit UPFs) for schools, Government agencies, hospitals and clinics.
2. *Information*: governments have the power to regulate

advertising, food labelling, marketing and commercial promotion of unhealthy, low-nutrient, ultra-processed foods, especially to children, in all forms of media.

3. *Incentives*: governments can use economic tools to disincentivise unhealthy foods (through taxing harm) while using subsidies and pricing to incentivise healthier food purchase for all, especially low-income families.

Nourishing the future

Children won't learn well if they're hungry; they can't concentrate. School feeding schemes not only nourish growing brains and bodies, they increase enrolment and retention of children. In Ghana, a study found that the national school feeding programme led to a 14 per cent improvement in literacy scores, 13 per cent in mathematics, and 8 per cent in reasoning ability for girls.[2] Meals provide nutrients for developing brains, for preventing anaemia and stunting, and strengthening immunity, especially among girls and children from the poorest households. The school lunch may be the only cooked meal of the day for many children.

Food Fighter: Wawira Njiru

As a young nutrition student in Australia, Wawira Njiru had an idea. On her return to Kenya in 2012, the idea led to a fundraiser which generated enough cash to build a small kitchen out of corrugated iron in her hometown, Ruiru, near Nairobi. A few months later, the kitchen was feeding twenty-five schoolchildren with nutritious hot meals.[3]

But Wawira was just getting started. In 2017, she travelled to Bengalaru, India, to check out the school lunch programme set up by the Akshaya Patra Foundation which fed 2 million children daily. She wanted to know about the basic nuts and bolts of procurement, accounting, personnel. By 2023, her NGO, Food4Education, had delivered more than 21 million meals – tens of thousands of young children are now being fed well every day, keeping them in school, switched on, able to learn.

The initiative captured the attention of the Kenyan Government who are now partnering with Food4Education to scale it up.[4] Under the new scheme, 250,000 children from 225 primary schools and Early Childhood Development centres in Nairobi will receive a hot meal every day – the largest programme of its kind in Africa. Ten new kitchens will employ 3,500 people. The goal in Kenya is universal provision by 2030.

India is home to the world's largest and longest-running school meals scheme. Recent evidence from it has shown that nutritional benefits span generations, especially among the poorest households.[5] Cost-benefit analyses show that quality school food provision boosts economic productivity – school feeding pays for itself many times over in the long run.[6]

When I worked in India in the mid-Nineties with UNICEF, the default response by Government to any questions about child hunger was to point to the midday meals programme for school-kids. As if that was all that was needed. We struggled to make the case then for the youngest children – the first 1,000 days – *before* they started school. Later, we came to see the power of school feeding as an educational intervention. And if kids could be kept in schools longer, alert and actively learning, their health and nutritional status – and thus their future prospects – would be boosted. Not only theirs, but their children's too, given the strong links between maternal schooling and the nutritional wellbeing of their future children. School meals are a win–win for both education and nutrition, in the short and long run.

In Brazil, they've extended the benefits even further. The Government funds healthy meals for millions of students in public schools, a third of which need to be purchased from local farmers who practise organic, low-carbon farming. The programme has changed both the food environment and behaviours of the next generation, reined in junk food, enhanced the livelihood of local farmers and improved the health and wellbeing of students.

On a wider level, Brazil provides a fascinating case study – it's not often a progressive leader gets two chances of shaping national policy, twenty years apart. President Luiz Inácio Lula da Silva started his first presidential term in 2003 and his second in 2023. In 2003, he championed the *Fome Zero* (Zero Hunger) programme aimed at eradicating hunger and extreme poverty. Jair Bolsonaro scrapped it as soon as he gained power. But then, on his return in 2023, Lula relaunched the programme as *Brazil Sem Fome* (Brazil Without Hunger). This time, with two significant changes. First, there was a much stronger focus on *quality* of food, especially within school feeding. The second change was to focus on democratic governance and include the voices of the marginalised through deep participation; in this way, bullet-proofing the programme from later shifts in political power.[7]

School feeding – nourishing the developing minds of the future generation – is a no-brainer. In England, free school meals are a statutory entitlement for eligible pupils, provided by local authorities. In January 2023, 2 million pupils were eligible, representing a quarter of all state-funded pupils – the highest proportion since tracking began in 2006. However fractious party-political discussions are, surely a free school meal is the easiest and least contentious of all policies. You would think so . . . especially as this is the country that, over 120 years ago, passed groundbreaking legislation providing free school meals for children 'unable by reason of lack of food to take full advantage of education'. But then there are always politicians like Brendan Clarke-Smith who will challenge anything that looks nanny-state-ish.

Food Fighter: Marcus Rashford

'No child in the UK should be going to bed hungry. Whatever you're feeling, opinion or judgement, food poverty is never the child's fault. Let's protect our young.'

(Marcus Rashford)

In 2020, as Britain went into its first COVID lockdown, Manchester United and England footballer, Marcus Rashford, was having flashbacks. Just a decade earlier, as a schoolboy, he had relied on school meals to get him through the day. He was now worried about kids going hungry after schools shut down. He wrote an open letter to remind MPs that hunger wouldn't stop when schools did. Under huge media pressure, in June 2020, the Government reversed its earlier decision and committed £130 million to continue free school meals (via vouchers) through the summer.

Around this time, Henry Dimbleby was about to launch the first part of the UK National Food Strategy that he had been leading. On a whim he sent the report to Rashford, not expecting a response. But then . . . nothing ventured, nothing gained.

A month later, Rashford did respond. He had read the report and wanted to support its implementation. In September 2020, he formed the Child Food Poverty Task Force, a coalition of charities and food businesses calling on the Government to implement three recommendations from the UK National Food Strategy. Then, in October, he launched a parliamentary petition to #EndChildFoodPoverty that ended up being signed by over 1.1 million people and in November, following a major public campaign, the UK Government announced a funding package to help alleviate child food poverty.

Rashford continues to campaign as an ambassador with the Food Foundation to keep the issue of child food poverty in the spotlight and hold the Government to account.

Dimbleby was both thrilled to have such a high-profile campaigner in his corner, but also dismayed that the Government would be so myopic as to only act once they had been strong-armed by a famous footballer.[8]

Globally, the problem is that, like so much else, the school feeding safety net is weakest where it needs to be strongest, in the countries and communities hit hardest by malnutrition. Of the 300 million school-age children who are undernourished, more than half live in Africa where fewer than one in five children have access to school feeding programmes.

Momentum is building, however. School meal plans now operate in nearly every country in the world, reaching over 400 million children for about US$48 billion per year.[9] Eighty countries have come together in a global School Meals Coalition. The drive and the funding has come from Global-South governments, not aid donors.

Protecting children

There are at least seven ways a law can protect children from predatory marketing: by restricting power of industry (tactics deployed), regulating content (use of images and sounds in ads), exposure (how much children can see), technique (how companies use technology and information on children), age of child, environment of marketing and the product being marketed.[10]

For Guido Girardi, it was simple – children's right to food and health was being violated by ultra-processed foods and it was the Chilean Government's duty to protect them. A medical doctor who became a senator representing Santiago, Girardi spent sixteen years (2006–2022) struggling against fellow politicians and the junk-food industry to bring in regulation. Chile now leads the world in terms of its comprehensive package of measures that includes front-of-pack labels, restrictions on marketing to children, 18 per cent soda taxes and banning the sale and marketing of junk food in schools.

Big black octagonal labels – *Alto En Calorias* (high calorie), *Alto En Azucares* (sugars), *Alto En Sodio* (salt), *Alto En Grasas Saturadas* (saturated fats) – are slapped on food packages and drinks bottles every time a critical threshold is breached. Up to four ugly labels on any one item. Cartoon characters were taken off cereal packets – a 2018 *New York Times* headline proclaimed the slaying of Tony the Tiger by the Chilean Government.

Initially, in June 2016, TV ads were banned when more than 20 per cent of the audience comprised children below fourteen years old. Two years later, a new law was brought in to counteract the industry's push to adult programming (as kids were still being affected via parents). This time a total ban on daytime TV advertising of junk food was introduced. Within a year, children's exposure to ads for regulated foods and drinks had dropped by 73 per cent.[11] Sales of junk food declined, and within three years consumption of calories, salt and sugar from regulated products had fallen by 25–37 per cent.[12]

As well as Chile, front-of-pack warning labels are now on food products in Peru, Israel, Mexico, Uruguay, Argentina, Brazil, Canada and Colombia, with others in the policy pipeline, including in several major African and Asian countries.[13]

Industry doesn't take this sitting down. The Chilean Government received ninety-two formal challenges from industry to its proposed bill.[14] In Mexico, Kellogg's hired young men to wander around supermarkets with Tony the Tiger masks and T-shirts, while others have been employed to turn products around, so the black octagons face inwards and are not visible. Another ruse is to print a 'front' on both the front and back of the package (but only print labels on one side). Companies innovate in depressing ways – the ban on cartoon characters has led some to use clear plastic wrappers and print the characters on the food product itself.[15] In the USA, where labels are being discussed belatedly, there is always the option for corporations to actually sue the Government for infringing on their First Amendment rights! With tobacco, this tactic led to thirteen years of delay.[16]

Warning labels are the only approach with proven success in reducing purchases of junk foods (high in energy or added sugar, sodium, saturated fats). Other label options (Nutri-Score, traffic lights, Health Star Ratings) have not shown real-world impacts on purchases or consumption.

In July 2021, an independent review for the National Food Strategy for England concluded with a wide range of recommendations to improve the UK food system. Nearly all of them were ignored or delayed. In March 2023, the Food Research Collaboration (FRC) in the UK argued for a total ban on the media advertising of junk food and restrictions in all indoor and outdoor public spaces, including retail and dining outlets. Again, nothing happened.

And yet, this had already been done successfully in the UK when the Greater London Authority banned junk-food advertising on the Transport for London (TfL) network in 2019. The Netherlands has similarly banned ads aimed at children from the Amsterdam Metro, the Ministry of Health in Brazil has banned all junk-food advertising on health department buildings, and most recently, in 2024, Norway banned all advertising of 'unhealthy' food and beverage products to children.

The greatest benefit of such policies is felt where the problem is most severe – in communities most exposed and at highest risk – thus reducing health inequalities. This is what real levelling-up looks like. Good things *are* happening – we just need to learn from them and scale them up.

Taxing harm

In Mexico, the idea of introducing a soda tax had been kicked around for several years in the 2010s.[17] Self-regulation by the industry had failed, as it always does – but the big corporations were actively resisting governmental intervention. Coca-Cola corralled sugar-cane producers and they had former President/former Chief Executive, Vicente Fox, as an ally.

The activist community at that time was relatively small. But things were beginning to change. Dr Simón Barquera and his team at the Nutrition and Health Research Center at the National Institute of Public Health were marshalling and communicating the growing evidence of the links between soft drinks and obesity, diabetes and chronic diseases. Eventually the Government began to wake up.[18] When Enrique Peña Neito and his PRI party came to power in 2012, the soda tax issue resurfaced. By this time the activists were stronger, more streetwise, and they were now backed by international organisations like the Pan American Health Organization. The Bloomberg Foundation donated US$10 million to fund media campaigns which generated over 1,000 media articles in the months leading to the 2013 vote on the tax.[19]

Of course, industry resisted. Along with labour unions, they challenged the tax. Coca-Cola invested millions in campaigns in which they argued the tax would negatively affect the poor and result in job losses.[20] Legislators were aggressively lobbied, pro-tax ads were blocked in national media, retailers mobilised and legal challenges were made in the Supreme Court.[21]

In October 2013, the House of Deputies voted to pass the bill. A key factor was Mexico's dire economic situation – the tax could be a new source of revenue.[22] The first of its kind in the world, the soda tax was launched in 2014. All sugar-sweetened beverages (SSBs) were subjected to an excise tax (about 10 per cent of retail price).* Tax revenue was ploughed back into improving access to and affordability of healthy diets, including public awareness campaigns, as well as structural interventions to increase the availability of clean water in schools and communities. Two years later, sugary-drink sales were down 12 per cent, while water sales went up by similar percentages.[23] The biggest changes occurred among poorest households. Industry's aggressive lobbying had failed to stop it, as NGOs and academics formed a strong pro-tax coalition and the advocacy group El Poder del Consumidor initiated strategic campaigns.[24]

In Africa, the only country to successfully introduce an SSB tax is South Africa. Like Mexico, South Africa has extremely high rates

---

* Excise taxes are paid by manufacturers or distributors, unlike sales taxes that need to be administered by retailers and paid directly by consumers. Taxes could be levied on bulk sales of sugar and salt to manufacturers with the resulting revenue earmarked for improving access to healthy foods in low-resource communities. Food companies are more likely to be motivated to reformulate or ditch their products.

of adult obesity (40 per cent among women), high and rising levels of type 2 diabetes and other diet-related diseases like cancer, dental caries and heart disease. Black South Africans are hit hardest and many live in junk-food swamps where consumption of sugary drinks and UPFs is stratospheric (South Africa is one of the top ten global consumers of Coca-Cola products). Most South Africans cannot afford a healthy diet. Over half the population live below the upper-bound poverty line of US$79 per month, and a quarter below the food poverty line of US$1 per day.[25]

After apartheid was defeated in the 1990s, the new Government embraced neoliberalism and deregulation. SSB multinationals like Coca-Cola and PepsiCo aggressively targeted marketing at poor, mostly Black South Africans.[26] Sugar was more affordable. Corporate influence became entrenched. Economic impact assessments of regulation gave greater credence to the negative effects on business than to the potential health benefits for the public. Big Soda companies infiltrated key policy forums despite clear conflicts of interest. Profits soared as costs (to health and environment) were externalised and corporate tax was kept low.

Industry actors like the Consumer Goods Council South Africa, Coca-Cola Beverages South Africa, and the South African Sugar Association promoted self-regulation.[27] They positioned SSBs as a cheap source of energy for poor people and threatened to roll back investment and community support in the region (South Africa is an entry point to the African market). They also funded research to sow doubt on existing scientific literature.[28]

After a two-year delay caused by this opposition (despite strong support by civil society) a 10 per cent tax was eventually introduced in 2017. The ensuing reduction in sugary-drink consumption was larger than that in Mexico. SSB purchases declined by 29 per cent and sugar intake by 51 per cent in the first two years, even more among poorest groups.*[29]

Taxes work. In the countries in which taxes have been implemented and evaluated, they have all had an impact, with significant drops in SSB purchases.[30] As evaluation findings are published, more taxes are approved across the world.[31] By 2023, such taxes had been implemented in 118 countries covering 51 per cent world's population.†[32]

In just one decade . . . this is huge global success story!

As well as countries, many cities and subnational jurisdictions introduce their own taxes (as we'll see in Chapter 16). Most are applied to sugary drinks and less commonly to confectionery and fats. In most cases, sales of taxed products fell at least as much as the percentage of taxation.

Such taxes are potentially 'win – win – win' policies because they save lives and prevent disease while advancing health equity and mobilising revenue for the general budget. They can also be earmarked for specific priorities such as financing universal health coverage (UHC) or highly cost-effective yet underutilised population health measures.

---

* Another example comes from the UK where the Soft Drinks Industry Levy (SDIL), launched in April 2018, comprised a two-tier tax (over 8g total sugar per 100ml charged at 24 pence per litre and between 5–8g total sugar per 100ml, charged at 18 pence per litre). The SDIL led to a substantial reduction in sugar content, with limited financial impact on industry. The SDIL has been associated with decreased prevalence of obesity in Year 6 girls, with the greatest differences in those living in the most deprived areas. (Rogers, Nina, et al. 'Associations between trajectories of obesity prevalence in English primary schoolchildren and the UK soft drinks industry levy: An interrupted time series analysis of surveillance data'. *PLOS Medicine* [January 2023]).

† 105 at national level and 13 at subnational level. 88 per cent were excise taxes. 73 per cent taxes were in low- or middle-income countries, mostly in Asia.

So, we've seen positive experiences with sugary drinks, but what about ultra-processed or junk foods? Well, this also appears to be doable. Research by New York University and Tufts University has shown that taxes on junk food are administratively and legally feasible.[33] Forty-seven US laws and bills from 1991 to 2021 used several criteria to define foods, which include product categories (e.g. candy/sweets, chips/crisps), degree of processing, place of preparation or sale (e.g. home-made, farmers' market, vending machine), nutrients (e.g. levels of salt, saturated fat, sugar or calories) and serving size.

A two-step process is used: first, to differentiate between necessary or staple foods (e.g. bread) and non-staple foods (e.g. sweets and crisps); and second, to consider the degree of processing and/ or nutrient criteria to decide which products to tax. Colombia was first country in Latin America to introduce a tax on ultra-processed products in November 2023.[34] Any industrially produced ready-to-eat foods with high added sugars, salt or saturated fats are taxed at 10 per cent (rising to 20 per cent in 2025).

'Every time a country puts forward a new strategy such as this in our region, it becomes a model and is not just picked up but improved,' said Beatriz Champagne, Executive Director of the Coalition for Americas' Health, a Latin American advocacy group.

Since the tax was first proposed in 2017, opposition from food industry lobbies has included personal threats, intimidation, surveillance and censorship of campaigns. The health ministry stood firm and has now created an independent committee – free of industry influence – to monitor implementation. Big step forward.

Bringing a healthy diet within reach
The key with taxing harmful products is to also make healthier options more accessible and more affordable. This is the other

side of the fiscal seesaw. The benefit will be felt on both sides by reducing the amount of harmful products clogging up our food system and our bodies, while improving the access and affordability of healthy food. Creative policy will find options to improve demand and consumption of fruits and vegetables, legumes, pulses, nuts and seeds, high-protein, micronutrient-dense grains and safe milk. If this can be done while also supporting local farmers and small- to medium-sized businesses, all the better.

Tax revenues can be ring-fenced and channelled towards subsidising the purchase of healthy foods by low-income and vulnerable households and/or subsidising the marketing of local and sustainably grown produce (e.g. fruit and veg). It's all about using a portfolio of incentives and restraints to shift the food system to a more sustainable and healthier mode and ensuring the most marginalised can benefit.

Thailand is already doing it. The Government-initiated Thai Health Promotion Foundation channels UPF and tobacco tax revenues towards building the evidence base, developing campaigns and mobilising people to address the commercial drivers of unhealthy diets.[35]

The way Seattle used the revenues from its sugary-drink tax is another great example. Initiated in 2018, the tax itself was a big success. Sales of sugary drinks (including a 10 per cent excise tax) dropped significantly, and the US$22 million annual tax revenue is being invested in low-income communities to subsidise purchases of fruits and vegetables in groceries and farmers' markets. The tax dividend is used to subsidise childcare, bring sustainably produced foods from local farms to preschools, add fresh, local, culturally diverse foods to school menus, and establish water bottle filling stations in schools. Taxing harms can subsidise health and reduce inequalities.

In the USA, promoting fresh produce via media campaigns

and Government subsidies has the potential to prevent 230,000 deaths from cardiovascular disease per year.[36] New legislation is being proposed to expand the SNAP (Supplemental Nutrition Assistance Program). Worth US$3.5 billion over five years of the 2023 Farm Bill, and authorising US$100 million of discretionary funding annually for state and local government, the new 'Opt for Health with SNAP, Close the Fruit and Vegetable Gap Act of 2023' will support healthy-food access among nutrition-insecure populations, by funding state/local governments and non-profits to provide point-of-sale incentives for SNAP recipients to purchase fruits and vegetables.

Among the array of options for governments to shape food environments it's politically easier to bring in tax than introducing marketing, sales and labelling regulations. Tax appears to have stronger global and domestic support from civil society, it's more visible, generating political and social attention, and it also provides economic as well as health benefits. Strong industry pushback against soda taxes can actually contribute to a Government's commitment to it. Governments don't want to be seen to be weak and they want the tax revenue.[37] Advertising and labelling regulations, on the other hand, are more vulnerable to lobbying pressure and to the type of delaying tactics we explored earlier.[38]

How do governments figure out *how* to regulate food products? Policymakers need to find a balance between comprehensiveness and practicality in choosing criteria. Most countries use nutrient profile models which include criteria derived from the nutrient content of products (sugar, sodium, saturated fat). The Pan American Health Organization (PAHO) model is the first to capture ultra-processing as well. Diet Coke, for example, would be subject to regulation by the PAHO model (but not by others), as it contains non-sugar sweeteners which would pass under the radar of other models. The NOVA system (which differentiates ultra-processed from other foods) is supported by the UN Food and Agriculture Organization and is used in national dietary guidelines of France, Brazil, Belgium, Brazil, Ecuador, Israel, the Maldives, Peru and Uruguay.[39] Research continues to try to unravel what it is about ultra-processing that is harmful. As these results come online, criteria can be adjusted to ensure the greatest benefit to public health.

Before we leave the arena of food policy, it's worth highlighting a whole bundle of upstream options that governments can employ. On agricultural production, they can: invest in research on fruits and vegetables, nuts and seeds; balance support to farmers to connect with global chains and to supply local markets with diverse, fresh foods; support biodiversity-enhancing, environmentally sustainable production of nutrient-dense foods (nuts, legumes, fruits, vegetables) and small-scale livestock; and in any measure, seek ways to strengthen women's agency and control over resources (labour power, income, time). Governments can also improve infrastructure for processing, storage, and preservation to retain nutritional value and food safety and reduce seasonality and post-harvest losses.

Embedding nutrition in health systems

Most nutrition interventions delivered through the health system today are inherently double-duty in that they target both undernutrition and overnutrition. Many interventions also generate dual benefits in their focus on women and the first 1,000 days (nine months of pregnancy and first two years of a child's life). We have already seen how a life-cycle approach yields the highest gains.

One Thousand Days

The 1,000 Days campaign was launched in 2010 in response to groundbreaking scientific evidence (highlighted in the original 2008 *Lancet* Maternal and Child Nutrition Series) of a powerful window of opportunity from the beginning of a woman's pregnancy to a child's second birthday. What does (or does not) happen in this critical period will determine the long-term health and nutritional status of the children. 1,000 Days is an advocacy hub that champions new investment by advocating for greater action on maternal and child nutrition and catalysing partnerships across sectors to scale up programmes. Advocacy is orientated around four pillars: Building Brains, Building Health, Building a Fair Start, Building Prosperity. More than sixty countries have committed to scaling up a package of nutrition interventions targeting this window of opportunity.

Probably the single most powerful direct intervention in the entire nutrition arsenal is support to infant and young child feeding. This includes the promotion of exclusive breastfeeding for the first six months of a child's life and supporting safe and healthy complementary feeding. Like most approaches, this should be multipronged – everything from face-to-face counselling of young mothers at community level, to activist NGOs shining a light on violations of the 1981 International Code on the Marketing of Breast-milk Substitutes and agitating for proper maternity leave legislation. Political leaders need to recognise the pervasive and invasive nature of formula milk marketing and legislate to prevent Code violations (including plain packaging for formula and national expansion of the Baby-Friendly Hospital Initiative).[40]

Beyond childcare and feeding, nutrition can be integrated into universal health coverage at all levels of care – community, primary and tertiary. We know what works, and now have strong evidence on a package of community-level interventions focusing on micronutrient supplementation (vitamin A, zinc, multi-micro-nutrient powders, iron-folic acid supplements during pregnancy), iron fortification of wheat flour, salt iodisation, deworming of children and community-based management of severe wasting. Scaling up this package would pay huge dividends in the worst-hit countries. For every dollar spent on rolling this out, US$16 can accrue as intergenerational benefits. This is an extraordinary benefit – cost ratio – imagine an economic investment that could promise such a return.[41]

Disease is a complex interplay between the environment and the individual. Public health is all about *preventing* disease and malnutrition by reducing environmental exposure to risk, not treating or ameliorating existing conditions. With any public health crisis, a two-pronged approach (prevention and treat-ment) is needed, whereby those at the greatest risk receive individualised treatment and, simultaneously, population-level risk reduction strategies are deployed. There are multiple exam-ples; for instance, severely ill patients with COVID are hospitalised while other measures are used to prevent popula-tion-level transmission; lung tumours are irradiated while smoking is banned in public.

The same applies for people living with severe obesity. Weight-loss drugs like semaglutide (e.g. Ozempic, Wegovy) and tirzepatide (Mounjaro) significantly reduce appetite, with new drugs coming online thick and fast. These expensive, lifelong, individual-level treatments (with, as yet, unknown long-term effects) in no way reduce the need to *prevent* obesity among the wider population through tackling the obesogenic environment in which we all live. Both prevention and treatment require strong governmental action, just as they do for any other health condition.

Modern medicine continues to patch up bodies that have been broken by the same corporate system that produces the medicine. It's the same with the global food system as diet companies are purchased by the junk-food industry.

Providing a safety net

Poverty, structural racism, gender discrimination and other forms of injustice shackle people and threaten their food security, nutritional wellbeing and their health. People and communities who are marginalised and oppressed are also at most risk from climate, environmental and food and health crises.

Social protection comprises a raft of policies and programmes that protect vulnerable people from shocks, reduce their poverty and promote their welfare and livelihood. Food or cash transfers, vouchers, fee waivers (for health or education), employment guarantee programmes, vocational training, school feeding, drought insurance and targeted subsidies (e.g. for food, fuel) are other options in the toolbox. Interventions like these act as a safety net. A simple cash transfer (e.g. *Bolsa Família* in Brazil) ensures people can eat if they cannot work (e.g. due to illness) and helps keep children in school.

Beyond cash or food transfers, there are other, more transformative, forms of social protection that address social injustice. Legislation to ensure adequate conditions of food system workers (including African migrants in Almeria) is one example.

Bolsa Família

Brazil's *Bolsa Família* is the world's largest conditional cash transfer programme for poverty reduction designed specifically to promote health.[42] Initiated in 2003, *Bolsa Família* had distributed funds to more than 25 per cent of Brazil's population by 2011. As of 2020, the programme covered 13.8 million families and paid an average of US$34 per month, in a country where the minimum wage is US$190 per month. Cash is transferred to eligible households on condition children attend school, where they get at least one meal per day, routine vaccinations, health check-ups and growth monitoring. Their mothers attend postnatal care services and receive health and nutritional education. Mortality among young children decreased as programme coverage increased, with the biggest impact on poverty-related malnutrition and diarrhoeal disease. *Bolsa Família* was a key driver of a 28 per cent reduction of poverty during President Lula's first term. In 2021, Jair Bolsonaro killed it when he assumed the presidency. But two years later, after Lula's re-election, *Bolsa* was relaunched.

Food banks are another form of safety net. In the words of Olivier De Schutter, UN Special Rapporteur on Extreme Food Poverty, food banks 'are a testimony to the failure of public authorities to deliver on the right to food and should be neither a permanent feature nor a substitute for more robust social programs'.

In the UK, one of the richest countries in the world, nearly 3 million people received emergency food parcels (from the Trussell Trust alone) in the year up to April 2023.[43] This compares to

26,000 in 2008/09 – more than a hundredfold increase in just fifteen years! Food banks were intended to be temporary. But there are now nearly 3,000 of them – twice the number of McDonald's restaurants.

This astronomical rise shows how the British State, over the last decade and a half of Tory Government, effectively abrogated its responsibility to protect the right to food. Food aid is now dispensed by the charity sector; the post-Second-World-War concept of the social contract is a distant memory. Do-nothing, look-the-other-way politics became normalised as the Welfare State was progressively replaced by charities who depend on public beneficence. Food banks are a great example of both community solidarity and governmental failure. *

Joining up

Malnutrition is multicausal. Its roots lie in several sectors that need to come together to address it. Agriculture needs to work in harmony with social protection to protect the nutrition and health of poor smallholder households as they grapple with seasonality and climate shocks. Improved water, sanitation and hygiene can increase nutritional benefits by reducing disease and enhancing nutrient absorption. And we've seen how linkages between local agricultural production and school feeding can generate 'win–win' benefits: income for local farmers, and nutrition and cognitive gains (and future income) for school-age children.

Large, multi-country studies have shown that the pursuit of

---

* A failure which some Government ministers seem bizarrely to be proud of: 'I have the privilege of some wonderful foodbanks in my constituency' (then-UK Health Secretary Victoria Atkins, February 2024). https://twitter. com/implausibleblog/status/1760317238068785585

wider goals – health equity, poverty reduction, water and sanitation, parental education – is critical for combating malnutrition.[44] The biggest improvements were consistently seen in programmes that delivered multisectoral interventions using different delivery platforms.

At the most fundamental political level, key success factors included high-level political commitment, strong leaders who mainstreamed nutrition across sectors in a joined-up approach, investments in data to see what was happening, vertical (national to community) coherence and the strengthened capacity of front-line workers in villages and cities.

Being accountable

Beyond the policies and programmes, the actual approach to governing – governance – is profoundly important, especially in the context of a food system that's controlled by commercial forces. Political parties make pledges and promises to get elected. Once elected, as the new government, they need to be held to account for what happens next . . . or what doesn't happen.

Conflict of interest is a big issue in food system governance, as Erik Millstone and Tim Lang discovered in their 2023 review of scientific advisory committees in the UK.[45] These committees were created to ensure a separation of science from policy. Ministers often insist – most likely after a bout of lobby pressure – that company reps are included on such committees, arguing that their knowledge is useful.

But this makes no sense. Any company can submit evidence and recommendations to committees, but if they sit at the policy table where discussions and decisions are made, it is a conflict of interest. And we know that generates biases in favour of industry.

Declared conflicts provide an indication of the extent to which independence may be compromised, as they can influence judgements about what should and should not be counted as a relevant risk to public health, how evidence is selected and interpreted, the height of the evidence bar, and who gets the benefit of the doubt.

Disclosure is not enough. A conflict of interest doesn't magically disappear if and when it's declared. In 2021, the UN Human Rights Council released a report addressing the role of science on toxic substances which stated: 'In order for the science that forms the basis of policy to be trusted, conflicts should be *avoided* rather than simply managed through disclosure processes.'

Governments should institutionalise clear and robust guidelines for assessing, monitoring and avoiding conflicts of interest. Tougher rules are needed on lobbying (including detailed disclosure of all interactions) and on spending and election campaign financing. This could be extended to shedding more daylight on international and bilateral trade and investment negotiations, with active involvement of those most likely to be impacted.

Accountability requires transparency. One of UK National Food Strategy's recommendations in 2021 was the Food Data Transparency Partnership aimed at setting targets, providing information to the public (including the health and environmental footprints of products), and incentivising industry to produce healthier, more sustainable food. Mandatory reporting by retailers and out-of-home suppliers on percentage sales and promotion of healthy vs. unhealthy food and drink could bring a step change in accountability. Public relations and communications agencies would also be required to report the proportion of support they provide to healthy vs. unhealthy food promotion. Such full disclosure would help citizens make informed choices and drive demand for healthier products. Unfortunately, after various delays (I wonder why) the plans were watered down. No longer would reporting be mandated, it would be voluntary. Will the new Labour Government bring back the mandate? Let's see . . .

Breaking up

Finally, if large corporations resist governmental attempts to rein them in, there is always a nuclear option available to a standing Government.[46] Political power legally trumps commercial power. Governments have three levers to address excessive corporate power. First, dispersion – the decentralisation and redistribution of concentrated corporate wealth and power using antitrust (competition law) to prevent and break up monopolies.[47] Second, democratisation in which corporate decision-makers are compelled to take into account the interests of all actors (e.g. via diverse stakeholder representation on corporate boards). And third, if all else fails, dissolution – the complete revocation of privileges, if and when corporations fail to disperse or democratise.

Breaking up is not hard to do. It's a political decision that can be made by any government with teeth. If supermarket cartels are driving farmers to the wall, the Government has to step in.

And change is happening. On 5 August 2024, a federal judge in the US ruled that Google had violated antitrust law.[48] US regulators are also seeking to break up Amazon and Meta, while the EU is threatening to escalate an antitrust case with Google. As Nicholas Shaxson, co-founder of the Balanced Economy Project, says, 'think of breakups not as a hammer smashing perfectly good firms into pieces, but as a Swiss army knife.'[49]

16

A Tale of Four Cities

Yes, we form the cities, but then the cities form us.
Jan Gehl, architect

Today, most people on the planet – six out of ten of us – live in cities. By 2050 it will be 80 per cent, with most of this expansion in Asia and sub-Saharan Africa.[1] In cities, inequalities and food injustice are often more pronounced. Food chains are longer, which makes fresh and healthier foods more expensive and more vulnerable to supply-side shocks. Food safety, sanitation and pollution can be big challenges. Big Food is also hyperactive in urban areas, targeting marketing to a high-density, captive population of consumers, many of whom lead solitary lives, looking for convenience.

Cities have traditionally engaged with the food system to ensure food safety through regulations, inspections and certification of service businesses and by managing food waste. But more is needed and there are big opportunities for cities to take the lead. Decentralisation has accelerated in many countries in recent decades, but for real autonomy, city authorities need at least three forms of power: fiscal, political and administrative.[2]

Cities have advantages too – dense social networks, strong

connectivity among organisations pursuing food justice, high literacy, political awareness, access to information and ideas. And there are long histories and traditions of urban resistance, including activist social movements. Although no country or national Government has yet managed to reverse a rising obesity trend, cities are now driving change and getting results.

Brighton

Along the coast from where I live, Brighton is a prosperous city of nearly 300,000 people, with pockets of real food poverty. The Brighton and Hove Food Partnership (BHFP) is an independent non-profit organisation working to make the city's food environment more equitable. In partnership with others, the BHFP runs cookery classes, community food groups, training, communications, campaigns and policy advocacy. In 2006, it published the first comprehensive city-wide action plan on food, later updated in 2012 and 2018. The latter included a consultation process with 600 participants and contains 200 actions which involve almost 100 partners and twenty-six separate council departments.

The whole-systems approach works. In 2021, Brighton was the first place in the UK to be awarded a Gold Sustainable Food Place Award. Data from the National Child Measurement Programme (NCMP) shows that levels of child overweight and obesity in Brighton are lower than national and regional levels. In December 2023, the Brighton and Hove Council announced a complete ban on fast-food adverts on over 200 council-owned bus and taxi shelters. Others are following now.

Several factors have been pivotal in the city: devolved power from the national level, political commitment from council leaders that was sustained across Labour Party and Green Party administrations, commitment of key individuals within the local authority and the city's voluntary sector, particularly the BHFP, solidified in a city-wide Food Strategy.

The strategy recommended a focus on the youngest children, including breastfeeding promotion; targeted school-based interventions, particularly in more deprived areas; strong inclusive cross-sectoral collaboration; and the use of local data to target support – for example, to individual primary schools.

London

In London, a study by dietetic students at King's College found that 69 per cent of food advertising across the boroughs of Greenwich, Havering and Merton was for 'unhealthy' products.[3] At that time, obesity was rising across the capital but with significant variation: Barking and Dagenham's prevalence (28 per cent) was more than twice that of Richmond and Thames (12 per cent).

In 2018 Transport for London (TfL) reported a deficit of £1 billion due to a fall in passenger numbers and reduced Government grants. Despite being under pressure to increase advertising revenue to avoid increasing fares, a ban on advertising food and drink high in fat, salt and sugar (HFSS) came into force across the TfL network in February 2019.

The restrictions led to a 20 per cent reduction in confectionery purchases and 1,000 fewer calories per household per week of unhealthy foods and drink.[4] This was estimated to lead to 100,000 fewer obesity cases, 3,000 fewer type 2 diabetes cases and 2,000 fewer heart disease cases across London, as well as saving the NHS £218 million.

A pivotal factor in pushing this through was the strong political support by Sadiq Khan, the Mayor of London. Khan decided any financial hit from banning HFSS ads was justified given the long-term costs of the child obesity epidemic. Close co-operation between the Greater London Authority and TfL, including support from the London Food Board and the Local Government Declaration on Sugar Reduction and Healthier Foods, provided impetus for parallel action on the part of boroughs. Retailers soon shifted to advertising healthier products. TfL's advertising revenues actually increased by £2.3 million in the first year after the policy was implemented.[5]

Niterói

In 2023, in Brazil, 30 per cent of children were overweight when the city of Niterói (with 37 per cent overweight) passed a law prohibiting the sale, marketing and distribution of ultra-processed products (UPPs) in schools. Six months later, Rio de Janeiro followed. More than 1 million students stand to benefit.

Both laws provide a legally codified definition of ultra-processed products (UPPs) for the first time in the country, including qualifying ingredients, additives, production processes and specific examples of products that should be prohibited (e.g. soft drinks, sweets, ultra-processed cakes and biscuits).

The food industry strongly opposed the inclusion of the UPP term, but the Rio legislation contains specific provisions and penalties for non-compliance with the law.

In support of Rio's bill, the Desiderata Institute, a non-profit, engaged in many rounds of discussions with city councillors to counter industry opposition. The Global Health Advocacy Incubator (GHAI) supported Desiderata by providing training on grassroots mobilisation and supporting advocacy and communications.* The Rio bill received unanimous support from the

---

* Drawing on decades of experience working with global civil society organisations across public health issues and political systems, GHAI provides strategic support to advocates working to implement laws that improve public health. As well as Niterói, GHAI supported advocacy, research, legal and communications action to persuade

city council and was enacted in July 2023. This led to a similar bill being introduced in São Paolo; other municipalities and states are now following.

Curitiba

South of Niterói and Rio, the city of Curitiba runs two programmes to ensure all city residents can buy fresh fruit and vegetables at fixed per-kilo prices that are 40–45 per cent below conventional retail. The Sacolão da Família and Nossa Feira programmes, which operate out of fixed stores and mobile markets, respectively, were developed because low-income groups were unable to afford fresh produce at supermarket prices, and many neighbourhoods lacked affordable alternative sources. Both extremely popular, they have a regulating effect on prices across the city. Nossa Feira also helps support the livelihoods of regional food producers by providing a guaranteed urban market for produce straight from the farm. A similar 'win–win' model to the partnership between schools and local farmers.

Other cities are also fighting back – Medellín in Colombia, Belo Horizonte in Brazil, Quito in Ecuador, Nairobi in Kenya, Dakar in Senegal – to name a few leading lights. In Europe, Amsterdam, Birmingham and Bristol. In North America, Philadelphia, Colorado and New York City have implemented reforms to food environments.

International organisations like the Milan Urban Food Policy Pact (MUFPP) are mobilising cities to transform their food

---

policymakers in Colombia to support food policies, to mobilise civil society support and to counter industry tactics. It's also active in Argentina, Ghana, India, Indonesia, Kazakhstan, Nigeria, Pakistan, Saint Kitts and Nevis, Uruguay, Vietnam, El Salvador, Costa Rica and Guatemala.

systems. More than 280 cities have now joined the Pact by signing a commitment to 'address non-communicable diseases associated with poor diets and obesity, giving specific attention where appropriate to reducing intake of sugar, salt, trans-fats, meat and dairy products and increasing consumption of fruits and vegetables and non-processed foods'.[6]

In 2023, I was involved with the Food Foundation and Birmingham City Council in an initiative to develop a food justice toolkit for use within the MUFPP and Eurocities networks.[7] It was an eye-opener for me. I had no idea so much was happening at the municipal level. Birmingham's food strategy is state of the art.[8] All the cities involved have mainstreamed food justice and self-governance into their strategies and plans, and they're all keen to share their experiences and learn from others. National governments are beginning to pay attention. A movement is being created.

17

Activate

What we think or what we know or what we believe is in the end of little consequence. The only thing of consequence is what we do.

John Ruskin

Consumers. To the food industry we're consumers – bodies at the end of the food chain that exist to buy the products they manufacture. But we are citizens, first and foremost. Citizens with agency that we sometimes forget we have. We need to use it. In this context, and at this time of cascading crisis, citizens, civil society organisations and networks must become more active and more activist. We need to shine a light on harms, challenge governments to do the right thing, hold them to account for their actions (or inaction) and raise wider public awareness. We need to be more vocal about food and public health and demand change from the political leaders we elect.

Citizenship sounds like a state of being, something you're born with, or you acquire over time. But it's really more a proactive process of engagement through which we empower ourselves.

Empowerment is a composite of choice, voice, challenge and change, the ability to choose, to voice your interests, to challenge the status quo, to change. And then there's a fifth ingredient –

self-confidence – the ability to recognise your own power and to assert yourself. This 'power within' (individual) is pivotal in realising the 'power with' (group). The self-confidence of individuals paves the way for a powerful collective and it is through the latter that we will have the greatest impact.

Citizen activism has exploded in the Global South in the twenty-first century, driven by rapid urbanisation, improved literacy and access to education (especially for women), a greater openness to political activity and the spread of new norms on rights and justice, including via social media.[1]

This chapter is the antidote to corporate capture and the dark arts – a public health playbook to help us shape a better future. Individually and collectively, there are many pathways to change, many tools and tactics to deploy. We can expose and oppose harmful products and practices and use evidence and experience to educate the public and advocate for stronger governmental action. We can monitor commercial and political practices and we can build social movements to disrupt 'business as usual' and hold industry and governments to account. All the while staying focused on the higher goal of improving access to healthy diets for all.

Expose, inform, advocate

Civil society organisations can draw on mounting scientific evidence and experiential insight to expose the harms caused by industry and the way the discourse has been polluted by the tactics that corporations use to deflect from their malnourishing products and practices. Pro-industry framings are spread through corporate social-responsibility initiatives and through front groups and paid-up researchers with whopping conflicts of interest. Sunlight is the best antiseptic. By exposing the source of spin and its motivation, corporate arguments can be debunked and harmful practices denormalised.

The corporate playbook includes arguments, rhetorical tricks and devices that we explored earlier. Companies portray themselves as benevolent providers. They push back against intrusive Government. They point the finger of blame at ignorant consumers for making poor choices. Neoliberalist ideology is so embedded that such positions begin to sound like self-evident truths. A counter ideology needs to be centred on equity and the root causes of the problems we face.[2] The social, political, and economic drivers of malnutrition are structural, not behavioural. They require Government action and they usually require us – citizens, the electorate – to make them act.

Evidence of what malnutrition does to individuals (and cumulatively to societies and economies) and the best mix of policies and programmes to combat it, is key. But it's not enough. We need to find better ways to counter the pollution of discourse on food and health and to tell the stories that really matter. One part of this is to inoculate the public by exposing the commercial origins of language used to distract from real causes. Words like 'litterbug', (carbon) 'footprint', 'nanny state', 'lifestyle', 'climate change' (not *crisis*), 'global warming' (not *heating*) all originate from industries keen to pass the buck.

Advocacy efforts that focus on the problem of obesity alone reinforce negative attitudes and generate stigma. By implying individuals have brought it on themselves, corporations and policymakers frame obesity as a moral failing. A more accurate narrative portrays individuals as protagonists who have agency but who are heavily constrained by the obesogenic environments in which they live, and over which they have limited control. This is another reason why a focus on the goal of reducing malnutrition in all its forms (including undernutrition, overweight and obesity) is preferred, and/or a focus on improving access to a healthy diet for all.

Advocates can also appeal to the law. Laws empower individuals and communities and can impel governments to act in the public interest. Legal settlements against the tobacco industry, opioid manufacturers and pesticide producers have all shown the power of litigation in naming and shaming, and in changing social norms towards industry. New research that shows how junk food is addictive, along with research into the damage it causes to our microbiomes, is frightening the industry. If emerging findings are confirmed, then lawsuits will follow.

Food Fighters:
The McLibel Two, José Bové and Cristiano Ronaldo

Round 1 (1997)

Where: London High Court (then European Court of Human Rights, Strasbourg, 2004)

Who: Environmental activists: Helen Steel and David Morris ('The McLibel Two')

What happened: The longest-running trial in British legal history. Steel and Morris questioned McDonald's claims that their burgers were both healthy and good for the environment. McDonald's took offence and the case went to court. The initial ruling went in part against Steel and Morris, but Justice Bell found the company had 'pretended to a positive nutritional benefit which their food didn't match' and 'exploited children in its advertising'. McDonald's had earlier threatened to sue more than fifty other organisations for libel,

---

including Channel 4 and several major publications, creating a climate of fear that chilled further legal challenges.[3]

Round 2 (1999)

Where: Building site in France

Who: José Bové and four other farmers

What happened: In a fight over American imports and tariffs Bové and his pals took a stand against US-imported hormone-treated beef and issued a passionate call to support local produce. The farmers demolished a partially built McDonald's restaurant, causing over 100,000 euros of damage, while hosting an impromptu cheese (Roquefort) tasting. Bové was jailed before later becoming a popular environmental hero, MEP and Green Party activist.[4]

Round 3 (2021)

Where: Euro Finals press conference, sponsored by Coca-Cola

Who: Cristiano Ronaldo

What happened: Ronaldo swept a bottle of Coke off the press conference table and replaced it with water, shouting '*Agua!*' to the banks of reporters. Coca-Cola's share price fell off a cliff, before climbing slowly back after other footballers were immediately banned from following his lead.[5] Three years later, Coca-Cola sponsorship of the Paris 2024 Olympics was met by a barrage of criticism, a new campaign 'Kick Big Soda Out of Sport' and a petition (with over 255,000 individual signatories and ninety-three organisations) that was presented to the Olympic Committee at the close of the games.[6]

Civil society can send transformative signals to industry if a large enough group of citizens (amplified by social media) creates a step change in demand for healthy, sustainable products and stops buying ultra-processed junk. Organised boycotts and buycotts (mass buying of the alternative) can, over time, have a big impact.

Advocacy can also target investors, a hybrid species being both public citizens and private co-owners. Compelling issue-framing can highlight the financial risks of investment in harmful industries and promote alternative investments. Better ones.

We know more now about what makes a corporation change. CEOs will ask: How much does it cost? Is our brand protected? Is it enhanced? Are we on the right side of history? Is the Government about to force us to do this? (Should we jump before we're pushed?) Will we gain a commercial edge if we do this? Advocacy should use these questions to expose differences between companies and leverage power against power. Such initiatives have led to the disinvestment of hundreds of billions of dollars from the tobacco, fossil-fuel and firearms industries. Junk food has to be next.

Public health and nutrition advocacy is now more evidence-driven and experience-informed than ever before. Reports, journal articles, policy briefs and multimedia campaigns convey ideas and lessons which are widely disseminated, both physically and digitally. We can break down success factors in political advocacy into three categories: problem, rationale and solutions.

First, with regard to the problem, use existing evidence (if it changes, so should you), expose the human drama, focus on the main causes and external barriers people face; use killer facts, elevate the signal from the noise. Another tactic is to emphasise how ultra-processed food is corporate bait to boost profits at the expense of children's health. A campaign that highlights how junk-food marketing aims to get us hooked on a product taps into teenagers' natural tendency to rebel, their resistance to being tricked or coerced. Much more effective than simply giving them information on healthy eating, according to a University of Chicago study in which 362 mid-teenagers in Texas were split into two groups. One group was given an investigative report on marketing tricks used by food companies, and the other was given simple advice on the benefits of healthy eating. Using follow-up surveys for the rest of the school year, researchers found that junk food was shunned more by the 'marketing tricks' group. Inspiration for the experiment came from the anti-tobacco campaigns of the 1990s, which had also highlighted the nefarious tactics of big firms to get people hooked on cigarettes.

Second, on the rationale for action, frame issues around equality and justice (caring is necessary but not sufficient), on the need to protect children, appeal to a sense of fairness (no one held back), connect personal with social (highlight how everyone benefits), stress that positive change is not only needed, it is within our reach.

Third, on solutions, present specific, feasible actions, target those in power with the media they use (not academic journals), frame solutions as better options, not less choice, identify quick wins, but prepare to play the long game, and finally, grow a rhinoceros hide – you'll be attacked if you challenge the status quo.

'Subvertising' is a new tactic gaining traction in bigger cities. Using art and wit to alter corporate advertising by creating parodies or spoofs to replace ads in public areas.[7] In 2022, a billboard in Brighton portrayed an apocalyptic climate dystopia of dead animals, toxic waste and burning forests, in the middle of which sat a Toyota 4×4. The slogan was 'Let's ruin everything'. A strip across the bottom read: 'In November 2022 Toyota were ranked the tenth-worst company in the world for their climate footprint and lobbying against climate action'. Founded in 2012, Brandalism is an activist artist collective in the UK that uses such protest art to demand governmental regulation of 'environmentally harmful products' and to call out blatant greenwashing by industry. It wasn't long before they targeted British Cycling following its insane decision to accept sponsorship from Shell.[8]

Watch

A growing number of organisations have developed corporate surveillance programmes to monitor harmful practices. Some – like Open Secrets, Transparency International, US Right to Know – have set up databases to systematically gather intelligence on the commercial and political activities of corporations and share this information widely.

Researchers are increasingly using freedom of information (FOI) requests. I filed one in 2023 (www.whatdotheyknow.com), as I was interested in the University of Reading's Food Science Department where I'd studied in the late Seventies. I was intrigued by the number of university staff who appeared to be happily taking funding from the ultra-processed food industry, either via associations like the British Nutrition Foundation (a long-time industry front) or directly to support their research. One professor was hyperactive on Twitter/X shooting down anyone who had the temerity to disseminate new research that revealed links between UPF consumption and various chronic diseases. The website suggested the department had some industry funding, though – unlike their public funding – it was not specified. During my three years in this department, nearly fifty years ago, I had become uneasy with the emphasis on working for the industry. I thought by now there would have been more of a balance with public health nutrition.

I lodged an FOI request, asking for the names and top three industry donors in the last five years. Several weeks of feet-dragging followed. The university first argued that it would infringe their commercial advantage and 'undermine its ability to fulfil its wider role as an institution dedicated to teaching and learning, which is clearly not in the public interest'. I argued that the primary public interest of any university department surely related to its academic independence and the quality of its work. Given the documented bias of industry-funded studies, the onus is on the university to be transparent. Eventually they backed down to reveal the top three donors – Mars Symbioscience, PepsiCo and Roquettes Frères – all UPF manufacturers. Total donations (2018–2023) amounted to £379,612, a tidy little sum.

Monitoring is also a way of holding governments to account to respond to any malpractice that's revealed. Examples include the International Network for Food and Obesity Research, Monitoring and Action Support (INFORMAS), which has developed methods and indicators to measure and compare food environments and policies across countries. Commercial databases such as Euromonitor Nutrition also now provide data on the volume, sales, nutrient composition, intake and brand share for UPFs across fifty-four countries, collated from primary and secondary data sources. Such data and evidence on what's being done, what could be done and the impacts of implemented policies are powerful fuel for advocacy.

Between 2013 and 2016, Oxfam's Behind the Brands campaign sought to drive more sustainable sourcing policies and practices among the ten biggest global food and beverage companies.[9] A scorecard was developed and used to assess agricultural sourcing policies and develop a league table. Within months all the corporations published new policies or assessments. A race to the top had been created – one that used both stick and carrot (challenging as well as praising). The scorecard was used by investors, pension-fund managers, industry peers and even companies to see the benefits of using the framework as a roadmap for their future social-sustainability policies.

To expose, track and counteract corporate tactics, we need to get organised. A global community of practice would help. This could encompass an online, interactive platform, a repository of evidence and experience, along with workshops (to connect people, share ideas and strengthen capacity) and a set of curated advocacy, communications and media resources. A one-stop shop for nutrition advocates and activists. The Governance, Ethics & Conflicts of Interest in Public Health Network is a great example. Adaptations of this chapter's 'counter-playbook' could include a regional or national focus, a focus on a particular industry or commercial organisation, and on tools and tactics for addressing a particular commercial practice. Systematically identifying examples of best practices around the world could complement ongoing work to understand and develop mechanisms to challenge the dominance of transnational corporations.

Organise, mobilise

Dr Jay Naidoo is an anti-apartheid activist from South Africa who now campaigns for the right to food. He often recalls a three-word lesson – 'Organise or starve' – passed down to him from his great-grandfather, an indentured labourer who came from South India to work on the sugar plantations of KwaZulu-Natal.

Nelson Mandela also knew something about the power of organised resistance. Throughout his life, he adhered to 'Ubuntu', a philosophy that supports collectivism over individualism, highlighting the interdependence of humans on each other and our responsibility to the world around us. ('I am, because we are'.)

Getting organised, building alliances and networks to amplify our collective power, can turn the key and convince policymakers to act. There are multiple examples through history of the power of social movements: the establishment of a Welfare State in the UK following the Second World War; the introduction of female suffrage following years of the suffragette movement; the trade union movement fighting for an eight-hour working day; the anti-apartheid movement; HIV activists taking on Big Pharma, forcing them to reduce drug costs.

We also now know that the public wants action, as opinion polls in different countries show support for Government regulation of junk food. But this support is usually quiet, passive, hidden. Just Stop Oil disrupts: it's highly visible, splashing orange paint around London. But nobody is marching in the streets to improve our diet. There is no Just Stop Junk . . . yet. Why is this?

Civil society organisations have real passion and commitment, but they often don't have sufficient power to challenge governments and the commercial food sector, and they may be fragmented and poorly funded. Without public pressure, governments are more likely to simply do nothing. Inertia and inaction means business as usual.

Brian Eno speaks about social revolution happening in two phases.[10] First, people realise the current system isn't working, and then they realise that everybody else has realised it too. This is when things start to take off, when people come together, energies converge and coalesce and a movement is born.

The American civil rights activist and writer Audre Lorde said, 'There is no such thing as a single-issue struggle because we do not live single-issue lives.' We need to link up, but also build on the past to learn countertactics from other activist organisations. Collective solidarity can be fostered by building coalitions. In turn, this means we need to break out of our professional or disciplinary silos. Tribalism confers identity and meaning but it can also stop us thinking for ourselves, and it can stifle the innovation that comes from crossing boundaries. We spend too much time in echo chambers where wholesale pre-packaging of positions is rife. Being a member of one group should never disqualify you from aligning with others. Social media forces us to entrench, rather than examine our own positions.

And there's so much to learn from other social movements. Synergies are forged across diverse movements to improve health, social justice and environmental outcomes. The fight for access to antiretroviral HIV therapies, for example, showed the power of mobilisation and organisation. South Africa's Treatment Action Campaign and other activists like ACT UP played good cop/bad cop, a twin-track strategy of working on the inside while applying pressure from the outside – sitting at the policy table and marching on the streets.[11] AIDS activists became extremely well-informed on the science and were always ready to get into the weeds. Throughout their struggles with Big Pharma and with governments, they highlighted their agency and ownership ('not about us, without us'). When business as usual is killing people and the planet, it's our moral right and civic duty to fight back.

But disobedience has to do more than disrupt. It must enlighten people and enable them/us to see the problem as well as the (potential) solution, and how our futures are connected. Confrontation without communication is just a mass vent, not progressive change.

In *No Is Not Enough* Naomi Klein impels coalitions of the 'no' to develop a collective vision of the 'yes'.[12] To connect, not compete. 'My crisis is bigger than yours' will never work in the long run, especially when it's clear the crises interact. It behoves us to deal with the crisis cascade as a multilayered, interacting challenge.

The co-founder of the UK's Reclaim the Streets movement, John Jordan, argues that resistance and alternatives are 'the twin strands of the DNA of social change'.[13] Change needs resources and space to develop. Roger Hallam, co-founder of Extinction Rebellion and Just Stop Oil, cites other cases in history where relentless non-violent civil obedience kept an issue in the limelight. And then something snapped, a tipping point was reached, a threshold breached, triggering sudden revolutionary change.

To challenge corporate power, we need to shine a laser light on its modus operandi, its strengths and weaknesses. Training, orientation and capacity-strengthening can be built into the process of coalition-building (learning from the success catalysed by Global Health Advocacy Incubator in Latin America.) The same needs to happen at academic level – graduate schools of nutrition and public health can offer classes on commercial determinants of nutrition and health (see Chapter 19). Why is food and nutrition so far behind the health community in this?

Public interest organisations often struggle for funding compared with industry-established and funded think tanks, front groups and fake grassroots ('astroturf') organisations. Bloomberg Philanthropies bucked this trend by investing in civil society action and research in Mexico. The funding had a big impact in raising public awareness and compelling Government to levy a tax on sugary drinks – and in supporting researchers to evaluate the impact of the tax. Its huge success led to a call for an investment of US$1 billion from philanthropic and other sources to support 100 countries to adapt and apply the Mexican approach.[14]

Shareholder activism
Half the world's money is held in pension funds. In the UK, it's £2.6 trillion, enough to buy everything produced in the country

for a whole year. Companies rely on our pensions and fund managers have a huge amount of dispersed power. If they use this power to invest in companies that generate financial returns but significant harms, they're investing in ill-health and the climate crisis on our behalf.

Pension funds could be invested in companies who aim to benefit (or at least, not harm) people and planet. As shareholders/co-owners/stewards, fund managers could engage with companies to help them move in this direction.

Responsible investment goes beyond environmental, social and governance (ESG) investing, which seeks to optimise financial returns within existing regulatory frameworks. ESG does not require investors to take responsibility for the impacts of their investments on people and planet. Responsible investors, on the other hand, are transparent in how they assess and trade off impacts against financial risk and return; they take a long-term approach and they take full responsibility for all impacts of their investments, negative and positive. *All* impacts are important; it's not just about financial risk and return. Of course, this brings tensions – how far are investors willing to go to reduce financial returns to avoid harming people and planet?

But we can all act, by asking questions and joining the conversation. Just ask your employer about your pension fund, check its website, figure out which companies they invest in and what they're doing. It's your right, it's your money.

Shareholder activism is gaining traction. By purchasing shares in companies and acquiring voting rights, non-governmental organisations can influence the actions of the company from the inside. One example was a proposal from Oxfam for Amazon to put an hourly warehouse-floor worker on its board of directors. In another campaign in early 2024, Dutch shareholder activists called for Shell's 'Follow This' climate resolution to align its emission targets with the 2015 Paris Agreement. As a result, twenty-seven big investors agreed to back the resolution, including the National Employment Savings Trust, which manages pensions for a quarter of UK workers. *The Guardian* (16 January 2024) reported a shareholder rebellion was now underway after Shell abandoned its plans to reduce oil and gas production before the end of the decade.

ShareAction

A non-profit, based in London, ShareAction promotes responsible investment by working with investors (including asset managers and pension funds) to push for action on climate, equality and health. It has three interconnected goals:

1. Unlock the power of investors to drive up standards for responsible investment.
2. Work with policymakers to set the legal frameworks for a finance system for people and planet.
3. Build a movement of citizens who are proactive in deciding where their money is invested, who come together to realise their collective power.

The organisation provides investors with examples of objective, coherent mechanisms to ensure all impacts are considered, not just financial risk and return. Responsible investors state how they calibrate return against impacts as well as the red lines – the negative impacts that are to be avoided at all costs.

As it holds shares in the biggest companies, ShareAction is able to table questions at annual general meetings (AGMs), challenging companies to reorientate their investments. Through its convening power, it gathers individual and institutional investors to co-file resolutions on specific topics to demand change.

In 2023, it persuaded Tesco to report on the percentage of its profits that derives from healthy foods. Unilever soon followed suit.

In March 2024, supported by a group of large shareholders including Legal and General, ShareAction called on Nestlé to reduce the proportion of unhealthy foods in its portfolio. The goal was to get the issue on the agenda, get the debate going. At the 18 April AGM in Lausanne, only 11 per cent of shareholders voted for it. 'Disappointing,' said ShareAction CEO Catherine Howarth, 'but it's a foot in the door.'

(Interestingly, this seems to be par for the course for AGM challenges by activist shareholders; in 2022, for example, 89 per cent of Coca-Cola's shareholders, 86 per cent of PepsiCo's and 87 per cent of McDonald's voted against proposals to improve public health and environmental impact.[15])

An earlier climate-related resolution proposed by ShareAction at Barclays in 2020, which led to 34 per cent of shareholders voting against the board, shocked the bank, who later released a net-zero strategy in response. An HSBC resolution demanding the bank stop financing fossil fuels led to significant changes even before the vote took place. When companies feel growing shareholder pressure, they will act . . . eventually.

The path of most resistance

The 'food citizen' concept emerged in the early 1990s alongside food democracy and food sovereignty – aimed at emphasising the agency and legitimacy of citizens in improving food systems.

In *Citizens*, Jon Alexander highlights the legalisation of abortion in Ireland as an exemplar of citizen power.[16] The decision was only taken after the Government admitted it was stuck and commissioned Citizen Assemblies.

Would a government ever commission such deliberations on junk food? Do we need activism to raise the issue to a point where it has to do this? Can we 'press all the buttons' and work on multiple fronts at the same time, using conventional activism to force Government to regulate and legislate, while demanding more power for citizen-led action and convening Citizens' Assemblies?

In our 'Stories of Change' initiative, we found that the spark that ignited the mix of success factors was leadership.[17] Influential individuals – nutrition champions – had knowledge and experience, but they were also adept at figuring out entry points, stories and angles to make the case for nutrition, depending on who they were speaking to. They knew how to adapt their language and behaviour and the way they framed a problem to catalyse action. They never called malnutrition a *problem*, they called it a *challenge*, one that the person they were speaking to, at that point in time, could help solve. These leaders were trusted in both formal and informal networks in which they operated. Some were naturally charismatic, but many had worked on face-to-face communications and they had improved over time.

In this work, we figured we needed to dig deeper to understand who these leaders really were, how they emerged and what made them effective. In a linked study, we interviewed eighty-nine influential decision-makers in four countries with high levels of undernutrition: Bangladesh, Ethiopia, India and Kenya.

These individuals opened doors, turned keys in policy processes and inspired others. They weren't hierarchical; this was 'lateral leadership' – the ability to work successfully across sectors, bridge disciplinary divides (e.g. between agriculture and health), build collaborations and alliances, and communicate effectively.

Leaders often work behind the scenes. In Peru, the country's record-breaking reduction of undernutrition in 2005–2011 has been attributed to the executive leadership by Peruvian politicians on all sides, particularly in the adoption of the electoral campaign '555' (reduce stunting for the under-fives by five percentage points in five years). But this was not the whole story. '555' started life as a pledge that had been extracted from all presidential candidates in the run-up to elections by a concerted campaign waged by a coalition of civil society groups. Different strategies for different people, depending on who they are, where they are and what they're facing.

In 2021, Scottish MP Kirsty McNeill called for a leadership revolution – again, not the usual hierarchical, patriarchal top-down style, but one in which leaders create the *conditions* for change. Leaders who are relentless champions for equity, who bring people together, build coalitions and movements before becoming their trustees, who hand the mic over, hold themselves accountable, and who adhere to the basic Nolan Principles for public-office holders of selflessness, integrity, objectivity, accountability, openness, honesty and leadership.[18]

Long haul

We do not inherit the land from our ancestors, we borrow it from our children.

Chief Seattle, leader of Duwamish and
Suquamish peoples

What we do or don't do now – as individuals, organisations and governments – has immense implications for future generations.

Structural racism and institutionalised discrimination against Indigenous peoples has generated a twenty-first-century form of food apartheid in many parts of the world.

But it goes beyond that. We're colonising the future too, because we're consuming it and we're repeatedly kicking the can down the road. Capitalist systems are depleting planetary resources in ways for which future generations will have to pay. This intergenerational theft is another form of corporate laundry – 'longwashing'. Of course, politicians do it too, selling short the next generation by shackling them with the implications of their decisions. Brexit and high-interest student loans are just two examples.

In *The Good Ancestor,* Roman Krznaric traces the history of our colonisation of the future.[19] Starting in the eighteenth century, he describes how Britain colonised Australia, considering it to be *terra nullius* ('nobody's land') ignoring Indigenous peoples' claims. We are now behaving in a similar way with time. Political and economic systems consider the future to be *tempus nullius* ('nobody's time'). Our temporal horizons have collapsed inwards, driven by short-term, dopamine-triggered feedback loops. Krznaric distinguishes between the 'marshmallow brain' – routinely hijacked by the digital distraction industry that has weaponised smartphones and social media platforms to steal time – and the 'acorn brain' that thinks long-term and considers the intergenerational consequences of actions taken today.

Reading this, I saw a lot of connections with food and nutrition. We had known for years about the way undernutrition persists through the life-cycle, and even across generations. But more recently, the new science of epigenetics was showing how our behaviours and environment can change the way our genes work. What we do now, therefore, can have major implications for the health of our future children, and for the health of their children.

The junk-food industry knows all about our marshmallow brain and has been manipulating its addictive and impulsive traits for decades. Politicians prefer marshmallows which are well suited to their narrow time horizons, linked with their limited time in office. Getting politicians to use their acorn brains and think long term is the big challenge.

We need to act now but think long term. To learn from Native American populations, who have long acknowledged their deep responsibilities to their great-grandchildren and beyond. The Iroquois code of 'seventh-generation decision-making' requires decisions made today to factor in the consequences for the next seven generations. A long-term 'do no harm' approach: do unto future generations as you would have past generations do unto you.

But we also need to be realistic. How can anyone 'think long' or plan for the future if they can't even nourish their families today? Food, nutrition and health *security* in the present are foundational for a better future.

18

Decolonise

As a discipline, international nutrition has always operated at the interface of health and food systems, both of which have deep roots in colonialism. Many of us bang on happily about nutrition being both a *marker* (of deprivation) and a *maker* (of development), but we seldom revisit a history when nutritional science propped up colonialism, racism, inequity and injustice.

White supremacy (and its white saviourism progeny in international development) goes well beyond the consolidation of the 'pale, male and stale' in positions of leadership. It manifests in what does (or does not) happen between countries, and groups and individuals within those countries.

After joining IFPRI in 1999, I worked on 'capacity-building for nutrition'. At that time the finger of blame for the failure of large-scale nutrition programmes pointed to insufficient, unsustainable capacities within communities and organisations responsible for implementing them. But many of us failed to take the next step. Inadequate capacity is not the cause of failure, it's the *symptom* of a larger failure that has its roots in colonialism and intergenerational injustice. The proper response is not to launch a capacity development programme – it's to dig deeper, to uncover and unravel the structural causes.

Digging Deeper

My alma mater, the London School of Hygiene and Tropical Medicine (LSHTM) was in the news a lot in 2020, as it was at the forefront of the COVID response (Chris Whitty was an alumnus). The School had been founded at the end of the nineteenth century by the UK Government's Colonial Office to support Empire. It shows in the name, one of many, including Liverpool School of Tropical Medicine and Imperial College.

After George Floyd's murder in 2020, the LSHTM council commissioned a review.[1] I read all 164 pages of it. The findings were damning: 'LSHTM's world-leading research has benefited a great many people worldwide, but the colonial attitudes inherent in LSHTM's historical mission negatively impact students and staff of colour today'.

There were deep dives into the lives of pioneer scientists, including Cicely Williams (see Chapter 4), who I remember studying when I was at the School half a century after her. In 1938, she made recommendations for the treatment of malnutrition that managed to combine the progressive (focus on prevention, on the youngest children, on the need for collaboration between health and agriculture) with the white supremacist (the imperative to educate 'primitive people'). By pointing to the behaviour of the parents, the British colonial Government could obviate any responsibility for the deaths of their children. The wider imperialist dynamics that wrecked indigenous farming, causing famines and widespread malnutrition, were ignored.

> The School responded to the findings: 'We are committed to LSHTM being a place of anti-racist education, employment, research and partnerships. Racism has no place in our school or society and will not be tolerated at LSHTM'.

In 2020, the global anti-racism movement and the COVID pandemic combined to lay bare entrenched structures and systems of racism, discrimination and unequal power that have shaped global health, nutrition and development institutions for decades. In May of that year, the month in which George Floyd was murdered, nearly all of the medical staff who died of COVID in the UK were from minority ethnic groups. Throughout the pandemic, individuals from these communities were at greatest risk.

The resurgence of Black Lives Matter then was paralleled by an accelerating movement to 'decolonise development'. Different people had different views on what this actually meant. Seye Abimbola nailed it:

We can begin to truly decolonize global health by being aware of what we do not know, that people understand their own lives better than we could ever do, that they and only they can truly improve their own circumstances and that those of us who work in global health are only, at best, enablers.[2]

To me, decolonisation starts with a proactive re-viewing and rethinking of the past through a justice lens. Becoming more aware of who you are, where you stand, where you're coming from. Positionality. Decolonisation has to challenge the institutional hierarchy that determines whose history is told, and whose knowledge counts. Outsiders like me need to focus on the 'enabling environment' and structural issues, and be prepared to stand in solidarity with civil society organisations for the long haul, through thick and thin.

In a 2019 paper, Stephanie Nixon uses the metaphor of a coin.[3] The coin represents a social structure that produces and maintains various forms of inequality. If you're on the top of the coin you exist in a state of privilege, you have an advantage that you did not earn, that you have because of who you happen to be. The bottom of the coin represents a state of oppression, or disadvantage that you did not earn, that you suffer because of who you happen to be. The top exists because the bottom exists – privilege and oppression are literally flip sides of the same coin.

People are rarely on the top of the coin because of merit or worth. Just as the disadvantage received by people on the bottom of the coin is unearned and unfair, so is the advantage received by people on the top. When resources (salaries, funding, leadership) flow to people on top to design and administer programmes for those on the bottom, we are just perpetuating inequity.

Defining a decolonial pathway cannot be done by those who wield power, those on the top of the coin. Power has to be fought for, just as independence was. It will not be ceded. A fight for food justice is a fight for social justice. Those of us in the Global North can be allies to marginalised groups. But the system cannot be transformed by providing aid. Far too often, development aid blocks or delays structural change. Disempowers. Allies need to step aside, look, listen and learn – eyes and ears, not mouth.

Decolonisation is a process, not a tokenistic tick-box exercise. The goal is not to move people from the bottom to the top. The goal is to dismantle the system of oppression that's causing these inequities – to get rid of the coin altogether. Many of us in the Global North see our work in 'international development' as neutral, selfless, even altruistic. But *assisting* people on the bottom of the coin does not change the system that put them there, it just perpetuates it. In practical terms, outsiders need to become less oblivious, step aside and foreground the knowledge and experience of people affected directly.

The 'international development' project has always been freighted with colonial baggage, reflecting 'us–them' relationships between countries and between people. Organisations constantly revise and reframe the concept to shore up their legitimacy. It's a story predicated on myths.

One myth is that policy is rational and linear; that the gap between theory and practice – the 'know–do gap' – can be reduced by better policy and better programmes. In *Cultivating Development*, David Mosse blows this out of the water.[4] Policy, he argues, is designed to maintain political support – to *legitimise* practice, not orientate it. Development interventions are driven not by policy but by the exigencies of agencies and the need to maintain relationships. They're designed to generate political support. Whoever controls the story controls the definition of the problem and the way of measuring it. We're back to epistemic power – the power of ideas. Projects are designed to be amenable to whatever the donor currently favours as the solution. The hammer comes first, not the nail.

In this world, failure is really a failure of interpretation. Projects only fail if they *are failed* by wider networks of support and validation. Project metrics are chosen to demonstrate change, whether it's change that's valued by those affected by it, or not, so long as metaphors of participation, partnership, good govern-ance are mobilised.

Policy has become an end not a means in development. Just as evidence does not lead to better policy, policy often does not lead to action or impact on the ground. Actions are driven by relationships, interests and cultures – not by policy. And yet, development reproduces and stabilises policy models to ensure the money keeps flowing.

More than ever, the aid industry targets short-term, measurable results with attributable links between their investment and outcomes. I remember the mind-numbing task of completing a 'logframe' for every proposal. The logframe (logical framework) is the North Star in results-based management. A step-by-step, box-by-box grid of assertions and promises of how project inputs will be translated by project activities and processes into quantified outputs, outcomes and impacts. A linear chain with each step being measurable and attributable to the project. There's nowhere to hide when you're being judged by the logframe and there's no space for creativity or innovation (unless it's been pre-specified and tabulated). And this was before proposals required Gantt charts, the ultimate in micro-management, originally developed in the early twentieth century to monitor factory workers at conveyor belts.

In *Blind Spot*, anthropologist and physician Salmaan Keshavjee develops an intellectual history of international development assistance for the health sector in low-income countries centred on the idea of a 'trap of neoliberal programmatic blindness'.[5] Neoliberalism shapes the behaviour of both the donor and the recipient at every step of the way: from proposal to interpretations of evaluation results. The rules of the game are known to all who play.

Working in India in the mid-1980s, I questioned my own role: Why was I there? Who was benefiting, the villagers or me? Naxalite revolutionaries asked me this question after walking into my hut one day – seven guys with rifles, one of which was pointed at my chest. I started to doubt 'development'. It wasn't a word the Koya used – they spoke about justice. Development without justice made no sense. At worst, it seemed like a bit of a game.

Large-scale, intergenerational appropriation alongside the drip-feeding of small-scale projects and handouts. I see parallels today in the way small-scale corporate social-responsibility projects are designed to deflect attention from large-scale profiteering.

Our overarching goal, then, should be international and intergenerational justice, not development. Enabling and supporting change, not delivering charity. Justice has equality, morality and freedom built into it and it encompasses social, racial, gender, climate and intergenerational dimensions. They're all interconnected. Justice is a *universal* goal – it applies to all people in all countries.

19

Illuminate

Power in the world of research governs who sets the research question, who pays for the work, who decides on methods, who actually does the work, whose names are on the paper, who publishes it, who reads it and who decides on the next study to be done – or the next research programme to be set up and funded. Pretty much everything.

Parachute research (also known as helicopter, or even parasitic, research) is when power is held by someone else, somewhere else, usually researchers from the Global North. Parachute researchers are air-dropped into a Global-South country for a week or so, to check on data collection before returning home to wait for the data to be sent. They then run analyses, publish the report, often with only their name/s on. Only then would they think – usually at the behest of the donor – to do something called 'outreach'. Outreach boils down to getting people back in the affected country to pay attention to the shopping list of recommendations at the back of the report. Involvement of local researchers is usually reserved for data collection, often in dangerous conditions. Historical power imbalances aren't disturbed and investment in sustainable research infrastructure in the study countries remains weak. This is scientific neocolonialism. It's better now though vestiges remain: why, for example, do international development organisations so often start their monthly newsletter with a list of travel destinations – Jeremy is going to Nairobi, Sophie is in Jakarta – as if this is the most newsworthy feature?

Decolonising research involves shifting control and leadership to academics and research organisations in study locations. Shifting power involves a lot more than granting co-authorship of papers with partners from study countries. Performative tokenism and a name on a paper does not equate with a meaningful involvement in a study. Insight and leadership of locals is needed throughout the research process. Local researchers are best placed to formulate relevant research questions, to understand local culture and to interpret and communicate findings in the most useful ways. It's basic ethics – researchers and communities should set the agenda where they live and work.

Researchers need to generate research questions before they get to work. But before that they need to ask some big questions about why they're doing research in the first place:

- *Why* study: to create generalisable knowledge for all? Or actionable knowledge on current challenges for people who demand or need it?
- *What* to study: clinical nutrition, nutrients, consumer behaviours? Or the deep-rooted structural drivers of malnutrition, and the political challenges in addressing it?
- *Who* to work with: vulnerable individuals (mothers, infants) or politicians, policymakers, businesses?
- *How* to study: detached, objective, hypothesis-testing, single-discipline research? Or embedded, participatory action-research that involves real people grappling in real time with challenges that they (not us) have identified? People with voice, volition, views.

Bridging the 'know–do' gap

In the early 2010s, nutrition's stock was rising. Part of this came from other crises becoming more manageable. The AIDS pandemic, for example, was being curbed as an effective triple therapy of antiretrovirals, supplemented with nutritional support, became more available and affordable.

A new *Lancet* Nutrition Series was released in June 2013, followed a week later by a Nutrition for Growth (N4G) Summit held in London that led to US$23 billion of pledges to tackle global malnutrition. The UK Government announced: 'World leaders sign global agreement to help beat hunger. Governments, businesses and charities make a historic pledge to end undernutrition in our lifetime at today's Nutrition for Growth event'. The week after that, the G8 Summit was held at Lough Erne, Northern Ireland, chaired by David Cameron. The G8 endorsed and 're-committed' member governments to honour the pledges made at the N4G. After that, new initiatives seem to be springing up almost weekly. A raft of 'Sustainable Development Goals' (SDGs) had been agreed by UN member states, one of which was 'to end all forms of malnutrition by 2030'. The UN designated 2016–2025 as the Decade of Action on Nutrition.

It all sounded like progress . . . until you checked the reality on the ground. Coverage of nutrition interventions was poor where they were most needed.[1] So was the state of underlying preconditions: food security, women's status, equity, access to adequate health-care services, water and sanitation. We had evidence of the problem, its causes, its consequences. We knew what worked and we had high-level commitments to act.

But something was missing.

Evidence and experience are different components of knowledge. We needed to understand experience, and learn from it. You don't learn to ride a bike by reading a manual. You jump on, fall off and get back on again, until you figure it out. Manuals provide information, not experience.

The 'know–do gap' – the disconnect between knowing what to do and actually doing it, between words and actions – was blocking progress. To bridge this gap, we needed better advocacy and better stories.

In the mid-2010s, we were hearing more calls from countries for experiential knowledge, on *how* nutrition improves, and *how to* (proactively) improve nutrition outcomes. Learning-by-doing had become a bit of a development cliché. But learning from someone else's 'doing' is also possible, so long as it's documented and conveyed in a compelling story. By showing connections, cutting through complexity, bypassing defence mechanisms, stories motivate us to believe 'yes, we can'. They can both inspire and inform action.

This is what propelled our team in 2015 to launch 'Stories of Change.'[2] We started with a first wave of six countries that had punched above their economic weight in reducing child malnutrition – 'positive-deviants' in ugly development-speak. Three were in South Asia (Bangladesh, Nepal and the state of Odisha in India) and three in Africa (Ethiopia, Zambia and Senegal). Each case study was led by a local research organisation that linked up with policymakers in quarterly meetings. Quantitative analyses were run and around 500 'key informant interviews' held (at every level from mothers and front-line health workers in villages to cabinet ministers), along with multiple focus-group discussions. We brought all this together in a series of consultations in all six countries.

The results were fascinating. Not all experiences we described were glowing success stories, and not all successes endured. It wasn't so much the 'what' that was important, but the 'how'. The key take-home was to think about the *process* (not necessarily any one intervention) and the enabling environment. Every setting was different, but in broad brush, we identified seven crucial interacting ingredients of progress: commitment, coherence, accountability, data, capacity, finance and leadership.

Change and challenge are almost the same words, and we saw that many changes were triggered by a challenge. Turning it round, changes also generate challenges – like crisis and opportunity, they are flip sides of the same coin.

A growing number of organisations, including UNICEF and London City University, are using similar 'lived-experience' research to shine a light on realities faced, and options for tackling malnutrition in different contexts. This can also help policymakers understand why a policy or intervention may not be working as expected and provide concrete recommendations on how to improve it.

Research and action . . . why is there such a tension between them, and between researcher and activist? Why this *ne'r the twain shall meet* dichotomy? I've often been puzzled by this. I came into this field as I wanted to try and make a difference. Research was a precursor to change, generating knowledge of the world to help us understand what's happening and how it might be improved. Discovery, understanding, change. So why has it become so divorced from the real world in which most of its subjects live?

Yes, research can improve action, but it works the other way too – action can enhance the relevance (and thus impact) of research. By researching real-world action, we see the roadblocks, the entry points, the windows of opportunity.

There is a quaint old notion that holding beliefs and values compromises research objectivity and neutrality. But silence and inaction are not neutrality. To work with a research organisation that is supported by another public or private organisation is to implicitly take a position. It's far better to be *explicit* about your positionality and values.

Academics/researchers and social movements have different theories of change, different pathways. But their goals are often the same. Most academics aim to generate rigorous evidence that, if presented properly to key policy actors, will result in decisions that improve the lives of marginalised communities. Social movements tread a different path – they aim to trigger change by building mass organisations that disrupt. Knowledge is for public action, to mobilise people – not for bureaucrats to design policies.

Collaborations between the two require these differences to be surfaced and discussed to enable joint action to achieve shared goals. Open debate is key to good research anyway, but it should be seen as an integral part of it.

In a 2023 blog post, Oxfam adviser Duncan Green shone a light on a new hybrid breed of 'pracademics', who are both academics and active practitioners.[3] He welcomed the crossover (if not the word!), but feared its professionalisation. There's a risk that institutionalising the concept would neuter it, would turn it into another box-ticking step in the next proposal. The clunky name won't stick, but the principle should.

In 1845, Friedrich Engels wrote *The Condition of the Working Class in England*, the first ever study of the commercial determinants of health in which he revealed the cost of the Industrial Revolution in terms of the health of its engine – working people.

Nearly 180 years later, some researchers do work on the commercial drivers of malnutrition, but relatively few. In the prevailing 'publish or perish' world they inhabit, the incentives are not there. Nor is the funding.

Studies that relate food system policies to governance and the nature of political decision-making are scarce. And digging into the way Big Food shapes food environments and infiltrates policy is a virtual no-go for many researchers.

The global health community is way ahead when it comes to investigating the drivers of ill-health that originate in wider structures, systems and colonial histories. Echoing Rupa Marya and Raj Patel's call for a 'deep medicine' approach, isn't it about time we engaged in some 'deep nutrition?'

Food equity will never be achieved unless action *within* the food system is combined with action *outside* it, to address deeply rooted sociopolitical drivers of food injustice. This requires addressing power asymmetries by holding the powerful to account and centring the interests and voices of those who are marginalised and excluded. There are knowledge gaps in all this which means this is an arena for research.

In 2024, Professor Angus Deaton dropped a bombshell in the International Monetary Fund's in-house magazine. His profession, economics, he wrote was in 'disarray', because it had, for so long, ignored the reality of power and inequity. Its policy recommendations were 'little more than a license for plunder'.[4] This was an extraordinary *mea culpa* from a Nobel laureate as he approached his ninth decade.

Researchers need to assess and analyse power to understand how it works in food systems and wider society, and who holds what type of power.[5] Informed by such a power analysis, practitioners and activists can select the right strategy to address imbalances: whether it's lobbying in the corridors of power, marching in the street, or providing low-profile, long-term support for grassroots organisations or public education.

At a minimum, we need researchers to apply their expertise to politics and commercial determinants – an arena which, after all, determines what gets done and what doesn't. This needs to pay attention to history. If colonialism, structural racism and inequity are considered to be off limits, we all lose. The 2023 UN Committee on Food Security report on reducing inequalities is a step in the right direction.[6]

Researchers can illuminate the path ahead by generating actionable knowledge, but they're rarely experts in communication. Connections need to be forged with journalists who are prepared to invest time and dig deep.

Food stories, at least in the UK, tend to default to scares about particular food items, restaurant reviews, *Bake-Off* highlights or air fryers. The coverage of poverty, inequity, corporate capture and the health and environmental cost of our food system is patchy and sporadic. If media coverage doesn't explore societal responses to food policy challenges, they are not on offer for the voting public. Politicians take their cue from media, especially in election years.

One groundbreaking initiative to redress the balance was an innovative collaboration in 2023, between the London College of Communication and the Refugee Journalism Project, led by Vivienne Francis and Simon Hinde. *Food: Responding to the Global Crisis* became an interdisciplinary meeting point for journalists, academics, activists and artists that culminated in a magazine and a public event.[7]

Stories covered asylum seekers in London, forced by British Government policy to subsist on £45 a week, and the struggles of agricultural workers in drought-affected Bihar, India, to feed their families. There were stories of innovation and progress by activists and organisations – like Made in Hackney, a vegan community meal service and cookery school in east London; the Om Sleiman community farm in Palestine; a profile of a Rwandan refugee who became a self-sufficient farmer in Uganda; and an in-depth look at India's massive free school meals programme, the largest in the world.

Plans are afoot for a global community of practice of journalists, researchers, filmmakers, podcasters, influencers, designers, photographers, illustrators, programmers, data wranglers, animators – anyone interested in telling stories about food, its politics and cultures.

20

Innovate

A thousand words will not leave so deep an impression as one deed.

Henrik Ibsen

The UK chocolate industry generates nearly £4 billion per year in revenue. West-African farmers who harvest the cocoa earn 23 pence a day (women) or 75 pence (men) – way below the international poverty line of £1.40 set by the World Bank.[1] Only seventeen out of eighty-two leading brands use chocolate from suppliers that pay farmers enough to live on.

Sixty per cent of the world's cocoa comes from West Africa, where one in two cocoa-growing households use child labour. That's more than 1.5 million children using dangerous chemicals, burning fields, wielding machetes and heavy-lifting when they should be in school.

KitKat maker, Nestlé, has been implicated in child labour, human-trafficking and slavery for decades. In 2021, former child slaves who were trafficked into Côte d'Ivoire filed a lawsuit against Nestlé USA who they accused of aiding and abetting the illegal enslavement of thousands of children on affiliated cocoa farms.[2]

Nestlé's lawyers did not deny there was slavery in its supply chain, but instead argued that corporations cannot be liable for violations of customary international law or human rights. Referencing the Nuremberg Trials extensively, they argued for immunity from punishment, stating that even the corporation that supplied the Nazis with the Zyklon B gas they used to kill millions was not convicted during that trial. The US Justice Department supported Nestlé, arguing that the case against the corporation could 'threaten foreign affairs interests' for the US Government.[3]

Tony's Chocolonely is a very different organisation to Nestlé. Its mission is to rid the *entire* chocolate industry of slavery – not just its own supply chain. Founded in 2005 by three Dutch journalists who'd been shocked to learn of Big Choc's use of enslaved child labour, Chocolonely builds direct long-term relationships with cocoa farmers in Ghana and the Ivory Coast, paying them a higher price and working with them to improve conditions. Through its 'Open Chain' platform, the company aims to share knowledge and tools with other companies who want to join up to rid the industry of slavery by using traceable cocoa beans, paying a living wage, strengthening farming co-operatives, and helping farmers improve crop yields, thus reducing the need to clear land to plant more cacao trees. A progressive people-first company that's broken the mould and is trying something new. This is what real innovation looks like.

'Innovation', however, is a word that's been purloined by the private sector, usually to refer to some technological change or a new product line to generate more profit. Of the Gates Foundation's list of 'six innovations in 2023' (showcased at the 2023 Grand Challenges Annual Meeting in Senegal), three were about AI access, two were about technologies (in-home malaria testing kit, bacterial vaginosis treatment) and one was about 'inclusion in scientific research'.

But real innovation happens at a much deeper level, when questions are asked about the purpose of business, when new business models are developed, when public benefit is written into company articles of association.

Many small- and medium-sized enterprises are moving in this direction. For example, a Kenyan firm has figured out a way to keep fast-food fast (i.e. convenient) while also ensuring it's healthy.[4] Kwanza Tukule pre-cooks beans and delivers them directly to street vendors — mostly women, who sell to low-income labourers — using a mobile app. In Ghana, the Banda Borae Cooperative transforms soybeans into ready-to-eat street food: grilled tofu kebabs.[5] In Madagascar, a social enterprise, Nutri'zaza, produces a fortified grain-and-legume flour that's sold in poor urban neighbourhoods.[6]

Prevailing politico-economic systems and regulatory structures have incentivised corporations in a race to the bottom, a race to 'add value' (for their shareholders) by developing and marketing an ever-increasing array of unhealthy ultra-processed foods. Their only accountability is to these shareholders. Performance is measured by financial indicators and regulated by corporate laws and accounting standards. Health and environmental damage is never factored into these business models.

Continuing such a carte-blanche approach of plunder and profit over people and planet is not tenable. We are a quarter of the way through this century in the middle of a decade that's pivotal for our future. Isn't it time to find a better way? A new approach to corporate governance in which people are viewed as citizens not just end-of-the-line consumers? An approach where shareholder primacy gives way to the creation of real value driven by public purpose?

Food Fighter: Emmanuel Faber

In October 2014, Emmanuel Faber became CEO of Danone, the multibillion-dollar manufacturer of yoghurt, soy milk and Evian water. He had earlier propelled Danone's strategy towards greater sustainability and increased compliance with ESG (environmental, social and governance) criteria, which often competed with financial criteria.[7]

Faber had turned Danone into an *'Entreprise à Mission'* – a new French category similar to an American B-Corp, whose purpose goes beyond profits and growth to incorporate social and environmental concerns. As part of his 'One Planet, One Health' strategy, he launched a carbon-adjusted earnings-per-share indicator that pegged the company's success directly to its environmental performance.

He went out on a limb. But it was all too much for his board of directors – he was sacked in March 2021 for poor financial performance.[8]

He had expected it: 'So far, ESG has been sort of an easy path for CEOs and boards that wanted to look good but weren't ready to really walk the talk.'

Old paradigms take a lot of chipping away, before they eventually collapse.

We need innovation in business models to ensure that food systems benefit health, sustainability, social equity and prosperity. Metrics that capture all four of these outcomes will be key for this new model; the era of solely counting and reporting on profit will be over.

Many company bosses say they would welcome Government

legislation designed to reduce junk-food sales.[9] They know the food they're selling is often terrible. They want to do the right thing, but they need a level playing field. Tim Rycroft, a spokesman for the Food and Drink Federation, has said: 'The industry has to be guided by the government. If the government says there is a reason why these [foods] are no longer acceptable, of course we will change'.[10]

On 15 July 2021, a group of investors, representing over £2.8 trillion in assets under management wrote to then-Prime Minister Boris Johnson:

> We call on the government to be ambitious in its response to the urgent challenges facing the food system. We believe that well-designed regulation creates an essential enabling environment for businesses seeking to build long-term thinking and sustainability into their business models.

They welcomed the strategy's recommendations for the *mandatory* reporting of nutrition and sustainability metrics (both backward- and forward-looking) for larger food sector companies. They agreed that voluntary reporting was not enough.

And yet, nothing happened. Or rather, things went backwards. Two years later, the UK Government (with Rishi Sunak as PM) announced that the proposed ban on multi-buy deals on food and drinks high in salt and sugar (including 'buy one, get one free', or BOGOF), would be delayed until October 2025. This was the second time the can had been booted down the road. The Government also pushed back proposed restrictions on unhealthy food adverts.

By this time, even some CEOs were getting fed up. Under constant pressure to deliver short-term results, they're reluctant to invest in developing technologies, which take time, when the goalposts are constantly shifting. Companies producing healthier alternatives, especially small businesses, had counted on receiving more funding from investors off the back of the legislation. Every vacillation reduces the likelihood and appetite for investors to make positive changes.

Shortly after Sunak's announcement of a delay, Sainsbury's and Tesco supermarkets vowed publicly to withhold volume-led promotions. This led to campaign groups including Sustain, Diabetes UK and the Obesity Health Alliance urging all UK food retailers to follow their lead.

A lot of oxygen is used in abstract discussions over partnerships and how 'the private sector can be part of the solution'. Most big companies just view such partnerships as part of their corporate social responsibility (CSR) efforts – an extension of marketing and reputational management.

Can we ever develop pro-nutrition, pro-health partnerships between public/governmental bodies and private companies? To me, this is a bit cart-before-horse. Before we get to that question, we need to see a clear shared purpose, articulated with actions not words. If there's no shared purpose, there is no point in discussing partnerships.

To find a new shared purpose, companies need to be willing to break the mould, to truly innovate. Part of this will involve the development of a stronger accountability model centred on health and sustainability targets and performance criteria that are independently specified, monitored and shared widely.

We need to see company data becoming publicly available, comparable and accessible to all. To date, accountability has meant financial accountability that's enshrined in law through mechanisms like quarterly reporting and auditing. Accountability for human and planetary health impacts is only partially regulated through labour laws and environmental protection laws.

Responsibility needs to be converted into accountability. This would involve setting a measurable 'account' of actions which one actor (the Government) is able to enforce compliance of another (the business) to meet. This will in turn require a major change of rules in how businesses operate and account for their actions.

The UK Food Foundation's 'Plating Up Progress' is a step forward; an initiative to assess the progress being made by UK businesses (retail, restaurant, caterers, dining chains, wholesalers) in moving towards a healthy and sustainable food system.[11] Regular reports provide dashboards that can be used by investors, the Government or businesses themselves, along with sector overviews and downloadable company data.

Another of the many great Food Foundation initiatives is the 'Investor Coalition on Food Policy', which advocates for regulation and standard-setting to promote greater transparency and accountability towards a heathier food system.[12] Over thirty investors with more than £6 trillion in assets have signed up. The focus for now is the UK, but there are plans to expand globally.

Finally, there is one big move that Big Food can make to contribute to food system transformation. Not to start something new, but simply to follow the rules set by governments and cease and desist from the Deadly Ds in Chapter 13. That would be a real game-changer.

21

Unite

*One hundred and twenty jumbo jets, full of young kids,
crashing every single day*
Attributed to James Grant, 1980

This was how the Executive Director of UNICEF caught the
attention of presidents and prime ministers in 1980. At that
time, 40,000 young children were dying each day from preventable causes.* James Grant was a straight-talking, laser-focused
American who, during the fifteen years of his tenure, galvanised
the international community to focus on children like no one
before. Or since.

Jim Grant spoke about jumbo jets, but he also spoke about
human rights, the original founding principle of the United
Nations. Combating malnutrition wasn't a choice, it was an
ethical imperative. In just two years (1989–1990), under his leadership, UNICEF developed the UN Convention on the Rights

---

* In New Delhi, during meetings with parliamentarians, our UNICEF team
adapted the Grant approach for India. Our version was: 'Every hour of the day
and night on every day of the year, an Airbus, packed with small children, crashes
in India. But we can prevent this happening – we have the knowledge, we have
the tools.'

of the Child (ratified by all countries except Somalia and the USA) and hosted the UN World Summit for Children in New York, the only global summit ever held on children.

UNICEF's mandate – child survival and development – was unbeatable. It still is. Who could argue against a better future for hundreds of millions of children? A child's future has to be the cornerstone of advocacy and agitation for change in food and health.

The Convention on the Rights of the Child that Grant championed is an international, legally binding agreement that states that children are individuals with their own rights. A rights-based approach is essentially a cascade of reinforcement – like protective layers of an onion with the child at the centre. Ultimately, governments (outer layer) have the duty of care, to respect, protect and fulfil the rights of the child, including the right to a healthy life, to develop in the best possible way, both mentally and physically, in order to reach their full potential. Adults (surrounding children in the centre) are responsible for ensuring children have access to food that is nutritious and healthy. Governments are responsible for working to reduce all forms of child malnutrition, including by controlling the products and practices of Big Food.

Since 2000, the UN has had a Special Rapporteur on the Right to Food whose job is to 'promote the full realisation of the right to food and . . . the fundamental right of everyone to be free from hunger so as to be able fully to develop and maintain their physical and mental capacities.' The current rapporteur, Michael Fakhri, a law professor from Oregon, reiterates that the right to food is not the right to be fed, it is the right to have access to an adequate quantity and quality of food (including access to land, time to cook). Food is not a commodity, food is life, pleasure, culture – it's how we define ourselves. Unless and until power imbalances in the food system are addressed, it will be impossible to realise human rights. It's basic. To protect and fulfil the right to food we need to focus not just on the 'ends', but crucially also on the 'means' – the *processes* that are driving change.

In October 2019, along with 179 other health and nutrition professionals from thirty-eight countries, I signed an open letter to the UN High Commissioner for Human Rights and the Director General of the World Health Organization. Published in the *British Medical Journal*, the letter called on them to initiate an inclusive process to develop guidelines on human rights, healthy diets and sustainable food systems because: 'the status quo is untenable and bold actions are needed. Market forces, alone, are failing to deliver healthy diets and sustainable food systems'.

Nothing happened, not even a response to the letter.

Comparing the UN World Summit for Children in 1990 with the UN Food Systems Summit in 2021 shows how the private sector has progressively worked the UN system. The ethical imperative is no longer the default.

Colliding worlds

There are tens of thousands of international organisations. The UN and its various agencies, the World Bank Group, the International Monetary Fund (IMF) and the World Trade Organization (WTO) sit at the centre of this web.

Many of the governmental actions (policies, programmes and legislation) that we explored earlier can and should be supported by international organisations, including the UN. There are different ways the UN can use its soft power, from evidence compilation, normative guidance, advocacy and communication, to mobilising finance.

Apart from the Security Council, the UN operates on a 'one

country, one vote' principle aimed to empower low- and middle-income countries. The World Bank and the IMF, on the other hand, operate 'one dollar, one vote', thus privileging richer countries, especially the USA (both the Bank and IMF are located in Washington DC). By setting the rules of global trade, the World Trade Organization (based in Geneva) has a big impact on food, nutrition and health, despite these not being their priorities.

International organisations exert soft power (discursive, epistemic) as knowledge brokers in various summits and global conferences where ideas get kicked around and norms shaped. The most pressing challenges facing humanity – climate, malnutrition, pandemics – are collective-action, *supranational* problems that straddle borders and demand international co-operation. All the more so when they get snarled up in cascading crises.

The big agencies don't always get on well. The 1980s saw a clash of ideologies between international agencies around competing narratives on the provision of health care and on development. The promotion of structural adjustment – the neoliberalist, free-market, austerity-led approach to development – by the World Bank and the IMF did not sit easily with the World Health Organization's push for universal access to primary health care, following the groundbreaking 1981 Alma Ata Declaration.

UNICEF took on the 'Washington Consensus' (of the World Bank and IMF) that promoted structural adjustment in the 1980s. One of the leaders of the pushback was Sir Richard Jolly who at the time was deputy director of UNICEF. Jolly co-authored *Adjustment with a Human Face* (1987) which highlighted the huge human cost of structural adjustment.[1] Later, he founded the annual UN Human Development Report with Mahbub ul Haq, which pioneered a rethinking of poverty and development away from narrow definitions of economic performance towards a broader focus on the multiple aspects of wellbeing. It had a huge influence, including on the development banks.

Global trade and national public health don't go together well, with mandates and interests that often conflict. Negotiations for trade which ignore health implications create hurdles for national regulations to protect public health.[2]

Global trade liberalisation has increased the consumption of ultra-processed foods around the world.[3] International trade and investment agreements (TIAs) sanctioned by the WTO often threaten national governments that choose to rein in Big Food. Trade authorities are simply not concerned with malnutrition. TIAs include clauses describing 'investor-state dispute mechanisms', which permit corporations to challenge the legality of policies that threaten their profits.[4] These mechanisms effectively create veto points which a public health or food policy has to navigate in order to come into effect – a process that can dilute planned Government regulation or deter future moves to restrict harms generated by the industry.[5]

Thailand's move to bring in legislation to reduce children's consumption of unhealthy snack foods by labelling food items, for example, was challenged by WTO state members. The regulation was delayed and watered down.[6] Participation in US and EU free-trade agreements is associated with a significant reduction in the implementation of several WHO-recommended policies that target unhealthy foods (including on anti-competition grounds).[7]

National governments, however, *do* have the power to forge ahead and prioritise the health of their populations, even if this runs counter to international agreements and frameworks. When more of them do so – following India's lead (see 'India vs. USA' textbox) – norms will change. The health of people and planet will rise up the priority list, as it should have done long ago.

India vs. USA

For decades, the USA has used trade agreements to under-mine food and nutrition programmes. India has by far the largest number of hungry people of any country. The national 'right to food' movement has, over the years, been successful in ensuring food-security programmes protect the poor. These programmes guarantee a food safety net, free of charge, through public distribution centres. The Indian Government collects rice, wheat and other crops from small- and medium-scale producers at fixed and fair prices, somewhat higher than free-market prices. Purchases go for distribution to the poor. It has been a great success, reducing poverty and food insecurity both for the farmers (via fair prices paid) and for the hundreds of millions of poor people who receive the benefit.[8]

The USA, however, has leveraged anachronistic trade agreements to file a formal dispute at the WTO to challenge the guaranteed prices offered to Indian farmers. The Indian Government is, they say, providing an excessive subsidy to farmers.[9] This from a country that has for many decades paid monumental subsidies to its own farmers, virtually none of whom are small-scale, poor and hungry. The hypocrisy is mind-blowing. India has stood its ground, so far.

Towards a food systems framework convention

One mechanism the UN uses to convene nations and solidify norms is by setting global goals. In 2015, the goal to eliminate hunger and malnutrition by 2030 was included as part of its Agenda for Sustainable Development.[10] Not only will we not reach that goal, but the position at the halfway point was actually worse than at the start of the Sustainable Development Goals (SDGs) era.

The SDGs did however break from historical tradition in that they were universal, for all countries around the world and not just for 'developing' countries. They also went beyond averages of a population to look at inequalities within them too. This was progress.

But there were controversial steps too. The last of the seventeen goals was to 'strengthen the means of implementation and revitalise the global partnership for sustainable development'. This goal encompasses a target for the development of 'multi-stakeholder partnerships that mobilise and share knowledge, expertise, technology, and financial resources'.

It sounds like a positive move. A dangerous precedent however had been set. By promoting multistakeholderism, the UN was kicking open the door for large corporations to participate in the policymaking processes . . . and that's what we're seeing now. Transnational corporations are part of the global economic system but that doesn't mean they should be invited to the policy table.

If there is to be goal on partnership, we need much stronger principles of engagement. One of the roles of the UN is to broker consensus on codes of conduct and agreements relating to global problems. We are calling out for an international agreement in which conflicts of interest are clarified and commitments made to avoid them in any partnership. The UN does have a Global Compact which outlines ten principles for businesses to advance societal goals, including human rights, labour, environment and anti-corruption.[11] Big Tobacco cannot be part of any partnership, but there's nothing about Big Food.

On the health side, some progress has been made. In 2017, the WHO released a draft tool for preventing conflicts of interest in nutrition policy and programming.[12] This was followed in 2021 by a roadmap brought out by the Pan American Health Organization (PAHO) to help ministries of health decide on whether and how to engage with any business.[13] Three years later, the WHO published a practical tool to aid decision-making on non-communicable disease prevention and control.[14] Positive steps, but more is needed to harmonise positions and approaches across the whole UN system.

There is one agency that's unequivocally nailed its colours to the mast. In 2023, UNICEF published its own in-house guidance on engaging with the food and beverage industry.[15] Among ten parameters, the agency stated it would 'avoid all partnerships with ultra-processed food and beverage industries' and 'advocate for food and beverage industry not to be included in public policy-making'. No fudging or fuzziness here.

Guidance on corporate engagement – when, where, why, how – is important, but perhaps it needs to be folded into a wider convention in the way that was done for tobacco. Launched in 2003, the World Health Organization's Framework Convention on Tobacco Control is a great example of how to protect public health policies from commercial interests.[16] The convention led to laws on smoking, graphic health warnings on products, bans on tobacco advertising, promotion and sponsorship, and hefty taxes.

In 2019, the *Lancet* Global Syndemic Commission recommended a Framework Convention on Food Systems to give teeth to a set of principles to rebalance power within food systems towards public health.[17] Current accountability mechanisms, including annual reports tracking nutrition and health commitments and actions, are too weak to enforce adherence. Five years later, the same recommendation for a framework convention was made by the NOVA architect, Carlos Monteiro, to protect populations from ultra-processed foods.[18]

Such a convention would apply to international organisations too. The World Trade Organization would be compelled to recognise WHO guidelines and standards for nutrient profiling, food and beverage labelling, and restrictions on marketing targeted at children. This would prevent repeated trade and investment law challenges by companies when countries try to create policies for healthier food environments.

Coalitions and movements form around policies, conventions and laws. In the early 2000s, the Framework Convention on Tobacco Control process stimulated civil society groups to create a network of 300 organisations from over 100 countries (the Framework Convention Alliance) to monitor Government adherence to the convention and exchange best practices. More recently, a coalition of over 350 civil society organisations – part of the #UNmute initiative – grew out of concern over the marginalisation of civil society voices at the UN.

In late 2023, I met Richard Jolly for a coffee below the South Downs, where we both live. Over thirty years had passed since we'd worked together on the UN mission to the Central Independent States, after the USSR collapsed. I was interested in his view of the United Nations as it approached its eightieth anniversary in 2025. As a six-year-old, Richard had been evacuated to North America to escape the war, returning aged ten in 1945, the year that the UN was founded. Most of his career has been spent in the UN and he's written many books. For one of these, *UN Ideas That Changed the World*, along with Louis Emmerij and Thomas Weiss, he'd interviewed seventy-three UN staff members from thirty-five countries. Many interviewees, he recalled, were hopeful for the UN's future despite having often felt frustrated. Nine big ideas had emerged – all of which were evolving, as the world was changing.

UN Ideas that Changed the World

1. Human rights for all: from aspiration to implementation.
2. Gender: from eliminating discrimination to promoting women's rights and empowerment.
3. Development goals: from national, regional to global.
4. Fairer international economic relations: from aid and mutual interest to global solidarity.
5. Development strategies: from national planning to governing the market.
6. Social planning: from sectoral to integrated perspectives.
7. Environmental sustainability: from environment and development to preserving the planet.
8. Peace and security: from preventing state conflict to protecting individuals.
9. Human development: from separate actions to an integrated approach.[19]

These nine ideas, I think, remain a useful checklist of the core purpose of the UN. I would just add a tenth on voice and inclusion, to ensure civil society and grassroots voices are heard and acted upon.

The United Nations was established eighty years ago to protect the world's growing population from existential threats including mass famine. We now have new global threats, but the best approach for the organisation to deal with them is to get back to basics, focus on human rights and reverse the slide towards corporate capture of our food and health systems.

22

Enable

The transformation of the food system requires an enabling environment, a key component of which is a well-resourced public sector. Economic stagnation, chronic debt and inflation have however squeezed the fiscal space for many countries. There are big questions about how governments raise revenues and how they use them better. And there are big questions about international aid.

Capitalism in the twenty-first century is relentless in its drive to grow money. The inexorable profit motive means that stuff that we need – energy, food, health care, housing – is eventually privatised, making it more expensive for everyone except the owners, who get rich. The rest of us feel poorer. Eventually we push back. The solution, we're then told, is more growth, which means more stuff to be owned. We don't actually need more growth, of course, but the system is there to persuade us that we do.

Look at capitalism and the climate crisis. Something has to give. Is green growth even possible? Can high-income/high-emission countries decarbonise fast enough to meet their obligations under the 2015 Paris Agreement, while *still* pursuing economic growth? Can growth be decoupled from carbon emissions? Jefim Vogel and Jason Hickel don't think so. In an analysis, they show that countries would on average take more than 220 years to reduce their emissions by 95 per cent, emitting twenty-seven times their remaining 1.5°C 'fair shares' in the process.[1] Decoupling rates would need to increase by a factor of ten by 2025 to meet Paris Agreement commitments.

So, the short answer is 'no' – high-income countries will need to pursue new strategies, reorientating the economy towards sufficiency, equity and human wellbeing.

What would this look like? In *Mission Economy*, Mariana Mazzucato lays out a plan to mend capitalism rather than end it.[2] Governments have immense power to make and shape markets but they're not using it. Mazzucato argues for a new form of capitalism that's infused with public interest not just private gain. Governments should not just wait to address inequality by redistributing income after it's been created (via taxes or benefits), they should initiate a programme of *pre*-distribution aimed at *preventing* inequality.

Another approach, by British economist, Kate Raworth – Doughnut Economics – seeks to create a balance between the needs of people and the planet.[3] Think of a doughnut (an unfortunate metaphor for us, but anyway . . .). There's an inner ring and an outer ring. The inner ring represents the minimum basic needs for a healthy life (food, water, health, energy, housing, income, education, equity, voting power, peace, justice, etc.). The outer ring represents an ecological ceiling, the planetary limits within which we must all live if we are to survive and prosper into the next century.

The goal is to live in between the two rings (in the doughnut, as it were). This requires a set of principles centred on holistic wellbeing, regenerative circular economies that are much more localised, social and economic equity, and ecological sustainability.

Doughnut Economics requires regulatory frameworks that disincentivise overconsumption, and it requires interdisciplinary collaboration, involving economists, sociologists, ecologists and policymakers to collectively design strategies for people and planet.

Then there's Jason Hickel's more radical 'De-Growth' movement that seeks to reverse the creep of privatisation by decommodifying social goods (like health, energy, housing) to allow people to access them.[4] It's not possible to survive the climate crisis if we continue to pursue growth, he argues. So, the questions then are: What do we value socially? What do we need to improve? What needs to be developed? What should be scaled down or phased out?

Nothing grows forever. Anyone who's studied growth of any species in a circumscribed space knows about the S-shaped curve. I remember my white-coated days at university in the late Seventies, peering into Petri dishes as bacterial colonies ran out of space. The ultimate goal of most organisms is to thrive, not to grow. A tree grows to a height determined by its ability to channel nutrients from its roots to its highest leaves. Then it stops and spends its time maturing. We cannot expand the world. So, why is endless growth pursued and revered?

The growth default spills over into other fields. Neoliberalism is the ideological tool in which the State is co-opted to support growth via unfettered capitalism. Inequalities increase as we become 'both consumers and consumed'.[5] This ideology has, over the years, percolated through to all sectors. Economic growth, for example, was the basic *raison d'être* for the Nutrition for Growth (N4G) process that started in 2013. The rationale for preventing kids from becoming malnourished was economic – ethics and human rights didn't get a look in. Twelve years on, this sounds positively archaic and yet N4G continues.

On 9 November 2023, the UN's Special Rapporteur on Extreme Poverty and Human Rights, Olivier De Schutter, gave a talk, 'Wellbeing without Growth: A New Approach to Combating Global Poverty' in which he highlighted links between economic growth, inequality and unhappiness. The growth of inequalities is so serious in the USA now that life expectancy is dropping due to poor diet, chronic disease and rising rates of suicide.

De-growth, he says, is hard to sell as it sounds negative. Instead, he spoke of a 'post-growth' world. Income-tax revenues would drop, so the big question is, how are social services (health, education, care, etc.) to be supported? Taxes are needed but there are many options beyond taxing labour and income. A more equitable tax system would include taxes on profits, land, property, wealth and commodity speculation. The proceeds could be used to support the most marginalised in society. In Bolivia, every child in a public school, for example, receives a meal financed by a small tax on hydrocarbon exports. Other countries like Senegal, Tanzania and Mozambique could tax windfall gains from natural gas exports. The 'polluter pays' principle could be given teeth so that companies that make billions from products that harm people and planet pay much higher rates of tax.

In his 2024 book, *The Poverty of Growth*, De Schutter argued for a new approach revolving around 'triple dividend measures'. Similar in principle to double-duty actions to reduce all forms of malnutrition, triple dividend actions are capable of reducing poverty and environmental harm while providing goods and services that are accessible and affordable to those who need them most.[6]

This is what the future looks like. Economic 'business as usual' is untenable. The notion that a rising tide floats all boats no longer holds water. The only rising boats in recent years are the superyachts of the new billionaires.

Countries are already beginning to develop new political and economic systems that put people's wellbeing first. These frameworks measure commercial effects on health and the environment and encourage practices that promote health. Ways to do this include enforcing policies – such as sugary-drink taxes – that ensure corporations pay their fair share of taxes and are obliged to account for the full costs of the health, social and environmental harms caused by the production, consumption and disposal of their products.

Bhutan pioneered the Wellbeing Economy Movement, creating a Gross National Happiness Index in 2008, inspired by the Buddhist concept of 'The Middle Path'. Health, education, good governance, ecological diversity and community vitality are tracked through thirty-three indicators. Ecuador has developed a wellbeing vision based on *'buen vivir'* ('living well together'), a term used by the Quechua peoples of the Andes to describe an approach to life that is rooted in community, ecology, culture and spiritual connection to the land. *Buen vivir* was integrated into the Ecuadorian constitution in 2008 and the Bolivian constitution in 2009. Similar wellbeing strategies have been developed in Wales (2015), New Zealand (2019) and Norway (upcoming).

True cost of food

At the famous Bretton Woods Conference in 1944, gross domestic product (GDP) was adopted as the main measure of national prosperity and thereby the focus of political attention. GDP measures the monetary value of goods and services produced in a country in a given period (usually each year). A metric that – as we enter the second quarter of the twenty-first century – has become a tired old dinosaur.[7]

The public doesn't really get it, conceptually or financially. In *When Nothing Works,* Luca Calafati and colleagues from the Foundational Economy Collective showed that in all the growth of take-home pay between 1999 and 2020, the top 10 per cent of earners raked in 25 per cent, whereas the bottom 10 per cent brought home just 3 per cent.[8]

Equity is one thing, but there's a lot more to wealth than what we produce. As Sir Partha Dasgupta has reminded us, in addition to produced capital (measured imperfectly by GDP) there is human capital and natural capital.[9] The costs of the climate and ecological crises that we (governments and taxpayers) will have to pay for are not captured in the GDP metric. Nor do these costs trouble those who generate them.

We urgently need new metrics. We cannot transform food systems without better quantification of all the costs and benefits the system generates. If you trace the full life of a product from when it's conceived to after it's consumed, and the impact on the consumer and on the environment, everything in between should be costed. This is the true cost of food which would, in turn, provide us with its true price.

Why aren't companies paying for the harms they cause? Why don't polluters pay? Whether it is ill-health due to unhealthy foods or environmental damage caused by pollution or greenhouse-gas emissions, costs like these should be factored into decision-making. Failure to do this provides warped incentives affecting all of us. Harmful food products would cost significantly more if the cost of 'negative externalities' were included. And healthy foods would cost less. This is the essence of true cost accounting (TCA).

TCA involves the estimation of the hidden costs of our food

system, generated by market, institutional and policy failures.[10] TCA is a job for the UN and the FAO is taking the lead. It will take time. When it's becomes institutionalised – and Switzerland hope to go live with TCA before the end of the decade – we will begin to correct these failures and lay the basis for new, better agrifood systems. The initial challenge is the lack of high-quality data, on both hidden costs and the costs of taking action.

More than 70 per cent of the hidden costs of the agrifood system derive from unhealthy diets dominated by ultra-processed foods that cause illness, reduce productivity and lead to premature death.[11] Higher-income countries pay the bulk of these costs, but low-income countries are disproportionately affected. The hidden costs to their agrifood systems amount to more than a quarter of their GDP (compared to just 8 per cent for high-income countries). One-fifth of the total costs are environmental, created by nitrogen emissions, greenhouse gases, land-use change costs and water use.

The FAO initiative involves a two-phase assessment process, relying first on national-level TCA assessments to raise awareness (presented in the 2023 *State of Food and Agriculture Report*), and second on a set of evaluations of abatement actions (in the 2024 edition). TCA requires innovations in research and data, as well as investments in data collection and capacity-building, especially in low- and middle-income countries, so that it can become a viable tool for informing decision- and policymaking in a transparent and consistent way.

We already have some success stories. In Thailand, TCA was used to support the transition to organic rice farming. Fewer pesticides and less burning of fields improved air quality and reduced respiratory illness, leading to up to US$4 billion in potential health savings. In India, TCA supported the Andhra Pradesh State Government in a major shift towards agroecological farming, which improved crop diversity and yields, human health (from safer farming methods) and increased farmers' net income by nearly 50 per cent.[12]

Economic systems that are fit for purpose – that will keep us healthy and our planet habitable – need to factor in the true cost of food. Full disclosure would drive demand for healthier and more sustainable products and practices, and help citizens make informed choices. Of course, as in any systemic change, low-income households will need to be supported along the way.

Frankenstein subsidies

One of the strangest and most damaging anachronisms that besets our current global food system is the continuing subsidisation of staple-food production. This one seems positively antediluvian. The rationale for subsidising staple foods – to ensure food security and prevent famine – originated eighty years ago, in the postwar period.

The ongoing transfer of huge sums of public money to corporations (as subsidies and tax breaks), along with the huge sums of public money paid later to clear up the mess they cause, is not tenable. Not if we are to get anywhere near to achieving international goals on climate, diet nutrition and health.*

Current global agricultural support amounts to US$800 billion per year, most of which goes to the largest farmers in the richest countries.[13] On top of this, there's a mind-boggling US$5 trillion in subsidies to fossil-fuel companies.[14,15] A recent US

---

* In his excoriating critique of corporate shenanigans, Grant Ennis argues that 'the most dangerous killers on earth are government-subsidized,' highlighting how corporations reinvest corporate welfare money to lobby for more funds and for laws to help them tighten their grip on food systems (Ennis, Grant. *Dark PR*. Daraja Press, Quebec, 2023, page 21.)

census shows that Government payments to American farmers rose 17 per cent (between 2017 and 2022) to US$10.4 billion. The largest farms (with at least US$50,000 sales) received 64 per cent of the total subsidies – despite accounting for only 11 per cent of the beneficiaries. The smallest farms received just 4 per cent of total subsidies.[16]

Despite American dietary guidelines recommending at least 50 per cent of a person's diet being fruits and vegetables, less than 10 per cent of US subsidies go to farmers growing fruits and vegetables. The vast majority go to staples like corn and soy, which are used to feed cattle, or to manufacture ethanol or ultra-processed foods.

In the face of cascading diet, health and climate crises, a pivot towards the production and consumption of legumes, fruits and vegetables, and renewable energy innovations could pay huge dividends. Research suggests that just subsidising vegetables by 5 per cent could increase consumption by more than 3 per cent.

At the 'UN Food Systems Summit +2 Stocktaking Moment' in Rome in July 2023, the talk about financing was all about the need for businesses to step up, and for governments to create incentives for that to happen. No one spoke about the upstream subsidies.

It will simply be impossible to make real inroads in shifting the balance towards healthier foods and levelling the trade playing field globally, unless and until there is a radical repurposing of these subsidies. This won't be easy and there'll be big trade-offs and choices over whether to privilege climate or dietary goals.[17] But worst of all would be a continuation of 'business as usual'.

Wealth tax

We're living through an unprecedented inequality boom. Three factors are key. First, as asset prices rise much faster than wages, the rich are becoming a hell of a lot richer, a hell of a lot faster. Second, corporate profits are rocketing, as the average global mark-up (difference between the price of production and sale price) has risen from 7 per cent in 1980 to 59 per cent by 2020. And third, taxation regimes are a lot less progressive than they used to be (in 1979, the top marginal rate of income tax was 83 per cent in the UK and 70 per cent in the USA; now these rates are 45 per cent and 37 per cent, respectively).[18]

Ahead of the 2024 Davos meetings, Oxfam released their inequality report – always a highlight of the deep midwinter.[19] One headline highlighted the contrast between Elon Musk's 'true tax rate' of about 3 per cent with the 40 per cent tax rate of a flour vendor in Uganda, who makes US$80 a month.

The report concluded with a recommendation for an annual tax of up to 5 per cent on the wealth of the world's multimillion-aires and billionaires. This would raise US$1.7 trillion a year, enough to lift 2 billion people out of poverty, fully fund the shortfalls on existing humanitarian appeals, deliver a ten-year plan to end hunger, support poorer countries hit by climate impacts, and deliver universal health care and social protection for 3.6 billion people in low- and lower-middle-income countries. As usual, the hard analysis and straight-talking conclusions of this report were in stark contrast to the rampant halo-sharing fest that followed at the Swiss ski resort.

In July 2024, new research by the independent Resolution Foundation described the UK as a country of 'booming wealth but busted wealth taxes'. There is huge potential, the authors argued, for desperately needed funds (as much as £10 billion) to be raised by taxing the wealth of the rich.[20]

Debt threat

> *Debt is neocolonialism, in which colonisers transformed them-*
> *selves into 'technical assistants'. We should better say 'technical*
> *assassins' . . . Under its current form, that is imperialism*
> *controlled, debt is a cleverly managed reconquest of Africa . . .*
> Thomas Sankara, President of Burkina Faso, 1987

Forty per cent of the world's population (3.3 billion people) now live in countries where debt interest payments exceed national health and education expenditures.[21] With little domestic revenue, many governments rely on private and civil society partners to achieve food systems goals. Debt relief is usually conditional on the adoption of the neoliberal pillars of austerity, privatisation, deregulation, similar to the structural adjustment era.[22] Money continues to flow from the poorest countries to the richest.

The IMF and G20 did suspend debt servicing for the COVID pandemic. But the debt didn't go away, it just grew. Two years later, debt servicing resumed. In 2022, Organisation for Economic Co-operation and Development (OECD) members gave US$211 billion in overseas development aid – almost the exact amount they received in interest payments on outstanding debt held by these same countries. That's just the interest . . . not the original capital which stands at around US$9 trillion.[23] How are countries supposed to roll out food, nutrition and health programmes, prepare for future pandemics, mitigate climate change with this on their shoulders?

Recognising the injustice, the American Public Health Association (APHA) Resolution on Debt Cancellation has demanded the IMF and G20 cancel debt among the most debt-distressed nations, provide aggressive debt relief for others, reject austerity, and increase financing for public sector health systems and other social services.[24] Other groups are coming together to amplify the call. For countries that, for centuries, have been plundered though colonialism and its rapacious neoliberal offspring, this surely is just the first rung on the ladder of inter-generational justice.

Aid and corporate laundry

In 2018, Save the Children (UK) argued for a step change in aid to nutrition.[25] Countries should widen their revenue base through progressive tax reform, innovative financing mechanisms could be expanded (including the Global Financing Facility and the Power of Nutrition initiative) and aid should be better targeted to the most excluded children.

All of these initiatives, the charity suggested, would need to be driven by national nutrition plans that identify need and prioritise the most vulnerable. Financing should be a lot more transparent to strengthen accountability and the prevalent divide between humanitarian and development action needs to be bridged to lock in developmental gains and mitigate against recurrence.

The dominant narrative on nutrition financing – the World Bank Investment Framework – is useful, despite significantly underestimating the funding needed.*[26] Estimated nutrition-specific financing needs for select maternal, infant and young child global targets have increased from US$7 billion to nearly US$11 billion per year. Around US$3 billion of this is expected

---

* The World Bank's Global Financing Facility (GFF) finances investment in reproductive, maternal, newborn, child and adolescent health and nutrition by enabling countries to leverage donor funding into larger investments. US$4 of bank credits are provided for every US$1 of donor funding. Analysts suggest the GFF could be more equitable and effective by being less top-down in its operations, by shifting decision-making power towards recipient countries at the global level and improving inclusivity in national-level decision-making platforms.

to come from direct funding for nutrition-specific interventions (usually through the health system) – twice as much as has been provided in recent years.[27]

Most aid, when it is mobilised, goes to international NGOs not local organisations. As aid budgets are stagnant or declining, the gap is being filled by corporate social-responsibility initiatives in Africa and Asia – at times, aided by international organisations.

At the UN Food Systems Summit in 2021, the 'Zero Hunger Private Sector Pledge' was launched. As of January 2024, US$574 million had been pledged.[28] The largest pledge was from PepsiCo (US$100 million before 2030),[29] one of the richest companies in the world, responsible for a huge amount of ill-health and plastic pollution. This was a textbook case of 'nutri-washing' – the high-profile pledging of small amounts of funds to reduce undernutrition while big business heads in the opposite direction, at a much larger scale, causing obesity and ill-health.

But wait . . . how can US$100 million be called a *small* amount?

Let's do a quick back-of-the-envelope calculation. PepsiCo's profit for the twelve months ending 30 September 2023 was US$49.4 billion. To make life easy, let's round this up a tad to US$50 billion. PepsiCo donating US$100 million over a decade equates to US$10 million per year. That's about one five-thousandth (1/5,000) of its annual profit. Assuming you earned US$50,000 per year, this would be the equivalent of your donating US$10 per year – about the price of three coffees. That's how small. It's one drop in a fizzy ocean of soda, but something the company can point to for the next decade and say, 'Look! We care'.

The President of PepsiCo Foundation, C.D. Glin, stated his reasons for the pledge:

We do this because, simply put, without embracing a more sustainable food system . . . our ability to source the necessary ingredients for our products is at risk, as is the world's ability to reliably access safe and healthy foods.

Interesting order . . . company first, world second.

Big Phil

Alongside corporate nutri-washing, the reduction of power and influence of global agencies such as the UN opens up space for philanthropies. Philanthropy comes from the Greek for 'lover of humanity', though most philanthropists love power more. They may be happy to give away some of their wealth under certain conditions, but they will always hang on to the power that has accrued in the process of acquiring it.

Another jaw-dropping statistic from the 2024 Oxfam report was the combined wealth of the world's richest eighty-one billionaires being equal to that of 4 billion people. 'Every billionaire is a policy failure'.[30] Any political and economic system that creates so many billionaires – 3,194 as of November 2023 – and in which half the world's wealth is owned by the richest 1 per cent, is not fair or sustainable.[31] It can never be – no matter how many philanthropies pop up.

There are now around 100,000 private foundations warehousing US$1 trillion in assets.[32] Endowments generate billions of dollars in investment income most years, virtually tax-free, allowing Big Philanthropy to become even bigger. Big Phil spawns new adjuncts – they have their own lobbyists, research centres, conferences, consultants, think tanks, media and publications. In many ways, it's similar to corporate social responsibility – the cash flow has just gone through an extra step (usually a billionaire owner's bank account).

Anand Giridharadas in *Winners Take All* talks of the philanthro-capitalist obsession with the twin goals of 'doing well and doing good'. Philanthropists don't see any contradiction in making billions from an inequitable system that shackles the intended beneficiaries of its later largesse. Most of them want to change the world but only in ways that allow them to continue to profit from the status quo. No surprise then that their primary focus is on market-driven innovations which often equate with tech-driven magic bullets. Structural change is off-limits.

The Gates Foundation is now a quarter of a century old. Bill Gates continues to be one of richest people on the planet, with a private fortune of US$117 billion along with a Gates Foundation endowment of US$67 billion. In total, this is more than the GDP of most of the countries in which his foundation is active. Bill Gates's power is not just financial – his grants open political doors and help him shape norms in the way the UN used to do. Rich nations are pressured to co-fund Gates's projects, and poorer countries are pressured to accept donations for them.

In a 2023 book, Tim Schwab highlights 'a dirty little secret of billionaire philanthropy is that it is highly subsidised by the taxpayers'.[33] The credit however does not go to the taxpayers – it goes to the philanthropist. It's also a great move for reducing his or her tax bill by as much as 74 cents for every dollar donated (usually 'his' . . . nine out of ten billionaires are men).

Ninety per cent of Gates Foundation donations have gone to organisations based in rich nations (mainly, USA, Switzerland, UK), which are then tasked with executing Gates's charitable interventions in the day-to-day lives of the global poor. Power is entrenched: the Foundation stays in control and it chooses what is donated, where and when. Gates was quoted in an interview: 'I was able to find things . . . like malnutrition . . . that would not be solved without philanthropy'. I had to check that line. But, yes, he did actually say that.[34]

Is this transformation or more neocolonial command and control?

In an op-ed in *Scientific American*, 'Bill Gates Should Stop Telling Africans What Kind of Agriculture Africans Need', Million Belay and Bridget Mugambe from the Alliance for Food Sovereignty in Africa slam the Gates Foundation approach, citing the huge opportunity costs and collateral damage of their AGRA flagship.[35]

Whose Revolution?

In 2006, the Alliance for a Green Revolution in Africa (AGRA) was launched with funds from the Gates and Rockefeller Foundations. The aim was to use an industrial model of agriculture to replicate India's Green Revolution approach four decades earlier, in Africa. In India, productivity and yields rose but so did inequality, as richer farmers gained the most. Some smaller farmers went backwards into debt in order to purchase the crucial agrochemical inputs for the package.

Critics argued the AGRA approach was poisoning the soils with chemicals and leading to widespread debt that often led to the sale of land and assets to pay back loans. Then an independent evaluation showed that AGRA had failed to significantly increase farmers' yields or incomes. The natural resource base of communities, their indigenous food systems –with in-built resilience to shocks – have been eroded. Hunger has actually *increased* by 30 per cent in

AGRA countries since 2006.[36] Larger, wealthier and more commercial farmers (typically men) however, have benefited.

Ultimately, the biggest winners have been the multi-national corporations who sell fertilisers, pesticides and seeds that farmers have to buy every year. Celestine Otieno, who advocates for ecologically friendly practices in Kenya, calls it 'the second phase of colonisation'.

In 2022, as the evaluation results emerged, AGRA changed its name – dropping 'green revolution' altogether. Now it just hides behind its acronym. A year later, in 2023, Heather Day of the Community Alliance for Global Justice and Million Belay wrote an open letter to USAID impelling them to reconsider their support:

> You cannot claim to be providing 'aid' to Africa while partnering with AGRA. This continued relationship reflects and reinforces neocolonial relationships, in which many of the economic benefits are actually redirected and reinvested back into powerful and wealthy institutions in the US and Europe, rather than in Africa.

AGRA was impeding communities' ability to participate in the policy process, threatening food sovereignty and violating human rights to a nutritious, sustainable diet and a healthy environment. To address Africa's hunger problem, they argued, support needs to be targeted to small-scale farmers who use effective, agroecological practices. There are myriad examples from all over Africa now of such successes.

In 2023, realising the need to improve its public profile, AGRA announced it would co-sponsor an African Food Prize. The other co-sponsor? Nestlé.[37]

For several years in the 2010s, I wrote proposals and led projects that were funded by the Gates Foundation.* I did not bite the hand that fed me. I hadn't joined the dots then, but I was becoming increasingly concerned about what was 'in scope' for nutrition and what wasn't – and the types of projects that were being prioritised and funded. I wondered why no one was speaking about the obesity pandemic and the commercial determinants of malnutrition. Then I read the 2017 open letter to the WHO Executive Board questioning its relationship with the Gates Foundation.[38] 'Making up WHO budget shortfalls with funding from major investors in food, drug, and alcohol companies . . . further compromises the independence of the WHO'.

Why was the world's premier health organisation taking money from – and granting privileged status to – an organisation that was investing in unhealthy commodities? Little wonder that obesity and commercial determinants were taboo.

Philanthropy is not giving. A gift is unconditional, and giving should, if anything, reduce not magnify, power imbalances. Handouts with strings attached can never substitute for social justice. Changing the world is ultimately a political project. So, the question is: What's the process? Who's accountable, and to whom? Are the people whose lives will be changed represented – actively, equitably – in this process?

Elites can support democracy, or they can harm it. Self-selected initiatives crowd out the public sector, reduce its legitimacy and

---

* My former organisation (IFPRI) is a member of the Consultative Group on International Agricultural Research (CGIAR), which is increasingly reliant upon philanthropy. The Gates Foundation was the largest donor in 2022 at US$105 million (the US was the largest government donor at US$89 million).

efficacy, and replace civic goals with narrow concerns about efficiency and markets.

The more you look at it, the more Big Phil starts to resemble corporate social responsibility on a larger scale, a halo-generating redistribution of wealth that is not democratic. Redistributing wealth is not the same as redistributing power. Who holds the power, who decides on solutions, on what's to be funded, who tells the story, whose name is on it – these are the big questions. Can philanthropy transform the world that generates the massive inequities that lead to thousands of billionaire philanthropists? Or is it providing kudos and profile for them and a deterrent to any attempts to rein in their power?

Why have we organised our society to allow people like Bill Gates to become so obscenely wealthy in the first place? What about the ethics of accepting funds drawn from monumental, barely taxed profits that have been amassed in the same system that generates inequality and malnutrition? Why is it considered normal that multibillionaires are permitted to transform their wealth into unregulated political influence via philanthropy? Big Phil would not exist if there was economic justice – it wouldn't need to.

The world will not change overnight and billionaires will be around for a lot longer. So there's another question: Is there any form of philanthropy that could support positive change?

Perhaps so. After her divorce from Jeff Bezos, MacKenzie Scott received a 4 per cent stake in Amazon, worth US$38bn. She announced she would give the money away 'until the safe is empty'. Eschewing the usual philanthro-capitalist approach that demands months of hoop-jumping and bureaucracy to get access to circumscribed funds, she started handing out big grants with no strings attached. No big declaration, no new foundation – she's since handed out half her windfall. A new 'trust-based philanthropy' that does not require monthly bean-counting and 'key performance indicators' that kill innovation.

The approach that Bloomberg Philanthropies is taking is also interesting. For the last decade, Bloomberg has supported civil society advocates, activists and researchers in several Latin American countries – Mexico, Brazil, Colombia – to demand policy action. And they have been successful, as some of the case studies highlighted earlier have demonstrated (e.g. the sugary-drink tax in Mexico and the UPF ban in schools in Niterói and in Colombia).

Bloomberg supports NGOs to develop campaigns to drive change, and they fund researchers to provide the evidence to fuel such campaigns, as well as to evaluate the impacts of policy change they've influenced. They also fund social lobby groups to support the legislative process. The 2019 *Lancet* Global Syndemic Commission recommended philanthropic funders create a pooled fund of US$1 billion to support a similar approach in 100 countries (US$10 million on average per country).

If this is done in an arm's-length, unbranded manner, it avoids any one philanthropy from exerting its power and influence in unilateral ways. Every donor would need to give up some power to enable more democracy to come in. Would the new philanthropy take this on? Would the latest crop of billionaires be prepared to step out of the limelight and agree to fund initiatives that have been designed by 'intended beneficiaries' – marginalised people who are struggling with food injustice and malnutrition, day to day?

Conclusion: Food Future

The elephant hawkmoth caterpillar is a bit of a thug. Large and brown, it has what looks like reptilian scales. On the back of its head are two blotches which mimic eyes to scare away birds. In my childhood obsession with lepidoptery, I was fascinated by this creature. But the big drama happens later, when its pupa cracks open and a pink and green thing of wonder emerges. Beast to Beauty. A complete transformation. The moth is radically altered from its crawling avatar – different purpose, different capability, different function.

'Food system transformation' has become the mother of all development clichés in this decade.* The real goal of many who invoke it is not real transformation – it's more about fiddling on the fringe. To truly overhaul the food system, we need to see a major shift in the structure and dynamics of power. Unsurprisingly,

---

* Between 2016 and 2020 there were forty-two major food systems reports (Slater, S. et al. 'An analysis of the transformative potential of major food system report recommendations.' *Global Food Security* Vol. 32 [2022], 100610). Nearly one a month. Disturbing in itself, but then this analysis was aimed at comparing their stated goal (food system transformation) to the recommendations to achieve it. Result? A huge disconnect. Most studies were about incremental reform, not transformation.

those in power now don't really want such a shift, whatever they proclaim in conferences, interviews and annual reports. But they do want to be seen to be on the right side of history – thought-leaders, champions of change, game-changers – so they go through the motions. Transformation without political change, without a shift in power, is fake.

What's really being discussed in these conferences and reports is transition, not transformation. An incrementalist journey from one setting to another in the same system. In transitions, the driving force is 'innovation'. The problem, however, is that any emerging innovations will follow the evolutionary logic of the system – they will be technological, not social.[1] Corporations will retain control; it's still the same game. Any new policies and programmes will be in their image, with their imprint.

Real transformation, on the other hand, involves a radical over-haul, in which the system is reinvented and reshaped. In which purpose, power and governance change. Transformation cannot be engineered within the existing system by those who control it. It will require organised pressure from outside to challenge and disrupt the government-enabled corporate entrenchment of power.

Real transformation will need to be guided by a bold vision of a future food system that is just, sustainable and healthy. A shared vision that's shaped by principles of 'fair play, fair share, fair say'. A new definition of public value that's not solely commer-cial and economic but grounded in humanity and ethics. In short, one that is focused on people and planet, not plunder and profit.

In this new world, power in its different forms would be better balanced. Corporations would no longer privilege profit at any price. They would cease from interfering with policy and politics. Governments would govern and be held accountable for the decisions they make and those they don't. Not simply fixing things belatedly when they go wrong or after they've been named and shamed by the media, but proactively shaping markets and improving the lives of citizens. Citizens themselves would become more active, more organised, their voices heard.

The shared vision would be accompanied by a consensus on a set of principles that govern actions within the food system. This is what a manifesto for a better food future could look like:

1. Shared responsibility
Governments, international organisations, civil society and the private sector all need to act. Everyone has a role to play, individually and collectively, taking account of potential conflicts of interest. Governments are responsible for legislation, policies and programmes, but they need to promote the co-creation of solutions as well as being held accountable for those they instigate.

Civil society and community organisations can play an active role not only in challenging governments to do the right thing, but in building movements and informing decisions on actions. As for the food industry, we need to see it align its goals and modus operandi progressively and transparently with the new vision.

Just as crises interact, so can we forge synergies across diverse movements to improve health, environmental and social outcomes. Linking people working separately on obesity, undernutrition or the climate crisis is one of the big challenges in creating concerted local-to-global action. No transformative social movement yet exists that addresses malnutrition. It's about time.

2. Human rights and accountability
Food and health are universal human rights – we all have the right to be well nourished. Yes, conventions and frameworks exist, agreements are elaborated on paper. But these rights are rarely built into laws or enacted. We need to fight to make this happen.

Human rights are not policy *options*, they're fundamental, non-negotiable touchstones of an ethical imperative. Built into a rights-based approach is accountability: if you have the responsibility, authority and capacity to act when action is needed, you have to act. And be held accountable for that action.

Human rights are also designed to ensure all three key pillars of equity: social justice (fair play), distributional fairness (fair share) and political inclusion (fair say).

'Fair play' requires recognition that people become malnourished as a result of deliberate decisions that deny them resources – land, food, education, health care – and because of who they are, where they are. Equity cannot be achieved without tackling power imbalances and linked socioeconomic, racial and gender discrimination. Levelling-up as a policy principle is a bad joke unless and until it involves a shift in power.

'Fair share' requires a fair distribution of resources, benefits and costs. Fair wages for food system workers, fair access to productive land for smallholder farmers, fair returns from the food they sell. Fairness also applies to the distribution of impacts, as well as outcomes. Marginalised communities at greatest risk from the climate crisis (despite doing the least to cause it), for example, need to be protected.

And the last pillar – 'fair say' – requires the strengthened agency and active participation of those most affected. Their voices heard and acted upon. The global policy discourse dominated by corporate actors who bang on about multistakeholderism (the 'big tent') has drowned out grassroots voices for too long. It's not about tokenistic seats at the table, it's about the power to influence what's actually on the table that counts. Those most affected by decisions need to play an active role in making them. 'Not about us, without us.'

In *Citizens*, Jon Alexander speaks of 'liquid democracy' – a more fluid approach to governing for the public good than the blunt instrument of electoral representation. Citizen assemblies and deliberative dialogues can surface the ideas and views of people who are most affected.

'Fair say' has to include youth – intergenerational change-makers who will design and sustain food systems that work for them, that are capable of nourishing 10 billion people by mid-century. New activist youth organisations and social movements are emerging, like Bite Back 2030.

3. Knowledge sharing and continuous learning

'Fair say' is also about opening the door to stories and knowledge of people who are affected by food injustice. Policy and legislation that's informed by diverse knowledge, including Indigenous peoples' knowledge, would be richer and more empowering. Continuous learning and knowledge sharing across disciplines, countries and communities is key to identifying social innovations and accelerating progress. Learning-by-doing and by capturing the experiences of multiple actors through stories of change will be key. Researchers and journalists both have a big role to play here.

4. Diversity

A food system that's diverse is healthy, secure and resilient. Secure because there's an in-built insurance in having many options – when one fails, others can pick up the slack. Healthy because a healthy ecosystem is one with a rich biodiversity. A healthy diet has many food types, different colours, tastes, textures; a healthy microbiome has a variety of friendly bacteria. It's resilient because a diverse food system – with different ways to produce many different types of food – spreads risk. Opening up the space for a thousand flowers to bloom means if one gets blighted, another one flourishes. This is the difference between being reliant on one potato variant (Ireland during the Great Hunger) or a multitude (Andean communities of Peru and Bolivia).

5. Systemic and structural

To tackle cascading crises we need systemic and structural change. The connectivity between climate, food and health crises and their mutual reinforcement can be used to turn negatives into positives. Adversity becomes advantage; vicious cycles become virtuous.

Just as diversity is a benefit for food systems, so are multi-pronged approaches to policy and programming. There are no magic bullets. Both top-down and bottom-up approaches – Government-led and citizen-led – are needed. A nutcracker approach of positive reinforcement.

A pioneer of the 'press all the buttons' philosophy was Dr Pekka Puska, a physician and politician who masterminded a spectacularly successful programme in Finland that almost halved cardiovascular disease mortality among men in just five years in the mid-1970s.[2] Puska knew that, in complex systems in which problems have multiple, interacting causes, any single intervention will be limited in its impact. Much better to use the interconnections by targeting several nodes in the system, pulling several levers at once. The multiplier effects this can unleash mean the overall impact is greater than the sum of its individual effects. Two plus two *can* equal five.

Synergistic epidemics can thus be transformed into progress. Action needs to be multilevel. We attack the root causes of poverty (to improve people's ability to purchase healthy food) while we reshape food environments (clean up food swamps and ensure healthier foods are accessible to all). The decorative 'Xmas tree' approach of adding new projects or other forms of aid to compensate for damage caused by an anachronistic system just won't cut it.

6. Intergenerational

Just as our children are protected from tobacco, alcohol, traffic accidents or asbestos in schools, we want to see future generations protected from the harms of ultra-processed food and drink. We want governments to act and use their regulatory powers to protect children's rights. We want global food and retail companies to take full responsibility for ensuring their products and practices do not undermine children's rights, their growth, their health. Intergenerational ultimately means sustainable – securing and protecting the future, for people and planet.

7. Freedom

Nobel laureate Amartya Sen once said, 'freedoms are not only the primary ends of development, they are also among its principal means'. We need to reclaim this word. Free-market libertarians have hijacked 'freedom' to imply any individual is free to choose to buy what they want, and nothing can be allowed to infringe on this. It's a big con. Governmental action to regulate ultra-processed foods – the dreaded 'nanny state' – is anathema to them.

But freedom of choice today is a myth. Real freedom comes when *everyone* has a choice, and the ability to access, afford, prepare and consume a healthy diet.

Then there's another type of freedom. As George Orwell said: 'Freedom is the right to tell people what they do not want to hear.' The freedom to 'speak truth to power' is key for any type of transformation.

But where to start? Let's return to the first principle – shared responsibility. Everyone has a role. The power shift needed for this to happen will require both sticks and carrots.

First, governments need to govern and shape the enabling environment for change. Put people first. Drive proactive policy, including taxes on harmful products, laws on food marketing, labelling, advertising, ingredients. Get rid of archaic subsidies and tax breaks that warp incentives towards high-profit, low-health food products. Use competition law to break up monopolies and reverse corporate capture. There are many options to impel companies to reduce the junk share of their portfolios and switch their focus to nutrient-rich, healthy foods.

To ensure marginalised communities have access to healthy diets, governments can also roll out social protection measures, including subsidised food, targeted cash transfers, free school meals and other safety nets (using tax dividends). Governments can ensure universal access of their populations to primary health care (especially antenatal and mother–child health care), immunisation, sanitation and safe drinking water. All of this requires political commitment and leadership, strong governance, coherence across sectors (including ministries of agriculture, food, health, education, water and sanitation, welfare), accountability, a well-trained workforce and adequate funding.

Second, civil society and citizens can step up, become more activist. Shine a light on harmful products and practices, challenge governments to do the right thing, and hold them to account for their actions (or inaction) in both national and global arenas. Civil society organisations have an array of tools and tactics for raising wider public awareness – using stories and lived-experience profiles, for example, to highlight both problems and solutions. Not only to inform action but also to inspire it. Organising, mobilising and connecting social movements to disrupt 'business as usual'. Citizens can become more literate and vocal about food, and network to expose, oppose, organise, mobilise – to realise their agency and collective power in the face of this challenge.

Third, knowledge brokers and media. Researchers need to get more involved in studies of power, food justice and the commercial determinants of malnutrition and ill-health. To open up the black box of political decision-making and policy formulation. By studying real-world policy and action (or its absence), we can start to see the roadblocks, the entry points, the opportunities. Academics can also make an unequivocal commitment to refuse any form of sponsorship of research, events, conferences and initiatives offered by the ultra-processed food industry.[3] Journalists can connect with civil society groups on media campaigns and dig deeper to unearth the real food stories of people and organisations who are changing the system.

United Nations agencies need to become united across their global architecture, strengthen multilateral governance to free it from industry interference and go back to basics and fight for human rights and equity. New global targets would include a focus on the commercial determinants of health and the urgency to reduce harmful products and practices. Agencies can commit to support member states in a variety of ways – technical, operational, financial, legal, communications – to shape healthy food environments.

And finally, the food industry. Companies can develop new business models that lead to food products that are affordable, accessible and healthy. They can incorporate social benefit into their constitutions and generate buy-in from shareholders for this new purpose. They can commit to stay away from the policy table, and to cease and desist from the dark arts. We want action, not words. We are crying out for transparency and accountability that goes well beyond quarterly sales reports. The industry can elevate human and planetary health in decision criteria – which requires action on the part of all investors, as well as company CEOs.

The time to act is now, because our future is at stake. There's nothing linear about cascading crises – most impacts will be felt after critical thresholds or tipping points are breached and we rarely know when this will happen. The COVID pandemic, followed by fuel, food and cost-of-living crises and conflict have stressed food and health systems, and driven millions into extreme poverty. Inequalities have worsened. We have become more divided at a time when we need to seek common ground. We cannot continue to watch leaders dither and bluster, abrogating their responsibility as our children are under threat.

Thomas Kuhn spoke of the liminal period when we are between paradigms, between stories – a period of revolutionary chaos when change can happen very quickly.[4] That's where we are right now – in a pivotal moment. Neoliberalism has clearly run its course. People are fed up with the junk products and practices of multinational food companies; fed up with the do-nothing politics of governments who fail to act in our interests. But we have the knowledge, and we're realising our agency and ability to turn things around.

In 'Pandemic as a Portal', Arundhati Roy looked ahead to a new world as COVID slammed into India in early 2020. She saw the pandemic both as a crisis and a moment when a new future was possible, but one that would need fighting for.[5] That's the fight we have on our hands right now: to transform our food system to bring health for all, not wealth for a few. A food system fit for the twenty-first century.

The profession I chose forty odd years ago was food and nutrition. Time spent living and working in South America and India woke me up. I saw how people became malnourished when their rights to food, health care, water and sanitation were denied. Those worst affected were invariably the most marginalised – socially, economically, politically. Nutritional status was – and still is – a powerful indicator of freedom and justice, and of human and societal health. The difference now is we have a whole raft of proven actions from global to national, right down to the household level. We're more streetwise and better connected than ever before. We know what the problem looks like, what's causing it and what needs to be done. We just need to do it.

Notes

Introduction

1 A pandemic is a disease that is large-scale, moves fast across the world and has catastrophic impacts. When pandemics combine and interact, we end up with a *syndemic*. In the mid-1990s, *syndemic* was first used to connote the synergistic nature of ill-health, malnutrition and social injustice (Singer, Merrill and Clair, Scott. 'Syndemics and Public Health: Reconceptualizing Disease in Bio-Social Context'. *Medical Anthropology Quarterly*, Vol. 17, No. 4 (2003), pp. 423–41). Syndemics arise under conditions of inequality caused by poverty, racial and gender inequity, stigmatisation, stress and structural violence – factors which act together to increase physical and social vulnerability to disease. A classic example was the HIV–malnutrition–food-insecurity syndemic in Africa in the 2000s. In 2019, a *Lancet* Commission referred to the intertwined pandemics of obesity, undernutrition and climate change as a 'global syndemic' – one which is now, and will be into the foreseeable future, the dominant cause of human and planetary ill-health. (Swinburn, Boyd et al. 'The Global Syndemic of Obesity, Undernutrition, and Climate Change'. *The Lancet*, Vol. 393, No. 10173 (February 2019), pp. 791–846.) Other scientists have arrived at the same diagnosis from different angles, using different words. On the eve of a new millennium, *polycrisis* was used to refer to 'interwoven and overlapping crises', in which dysfunctional

global systems have knock-on effects that cascade (or spill over) into other global systems. Others refer to the 4Cs: conflict, climate, COVID and cost of living. Another linked concept is that of the *permacrisis,* though this denotes a static, entrenched situation, implying that crises can only be managed, not resolved (which I don't believe). All definitions highlight the interactions between crises in which the ensuing damage is greater than the sum of individual harms (2 + 2 = 5).

2 World Obesity. 'Economic Impact of Overweight and Obesity to Surpass $4 Trillion by 2035', 2 March 2023. <worldobesity.org>

3 Global Nutrition Report. Bristol: Development Initiatives, 2021.

I CASCADE

1. Overfed, Undernourished

1 Gillespie, Stuart and Haddad, Lawrence. *The Double Burden of Malnutrition in Asia: Causes, Consequences and Solutions.* New Delhi: SAGE, 2003.

2 WHO, 'Obesity and Overweight', 1 March 2024 <https://www. who.int/news-room/fact-sheets/detail/obesity-and-overweight>.

3 Food Foundation. 'A Neglected Generation', June 2024, p. 3. <https://foodfoundation.org.uk/publication/neglected-generation-reversing-decline-childrens-health>

4 NCD. Risk Factor Collaboration (NCD-RisC). 'Worldwide Trends in Underweight and Obesity from 1990 to 2022: A Pooled Analysis of 3663 Population Representative Studies with 222 Million Children, Adolescents, and Adults'. *The Lancet*, Vol. 403 (2024), pp. 1027–50.

5 Devlin, H. 'Surge in Number of People in Hospital with Nutrient Deficiencies, NHS Figures Show'. *The Guardian*, 21 December 2023.

6 Murray, J. 'Children Have Bowed Legs': Hunger Worse Than Ever, Says Norwich School'. *The Guardian*, 21 December 2023.

7 NHS. 'National Child Measurement Programme, England, 2022/23 School Year. Summary', 19 October 2023.

8 UNICEF–WHO–The World Bank. 'Joint Child Malnutrition Estimates (JME): Levels and Trends', 18 May 2023.

9 Victora, Cesar G. et al. 'Revisiting Maternal and Child Undernutrition in Low-Income and Middle-Income Countries: Variable Progress Towards an Unfinished Agenda'. *The Lancet*, Vol. 397 (April 2021), pp. 1388–99.

10 WHO. 'Obesity and Overweight', 1 March 2024 <https://www.who.int/news-room/fact-sheets/detail/obesity-and-overweight>.

11 US Centers for Disease Control and Prevention. National Health and Nutrition Examination Surveys (1960–2000).

12 World Obesity, 2023.

13 International Institute for Population Sciences. *National Family Health Survey (NFHS-5)*, 2019–2021. <www.rchiips.org/nfhs>

14 Alderman, Harold et al. 'Long Term Consequences of Early Childhood Malnutrition'. *Oxford Economic Papers*, 58, no. 3 (2006), pp. 450–74.

15 Aizer, A. and Currie, J. 'The Intergenerational Transmission of Inequality: Maternal Disadvantage and Health at Birth.' *Science*, Vol. 344, No. 6186 (23 May 2014), pp. 856–61; Perez-Escamilla, R. et al. 'Nutrition Disparities and the Global Burden of Malnutrition.' *BMJ*, 361 (2018), k2252.

16 Stevens, G.A. et al. 'National, Regional, and Global Estimates of Anaemia by Severity in Women and Children for 2000–19: A Pooled Analysis of Population-Representative Data.' *The Lancet Global Health*, Vol. 10, No. 5 (2022), pp. e627–e39.

17 Lumey, L.H. et al. '*Hongerwinter*. The Dutch Hunger Winter Families Study'. *International Journal of Epidemiology*, Vol. 36, No. 6 (2007), pp. 1196–1204.

18 Yajnik, C.S. 'Confessions of a Thin-Fat Indian'. *European Journal of Clinical Nutrition*, Vol. 72, No. 4 (April 2018), pp. 469–73.

19 Wilson, Bee. *The Way We Eat Now*. London: Fourth Estate, 2019, p. 79.

20 Driscoll, A.K. and Gregory, E.C.W. 'Increases in Prepregnancy Obesity: United States, 2016–2019'. NCHS Data Brief 392 (2020), pp. 1–8.

21 Farren, M. et al. 'The Interplay Between Maternal Obesity and Gestational Diabetes Mellitus'. *Journal of Perinatal Medicine.*, Vol. 43 (2014), pp. 311–317.

22 Starling, A.P. et al. 'Associations of Maternal BMI and Gestational Weight Gain with Neonatal Adiposity in the Healthy Start Study'. *American Journal of Clinical Nutrition.*, Vol. 101 (2015), pp. 302–309; Chen, L.-W. et al. 'Maternal Macronutrient Intake During Pregnancy Is Associated with Neonatal Abdominal Adiposity: The Growing Up in Singapore Towards Healthy Outcomes (GUSTO) Study'. *Journal of Nutrition.*, Vol. 146 (2016), pp. 1571–79.

23 Ibáñez, L. et al. 'Early Development of Adiposity and Insulin Resistance After Catch-Up Weight Gain in Small-for-Gestational-Age Children'. *Journal of Clinical Endocrinology & Metabolism.*, Vol. 91 (2006), pp. 2153–58.

24 Simmonds, M. et al. 'Predicting Adult Obesity from Childhood Obesity: A Systematic Review and Meta-Analysis', *Obesity Reviews*, Vol. 17, No. 2 (2016), pp. 95–107.

2. Damage

1 Seckler, David. 'Small but Healthy: A Basic Hypothesis in the Theory, Measurement and Policy of Malnutrition'. In: P.V. Sukhatme (ed.), *Newer Concepts in Nutrition and Their Implications for Policy*, Maharashtra Association for the Cultivation of Science Research Institute, Pune, 1982.

2 Gillespie, Stuart. 'Myths and Realities of Child Nutrition.' *Economic and Political Weekly,* Vol. 48, No. 34 (2013), pp. 64–67.

3 Swinburn, Boyd, et al. 'The Global Syndemic of Obesity, Undernutrition, and Climate Change'. *The Lancet*, Vol. 393, No. 10173 (February 2019), pp. 791–846.

4 Global Nutrition Report. Bristol: Development Initiatives, 2021.

5 Black, R.E. et al. 'Maternal and Child Undernutrition and Overweight in Low- and Middle-Income Countries'. *The Lancet* (June 2013), pp. 15–39.

6 UNICEF–WHO–The World Bank. 'Joint Child Malnutrition Estimates (JME): Levels and Trends', 18 May 2023.

7 Steele, Margaret and Finucane, Francis. 'Philosophically, Is Obesity Really a Disease?' *Obesity Reviews*, Vol. 24, No. 8 (August 2023) e13590

8 Yeo, Giles. 'Fat Cells Stretch, They Don't Multiply: Why Everything You Know About Weight Gain Is Wrong'. *Science Focus*, 2 April 2023. <https://www.sciencefocus.com/the-human-body/weight-gain-fat-cells>

9 CDC NHANES 1999–2022 (2022) <https://www.cdc.gov/obesity/php/data-research/adult-obesity-prevalence-maps.html>; O'Hearn, M. et al. 'Trends and Disparities in Cardiometabolic Health Among Us Adults, 1999–2018.' *Journal of American College of Cardiology*, Vol. 80, No. 2 (12 July 2022), pp. 138–51.

10 Popkin, B.M. et al. 'Dynamics of the Double Burden of Malnutrition and the Changing Nutrition Reality'. *The Lancet*, Vol. 395, No. 10217 (4 January 2020), pp. 65–74.

11 Ladher, N. et al. 'Challenges of Obesity and Type 2 Diabetes Require More Attention to Food Environment'. *BMJ*, Editorial 2023, Vol. 383 (October 2023), p. 2269.

12 Nettle, Daniel et al. 'Food Insecurity as a Driver of Obesity in Humans: The Insurance Hypothesis'. *Behavioral and Brain Sciences*, Vol. 40 (January 2017) p. e105.

13 FAO, IFAD, UNICEF, WFP and WHO. *The State of Food Security and Nutrition in the World 2018. Building climate resilience for food security and nutrition*. Rome: FAO, 2018.

14 Stinson, E.J. et al. 'Food insecurity is associated with maladaptive eating behaviors and objectively measured overeating'. *Obesity*, Vol. 26, Issue 12 (2018), pp. 1841–48.

15 Khalili-Mahani, N. et al. 'To Each Stress Its Own Screen: A Cross-Sectional Survey of the Patterns of Stress and Various Screen Uses in Relation to Self-Admitted Screen Addiction'. *Journal of Medical Internet Research*, Vol. 21, No. 4 (2 April 2019), e11485.

16 Abbar, S. et al. 'You Tweet What You Eat: Studying Food Consumption Through Twitter'. *Proceedings of the 33rd Annual ACM Conference on Human Factors in Computing Systems*, 18 April 2015, pp. 3197–3206.

17 Obesity Health Alliance. 'Weight Stigma: Position Statement', January 2024. <obesityhealthalliance.co.uk>
18 Sheng, J.A. et al. 'The Hypothalamic-Pituitary-Adrenal Axis: Development, Programming Actions of Hormones, and Maternal-Fetal Interactions'. *Frontiers in Behavioural Neuroscience*, 14 (2021), 601939.
19 Yeo, 'Fat Cells Stretch', 2023.
20 Swinburn, 'Global Syndemic of Obesity', 2019.
21 World Obesity, 'Economic Impact of Overweight and Obesity', 2023.
22 Ochoa-Moreno, I. et al. 'Projected Health and Economic Effects of the Increase in Childhood Obesity during the COVID-19 Pandemic in England: The Potential Cost of Inaction.' *PLOS ONE*, Vol. 19, No. 1 (2024), e0296013.
23 Jackson, T. 'The False Economy of Big Food'. Food, Farming and Countryside Commission, 15 November 2024.

II REGIME

1 McMichael, Philip. 'A Food Regime Genealogy'. *The Journal of Peasant Studies*, Vol. 36, No. 1 (2009), pp. 139–69. I draw on the concepts and principles underpinning Philip McMichael's 2009 genealogy, but with slightly altered dates for the three regimes I focus on.

3. Colonial

1 Johnson, Walter. *Soul by Soul: Life inside the Antebellum Slave Market.* Harvard University Press, 1999.
2 Muhammad, Khalil Gibran. 'The Sugar That Saturates the American Diet Has a Barbaric History as the '"White Gold" That Fueled Slavery'. *New York Times Magazine*, 14 August 2019.
3 Muhammad, 'Sugar That Saturates the American Diet', 2019.
4 Von Tunzelmann, Alex. *Indian Summer: The Secret History of the End of an Empire.* New York: Henry Holt, 2007.
5 Koram, Kojo. *Uncommon Wealth.* London: John Murray, 2023.
6 Koram, *Uncommon Wealth*, 2023.
7 Smith, Adam. *The Wealth of Nations.* London: W. Strahan and T. Cadell, 1776.

8　Malthus, T. *An Essay on the Principle of Population*. London: J. Johnson, 1798.

9　Mohla, Anika. 'Hunger Deaths'. *New Indian Express*, 14 June 2014.

10　McCall, F. 'The FitzRoy Report, 1904', 30 April 2021 <https://history.port.ac.uk/?p=2264#_ftn1>.

11　Nelson, E. et al. 'Historicising Global Nutrition: Critical Reflections on Contested Pasts and Reimagined Futures'. *BMJ Global Health*, Vol. 6 (2021), e006337.

12　Corning, J.L. *Brain Exhaustion, With Some Preliminary Considerations On Cerebral Dynamics*. New York: D. Appleton, 1884.

4. Cold War

1　United Nations. 'Universal Declaration of Human Rights', 1948. <https://www.un.org/en/about-us/universal-declaration-of-human-rights>

2　Byerlee, Derek and Fanzo, Jessica. 'The SDG of Zero Hunger 75 Years On: Turning Full Circle on Agriculture and Nutrition'. *Global Food Security*, Vol. 21 (2019), p. 54.

3　Khan, M.S. et al. '*The Lancet* and Colonialism: Past, Present, and Future.' *The Lancet*, Vol. 403 (March 2024), pp. 1304–1308.

4　Byerlee and Fanzo, 'SDG of Zero Hunger', pp. 52–59.

5　Gollin, Douglas et al. 'Two Blades of Grass: The Impact of the Green Revolution'. *Journal of Political Economy*, Vol. 129, No. 8 (2021), pp. 2344–84.

6　Sukhatme, P.V. 'Size and Nature of the Protein Gap', *Nutrition Reviews,* Vol. 28, No. 9 (1970), pp. 223–26.

7　McLaren, D. 'The Great Protein Fiasco'. *The Lancet* , Vol. 304 (July 1974), pp. 93–96.

8　Reutlinger, S. and Selowsky, M. *Malnutrition and Poverty. Magnitude and Policy Options*. Baltimore: World Bank by the Johns Hopkins University Press, 1976.

5. Corporate

1　George, Susan. *How the Other Half Dies: The Real Reasons for World Hunger.* London: Penguin, 1976.

2 Wise, T. 'US Misuses Trade Agreements to Undermine Food Sovereignty'. Opinion, Inter-Press Service, 11 December 2023. <https://www.ipsnews.net/2023/12/u-s-misuses-trade-agreements-undermine-food-sovereignty/>

3 Freeman, Andrea. 'The Unbearable Whiteness of Milk: Food Oppression and the USDA'. *UC Irvine Law Review*, Vol. 3 (2013), p. 1251.

4 Moss, M. *Hooked: How We Became Addicted to Processed Food.* London: W.H. Allen, 2010.

5 Chang, Ha-Joon. *Edible Economics: A Hungry Economist Explains the World.* London: Allen Lane, 2022.

6 Nkrumah, Kwame. *Neocolonialism: The Last Stage of Imperialism.* London: Thomas Nelson & Sons, 1965.

7 Rodgers, A. et al. 'Prevalence Trends Tell Us What Did Not Precipitate the US Obesity Epidemic'. *The Lancet*, Vol. 3 (April 2018), pp. e162–3.

8 Popkin, B.M. 'The Nutrition Transition in Low-Income Countries: An Emerging Crisis.' *Nutrition Reviews*, Vol. 52, No. 9 (1994), pp. 285–298.

9 Wilson, Bee. *The Way We Eat Now.* London: Fourth Estate, 2019, p. 101.

10 Van Tulleken, Chris. *Ultra-Processed People: Why Do We All Eat Stuff That Isn't Food . . . and Why Can't We Stop?* London: Cornerstone, 2023.

11 Gabarell, L. et al. 'How Nestlé Gets Children Hooked On Sugar in Lower-Income Countries'. *Public Eye*, April 2024. <https://stories.publiceye.ch/nestle-babies/>

12 Gillespie, S. and Hodge, J. 'On the Front Line: Community Nutrition Programming'. In: S. Gillespie et al. (eds), *Nourishing Millions,* Washington DC: IFPRI, 2016.

13 UNICEF. *Strategy for Improved Nutrition of Children and Women in Developing Countries.* New York: United Nations Children's Fund, 1990.

14 Scrinis, Gyorgy. *Nutritionism: The Science and Politics of Dietary Advice.* New York: Columbia University Press, 2015.

III UNRAVELLING

6. First Food Fight

1 *New Internationalist*. 'Action Now on Baby Foods'. Editorial, 1 August 1973. <https://newint.org/issues/1973/08/01>
2 Anttila-Hughes, J.K. et al. 'Mortality from Nestlé's Marketing of Infant Formula in Low and Middle-Income Countries'. NBER Working Paper 24452 (2023).
3 WHO International Code of Marketing of Breast-Milk Substitutes, 27 January 1981. <https://www.who.int/publications/i/item/9241541601>
4 Victora, C.G. et al. 'Revisiting Maternal and Child Undernutrition in Low-Income and Middle-Income Countries: Variable Progress Towards an Unfinished Agenda'. *The Lancet*, Vol. 397 (April 2021), pp. 1388–99.
5 Victora, C.G. et al. 'Breastfeeding in the 21st Century: Epidemiology, Mechanisms, and Lifelong Effect'. *The Lancet*, Vol. 387, No. 10017 (January 2016), pp. 475–90.
6 WHO/UNICEF. *How the Marketing of Formula Milk Influences Our Decisions on Infant Feeding.* Geneva: World Health Organization and the United Nations Children's Fund, 2022.
7 Crowther, S.M. et al. 'The resurgence of breastfeeding, 1975–2000.' In: S.M. Crowther et al (eds), *Wellcome Witnesses to Twentieth Century Medicine 2009*, Wellcome Trust Centre for the History of Medicine at UCL, London, 2009.
8 Alive and Thrive. 'Putting Babies before Profits', 2021 <https://express.adobe.com/page/uNwlQ5zsQ1Ccy/>.
9 *New Internationalist*, 'Action Now on Baby Foods', 1973.
10 Anttila-Hughes, et al. 'Mortality from Nestlé's Marketing of Infant Formula', 2023.
11 International Breastfeeding Action Network. *Breaking the Rules, Stretching the Rules*, 2017.
12 WHO/UNICEF, *How the Marketing of Formula Milk Influences Our Decisions*, 2022.
13 Vogell, H. 'The U.S. Government Defended the Overseas Business Interests of Baby Formula Makers. Kids Paid the

Price'. ProPublica, 21 March 2024. <https://www.propublica.org/article/how-america-waged-global-campaign-against-baby-formula-regulation-thailand>

14 Vogell, H. 'The Biden Administration Says Its Trade Policy Puts People Over Corporations. Documents on Baby Formula Show Otherwise'. ProPublica, 22 July 2024 <https://www.propublica.org/article/baby-formula-regulation-biden-administration-europe-taiwan>.

15 WHO/UNICEF, *How the Marketing of Formula Milk Influences Our Decisions*, 2022.

16 Chetley, A. *The Politics of Baby Foods. Successful Challenges to an International Marketing Strategy.* London: Pinter, 1986.

7. Fake Food Flood

1 Gillespie, S.R. et al. 'How Nutrition Improves'. ACC/SCN State-of-the-Art Series, Nutrition Policy Discussion Paper No. 15. Geneva: UN Standing Committee on Nutrition, 1996.

2 Pollan, M. *In Defense of Food: An Eater's Manifesto.* New York: Penguin, 2009.

3 Dimbleby, Henry and Lewis, Jemima. *Ravenous: How to Get Ourselves and Our Planet into Shape.* London: Profile Books, 2023, p. 72; Rauber, F. et al. 'Ultra-Processed Food Consumption and Risk Of Obesity: A Prospective Cohort Study of UK Biobank'. *European Journal of Nutrition,* Vol. 60, No. 4 (2021), pp. 2169–80.

4 Van Tulleken, Chris. *Ultra-Processed People: Why Do We All Eat Stuff That Isn't Food . . . and Why Can't We Stop?* London: Cornerstone, 2023.

5 Goudie, S. *Broken Plate.* London: Food Foundation, 2023. <https://foodfoundation.org.uk/publication/broken-plate-2023>

6 Wood, B. et al. 'What is the Purpose of Ultra-Processed Food? An Exploratory Analysis of the Financialisation of Ultra-Processed Food Corporations and Implications for Public Health'. *Global Health,* Vol. 19, No. 85 (2023).

7 Lane, M. et al. 'Ultra-Processed Food Exposure and Adverse Health Outcomes: Umbrella Review of Epidemiological Meta-Analyses'. *BMJ,* Vol. 384 (2024), e077310.

8 Mendoza, K. and Tobias, D. 'Editorial: Quantity and Quality of Evidence are Sufficient: Prevalent Features of Ultraprocessed Diets are Deleterious for Health.' *Advances in Nutrition*, Vol. 100157 (2023) pp. 1–2.

9 Puig-Vallverdú, J. et al. 'The Association Between Maternal Ultra-Processed Food Consumption During Pregnancy and Child Neuropsychological Development: A Population-Based Birth Cohort Study'. *Clinical Nutrition*, Vol. 41, No. 10 (2022), pp. 2275–83.

10 Borge, Tiril et al. 'The Associations Between Maternal and Child Diet Quality and Child ADHD: Findings from a Large Norwegian Pregnancy Cohort Study'. *BMC Psychiatry*, Vol. 21, No. 139 (2021).

11 Bandy, Lauren et al. 'The Development of a Method for the Global Health Community to Assess the Proportion of Food and Beverage Companies' Sales that are Derived from Unhealthy Foods'. *Globalization and Health*, Vol. 19, No. 93 (2023).

12 Evans, Judith. 'Nestlé Says Majority of Its Food Portfolio Is Unhealthy'. *Irish Times*, 31 May 2021.

13 Makortoff, K. and Jolly, J. 'KitKat Owner Nestlé Fights Off Push to Cut Back on Unhealthy Products'. *The Guardian*, 18 April 2024 <https://www.theguardian.com/business/2024/apr/18/nestle-vote-sugar-salt-fats?CMP=share_btn_url>.

14 Madruga, Mariana et al. 'Trends in Food Consumption According to the Degree of Food Processing Among the UK Population over 11 Years'. *British Journal of Nutrition*, Vol. 130, No. 3 (August 2023) pp. 476–83.

15 Colombet, Z. et al. 'Social Inequalities in Ultra-Processed Food Intakes in the United Kingdom: A Time Trend Analysis (2008–2018)'. *Journal of Epidemiological & Community Health*, 76 (2022), A6-A7.

16 Parnham, Jennie C. et al. 'The Ultra-Processed Food Content of School Meals and Packed Lunches in the United Kingdom'. *Nutrients*, Vol. 14 (2022) <https://www.mdpi.com/2072-6643/14/14/2961>.

17 Pries, A.M. et al. 'Unhealthy Snack Food and Beverage Consumption Is Associated with Lower Dietary Adequacy

and Length-for-Age Z-Scores among 12–23-Month-Olds in
Kathmandu Valley, Nepal'. *Journal of Nutrition*, Vol. 149, No. 10
(2019), pp. 1843–51.

18 CGIAR. 'SHiFT Symposium at Micronutrient Forum
Sheds Light on Adolescent Nutrition in Ghana and Viet
Nam', 2024. <https://www.cgiar.org/news-events/news/
shift-symposium-at-micronutrient-forum-sheds-light-on-
adolescent-nutrition-in-ghana-and-viet-nam>

19 Dicken, S.J. and Batterham, R.L. 'The Role of Diet Quality
in Mediating the Association Between Ultra-Processed Food
Intake, Obesity and Health-Related Outcomes: A Review of
Prospective Cohort Studies'. *Nutrients,* Vol. 14 (22 December
2021), p. 23; Bonaccio, M. et al. 'Ultra-Processed Food
Consumption Is Associated with Increased Risk of All-Cause
and Cardiovascular Mortality in the Moli-sani Study'. *American
Journal of Clinical Nutrition*, Vol. 113, Issue 2 (2021), pp. 446–55.

20 Julia, C. et al. 'Respective Contribution of Ultra-Processing
and Nutritional Quality of Foods to the Overall Diet Quality:
Results from the NutriNet–Sante Study'. *European Journal of
Nutrition*, Vol. 62 (2023), pp. 157–64.

21 This list drew on Hall, K.D. 'From Dearth to Excess: The Rise
of Obesity in an Ultraprocessed Food System'. *Philosophical
Transactions of the Royal Society B*, Vol. 378 (2023), 20220214.

22 WHO. 'Aspartame hazard and risk assessment results released',
14 July 2023. <https://www.who.int/news/item/14-07-2023-
aspartame-hazard-and-risk-assessment-results-released>

23 Lobstein, Tim and Brownell, Kelly D. 'Endocrine-Disrupting
Chemicals and Obesity Risk: A Review of Recommendations
for Obesity Prevention Policies'. *Obesity Reviews*, Vol. 22, No. 11
(November 2021).

24 University of Oxford, The George Institute for Global Health
and UNICEF. 'Developing a Reference Tool for UNICEF
and Other International Agencies to Inform Principles of
Engagement with the Food And Beverage Industry', 2023
<https://www.unicef.org/documents/nutrition/tool-inform-
principles-of-engagement-food-and-beverage-industry>.

25 Vitale, M. et al. 'Ultra-Processed Foods and Human Health: A
    Systematic Review and Meta-Analysis of Prospective Cohort
    Studies'. *Advances in Nutrition*, Vol. 100121 (2023).

26 Gearhardt, Ashley N. et al. 'Social, Clinical and Policy
    Implications of Ultra-Processed Food Addiction'. *BMJ* (October
    2023); Praxedes, D.R.S. et al. 'Prevalence of Food Addiction
    Determined by the Yale Food Addiction Scale and Associated
    Factors: A Systematic Review with Meta-Analysis'. *European
    Eating Disorders Review*, Vol. 30, No. 2 (2022), pp. 85–95;
    Yekaninejad, M.S. et al. 'Prevalence of Food Addiction in
    Children and Adolescents: A Systematic Review and Meta-
    Analysis.' *Obesity Reviews,* Vol. 22, No. 6, (2021), e13183.

27 Berridge, Kent C. and Robinson, Terry E. 'Liking, Wanting
    and the Incentive-Sensitization Theory of Addiction'. *American
    Psychologist*, Vol. 71, No. 8 (2017), pp. 670–79.

28 Fazzino, T.L. et al. 'Proof for Why We Need Cross-Industry
    Approaches to Research on the Commercial Determinants of
    Health'. *Addiction*, Vol. 119, No. 1 (2023) pp. 72.

29 Fazzino, T.L. et al. 'US Tobacco Companies Selectively
    Disseminated Hyper-Palatable Foods into the US Food System:
    Empirical Evidence and Current Implications'. *Addiction*, Vol.
    119, No. 1 (January 2024), pp. 62–71. <https://onlinelibrary.
    wiley.com/doi/10.1111/add.16332>

30 Thanarajah, Sharmili Edwin et al. 'Habitual Daily Intake of
    a Sweet and Fatty Snack Modulates Reward Processing in
    Humans'. *Cell Metabolism*, Vol. 35, No. 4 (2023), pp. 571–84.

31 Nestlé. 'Nestlé Enters Weight Management Market:
    Jenny Craig Acquisition Enhances Group's Nutrition,
    Health and Wellness Dimension', 19 June 2006 <https://
    www.nestle.com/media/pressreleases/allpressreleases/
    weightmanagementmarketjennycraig-19jun06>.

32 de Jeu, M. and van den Berg, I. 'Obesity as a Business Model:
    The Food Industry's Double Agenda', Follow the Money, 29
    August 2024. <https://www.ftm.eu/articles/obesity-as-a-
    business-model>

33 Lawinski, J. 'The Ozempic Effect Is Real: Study Zeroes in on

Glp-1 Users' Food Needs'. *Food Dive*, 8 May 2024. <https://www.fooddive.com/news/the-ozempic-effect-real-study-zeroesglp-1-users-food-needs/715549/?lctg=9072588>

8. Swamps and Deserts

1 Swinburn, B. et al. 'INFORMAS (International Network for Food and Obesity/Non-communicable Diseases Research, Monitoring and Action Support): Overview and Key Principles'. *Obesity Reviews*, Vol. 14, No. S1 (October 2013), pp. 1–12.

2 Swinburn, B. et al. 'Dissecting Obesogenic Environments: The Development and Application of a Framework for Identifying and Prioritizing Environmental Interventions for Obesity'. *Preventative Medicine*, Vol. 29, No. 6 (December 1999), pp. 563–70.

3 Tufts University. 'Food Prices for Nutrition: Diet Metrics for a Better-Fed World', <https://sites.tufts.edu/foodpricesfornutrition/>.

4 FAO, IFAD, UNICEF, WFP and WHO. *The State of Food Insecurity and Nutrition in the World*, 2024.

5 FAO, IFAD, UNICEF, WFP and WHO. *State of Food Insecurity and Nutrition*, 2024.

6 Morrison, J. et al. 'Supporting Transformation of Food Systems to Nourish People and Planet: Our Policy Focus', January 2024. <https://www.foodsystemsdashboard.org/>

7 FAO, IFAD, UNICEF, WFP and WHO. *The State of Food Insecurity and Nutrition*, 2024.

8 Food Foundation. Food Insecurity Tracking. Round 15, July 2024 <https://foodfoundation.org.uk/initiatives/food-insecurity-tracking>.

9 Goudie, S. *Broken Plate*. London: Food Foundation, 2023 <https://foodfoundation.org.uk/publication/broken-plate-2023>.

10 Rayner, Jay, 19 March 2018 <https://twitter.com/jayrayner1/status/975672927516491776>

11 Dimbleby, Henry and Lewis, Jemima. *Ravenous: How to Get Ourselves and Our Planet into Shape*. London: Profile Books, 2023, p. 91.

12 Top ten in the US are McDonald's, Subway, Burger King, Pizza Hut, Jack-in-the-box, Kentucky Fried Chicken, Taco Bell, Domino's Pizza, Wendy's and Little Caesars. It's not so different in the UK.

13 Thomas, T. 'Unhealthiest UK Restaurants and Takeaways "More Likely to Be Found in Deprived Areas"'. *The Guardian*, 8 March 2024. <https://www.theguardian.com/society/2024/mar/08/unhealthiest-uk-restaurants-and-takeaways-more-likely-to-be-found-in-deprived-areas?CMP=Share_iOSApp_Other>

14 Garduño-Alanis, A. et al. 'A High Density of Ultra Processed Food, Alcohol & Tobacco Retail Stores, and Social Inequalities Are Associated with Higher Mortality Rates of Non-Communicable Diseases in Mexican Adults: 2005 to 2021'. *PLOS ONE,* Vol. 19, No. 4 (2024), e0301387; Lovasi, G.S. et al. 'Healthy Food Retail Availability and Cardiovascular Mortality in the United States: A Cohort Study'. *BMJ Open*, Vol. 11, No. 7 (2021), e048390.

15 Brooks, P. 'Unavoidable Impact: How Outdoor Advertising Placement Relates to Health and Wealth Inequalities'. Adfree Cities, March 2024. <https://adfreecities.org.uk/unavoidable-impact/>

16 Currie, Janet et al. 'The Effect of Fast Food Restaurants on Obesity and Weight Gain'. *American Economic Journal: Economic Policy*, Vol. 2, No. 3 (2010), pp. 32–63.

17 Wilson, Bee. *The Way We Eat Now*. London: Fourth Estate, 2019, p. 184.

18 Carraher, M. et al. *Food Policy in the United Kingdom*. London: Earthscan, 2023, p. 144.

19 Carraher, et al. *Food Policy in the United Kingdom*, 2023.

20 Boyland, E. et al. 'Advertising as a Cue to Consume: A Systematic Review and Meta-Analysis of the Effects of Acute Exposure to Unhealthy Food and Non-Alcoholic Beverage Advertising on Intake in Children and Adults'. *American Journal of Clinical Nutrition*, Vol. 103, No. 2 (2016), pp. 519–33.

21 Thomas, Christopher et al. 'Under Pressure: New Evidence on Young People's Broadcast Marketing Exposure in the UK'. Cancer Research UK, March 2018.

22 Johnson, B. 'World's Largest Advertisers'. *Advertising Age*, 5 December 2017.

23 Outsmart. 'Out of Home Advertising Spend Analysis, 2021–23'. <20240208113456_Out_Of_Home_Advertising_Spend_Analysis_2021-23.pdf (outsmart.org.uk)>

24 Goudie, *Broken Plate*, 2023.

25 Bite Back 2030. *Fuel Us, Don't Fool Us.*, 2024. <https://www.biteback2030.com/>

26 Coates, A. and Boyland, E. 'Kid Influencers: A New Arena of Social Media Food Marketing'. *Nature Reviews Endocrinology*, Vol. 17, No. 3 (2021), pp. 133–34.

27 Bite Back 2030, *Fuel Us*, 2024.

28 Food Foundation. 'State of the Nation's Food Industry 2024', November 2024. <https://foodfoundation.org.uk/publication/state-nations-food-industry-report-2024>

9. Carbon and Plastic

1 Crippa, M. et al. 'Food Systems Are Responsible for a Third of Anthropogenic GHG Emissions'. *Nature Food*, Vol. 2 (2021), pp. 198–209.

2 Clark, M. et al. 'Global Food System Emissions Could Preclude Achieving the 1.5°C and 2°C Targets'. *Science*, Vol. 370 (2020), pp. 705–708.

3 Food systems drive 86 per cent of biodiversity loss worldwide, 90 per cent of deforestation and 70 per cent of global freshwater withdrawals. Pendrill, F. et al. 'Agricultural and Forestry Trade Drives Large Share of Tropical Deforestation Emissions'. *Global Environmental Change*, Vol. 56 (2019) pp. 1–10; Forslund, T. et al. 'Tackling Root Causes: Halting Biodiversity Loss Through the Circular Economy'. *Sitra*, No. 205 (2022). <https://www.sitra.fi/en/publications/tackling-root-causes/>; Ritchie, H. et al. 'Environmental Impacts of Food Production', Our World in Data, 2022. <https://ourworldindata.org/environmental-impacts-of-food>

4 Anastasiou, K. et al. 'A Conceptual Framework for Understanding the Environmental Impacts of Ultraprocessed

Foods and Implications for Sustainable Food Systems'. *Journal of Cleaner Production*, Vol. 368 (25 September 2022), 133155.

5 Tereza da Silva, J. et al. 'Greenhouse Gas Emissions, Water Footprint, and Ecological Footprint of Food Purchases According to Their Degree of Processing in Brazilian Metropolitan Areas: A Time-Series Study from 1987 to 2018'. *Lancet Planetary Health*, Vol. 5, No. 11 (November 2021), pp. e775–e785.

6 Changing Markets Foundation. 'Mighty Earth. Net-zero integrity: Nestlé's methane blindspot', 2023. <https://changingmarkets.org/report/net-zero-integrity-nestles-methane-blindspot/>

7 'Treating Beef Like Coal Would Make a Big Dent in Greenhouse Gas Emissions'. *The Economist*, October 2021.

8 Ritchie, H. *Not the End of the World*. London: Chatto and Windus, 2024, p. 162.

9 Edwards, R.B. et al. 'Causes of Indonesia's forest fires'. *World Development*, Vol. 127 (2020), 104717.

10 Neslen, A. 'Nestlé, Hershey and Mars "breaking promises over palm oil use"'. *The Guardian*, 28 October 2017. <https://www.theguardian.com/environment/2017/oct/27/nestle-mars-and-hershey-breaking-promises-over-palm-oil-use-say-campaigners>

11 Lawrence, F. 'Should We Worry about Soya in Our Food?' *The Guardian,* 25 July 2006. <https://www.theguardian.com/news/2006/jul/25/food.foodanddrink>

12 Soil Association. 'Why Are We Calling for Peak Poultry?', 2022. <https://www.soilassociation.org/causes-campaigns/peak-poultry/>

13 Mighty Earth. 'European Supermarkets Fail to Act on Deforestation-Linked Soy', 11 July 2022. <https://mightyearth.org/article/european-supermarkets-fail-to-act-on-deforestation-linked-soy/>

14 Statista. Topic: Plastics industry worldwide. <https://www.statista.com/topics/5266/plastics-industry/ (2023).>

15 Break Free from Plastic Movement. Brand Audit 2023 Report, February 2024. <https://brandaudit.breakfreefromplastic.org/brand-audit-2023/>

16 Allen, D. et al. *The Fraud of Plastic Recycling: How Big Oil and the Plastics Industry Deceived the Public for Decades and Caused the Plastic Waste Crisis.* Center for Climate Integrity, 2024.

17 Yates, J. et al. 'Trust and Responsibility in Food Systems Transformation. Engaging with Big Food: Marriage or Mirage?' *BMJ Global Health*, Vol. 6 (2021), e007350.

18 Qian, N. et al. 'Rapid single-particle chemical imaging of nano-plastics by SRS microscopy'. *PNAS*, Vol. 121, No. 3 (2024), pp. 1–12.

19 Cimmino, I. et al. 'Potential Mechanisms of Bisphenol A (BPA) Contributing to Human Disease'. *International Journal of Molecular Sciences*, Vol. 21, No. 16 (11 August 2020), p. 5761.

20 Ruggeri Laderchi, C. et al. 'The Economics of the Food System Transformation'. *Food System Economics Commission, Global Policy Report*, February 2024.

21 UN Climate Change IPCC reports 2018, 2019. <https://unfccc.int/>

22 Romanello, M. et al. 'The 2023 Report of the *Lancet* Countdown on Health and Climate Change: The Imperative for a Health-Centred Response in a World Facing Irreversible Harms'. *The Lancet,* 14 November 2023.

23 Oxfam. 'Survival of the Richest: How We Must Tax the Super-Rich Now to Fight Inequality', 2023.

24 Maitland, A. et al. 'Carbon Billionaires: The Investment Emissions of the World's Richest People'. Oxfam: Policy & Practice, 2022.

10. Pandemic

1 Gillespie, S.R. 'Potential Impact of AIDS on Farming Systems: A Case Study from Rwanda'. *Land Use Policy*, Vol. 6, No. 4 (1989), pp. 301–12.

2 De Waal, A. and Whiteside, A. 'New Variant Famine: AIDS and Food Crisis in Southern Africa'. *The Lancet*, Vol. 362, No. 9391 (11 October 2003), pp. 1234–37.

3 Loevinsohn, M. and Gillespie, S.R. 'HIV/AIDS, Rural Livelihoods and Food Security: Understanding and Responding'. *FCN Discussion Paper 157*, Washington DC: IFPRI, 2003.

4 Gillespie, S. et al. (eds). 'Poverty, HIV and AIDS: Vulnerability and Impact in Southern Africa'. *AIDS*, Vol. 21 (2007), Supplement 7.

5 Gillespie, S. et al. 'AIDS in Africa: Dynamics and Diversity of Impacts and Response'. In: Anke Niehof, Gabriel Rugalema and Stuart Gillespie (eds), *AIDS and Rural Livelihoods: Dynamics and Diversity in sub-Saharan Africa*, London: Earthscan, 2010, p. 7.

6 Byron, E. et al. 'Integrating Nutrition Security with Nutritional Support for People Living with HIV: Lessons Being Learned in Kenya'. *Food and Nutrition Bulletin*, Vol. 29, No. 2 (2008), pp. 87–97.

7 Gillespie, S. 'Epidemics and Food Systems: What Gets Framed, Gets Done'. *Food Security*, 12 (8 July 2020), pp. 895–98.

8 Gillespie, Stuart. 'Nutrition Policy and Practice: Unpacking the Politics'. In: Andrew Marble and Heidi Fritschel (eds), *Global Food Policy Report,* Washington DC: IFPRI, 2013, pp. 75–86.

9 Bregman, R. *Humankind: A Hopeful History.* London: Bloomsbury, 2020.

10 Fakhri, M. The Right to Food, Violence, and Food Systems. Eighth Annual T.M.C. Asser Lecture (2024) <https://www.asser.nl/asserpress/books/?rId=14037>

11 Sridhar, D. *Preventable.* London: Penguin, 2022, p. 327.

11. Shackled

1 Oxfam. 'Survival of the Richest: How We Must Tax the Super-Rich Now to Fight Inequality', 2023.

2 Stice, J. 'Workers reveal what it's really like to work at Taco Bell'. *Mashed*, 2 February 2023. <https://www.mashed.com/196485/workers-reveal-what-its-really-like-to-work-at-taco-bell/>

3 IPES-Food. *Who's Tipping the Scales? The Growing Influence of Corporations on the Governance of Food Systems, and How to Counter It*, 2023.

4 Haddaway, N. 'Almeria: The True Cost of our Fruit and Veg'. In: *Food: Responding to the Global Crisis, Artefact* magazine (2023), pp. 34–41.

5 United Nations Children's Fund. 'A Systems Approach to Improving Children's Diets: Learning from Lived Experience'. New York: UNICEF, 2022.

6 UNDP. '10 things to know about Indigenous peoples', 29 July 2021. <https://stories.undp.org/10-things-we-all-should-know-about-indigenous-people>

7 Gatica-Domínguez, G. et al. 'Ethnic Inequalities in Child Stunting and Feeding Practices: Results from Surveys in Thirteen Countries from Latin America'. *International Journal for Equity in Health*, Vol. 19, No. 53 (2020).

8 Batal, M. and Decelles, S. 'A Scoping Review of Obesity Among Indigenous Peoples in Canada'. *Journal of Obesity* (June 2019), e9741090.

9 Kelliher, A. 'Life Expectancy of Indigenous Peoples Is More Than Five Years Lower Than Non-Indigenous Population in the US'. *The Conversation*, 3 February 2023.

10 Temple, J.B. and Russell, J. 'Food Insecurity Among Older Aboriginal and Torres Strait Islanders'. *International Journal of Environmental Research and Public Health*, Vol. 15, No. 8 (2018), 1766.

11 Skinner, K. et al. 'Giving Voice to Food Insecurity in a Remote Indigenous Community in Subarctic Ontario, Canada: Traditional Ways, Ways to Cope, Ways Forward'. *BMC Public Health*, Vol. 13, No. 1 (2013), p. 427.

12 Arias, Elizabeth et al. 'Provisional Life Expectancy Estimates for 2022'. CDC Report No. 31, November 2023. <https://www.cdc.gov/nchs/data/vsrr/vsrr031.pdf>

13 Food Foundation. 'Food Insecurity Tracking', July 2024. <www.foodfoundation.org.uk>

14 Brones, A. 'Karen Washington: It's not a food desert, it's food apartheid'. *Guernica*, 7 May 2018. <https://www.guernicamag.com/karen-washington-its-not-a-food-desert-its-food-apartheid/>

15 FAO. 'The status of women in agrifood systems', 2023. <https://www.fao.org/3/cc5343en/online/cc5343en.html>

16 Rajagopalan, M. and Inzamam, Q. 'The Brutality of Sugar: Debt, Child Marriages and Hysterectomies'. *New York Times*, 24

March 2024. <https://www.nytimes.com/2024/03/24/world/asia/india-sugar-cane-fields-child-labor-hysterectomies.html>

17 D'Souza, A. and Tandon, S. 'How Well Do Household-Level Data Characterize Undernourishment? Evidence from Bangladesh'. *SSRN Scholarly Paper 2657617*, 2015; Harris-Fry, H.A. et al. 'Status and Determinants of Intra-Household Food Allocation in Rural Nepal'. *European Journal of Clinical Nutrition*, Vol. 72, No. 11 (2018), pp. 1524–36; Gittelsohn, J. 'Opening the Box: Intrahousehold Food Allocation in Rural Nepal'. *Social Science & Medicine*, Vol. 33, No. 10 (1991), pp. 1141–54.

18 Marya, R. and Patel, R. *Inflamed*. London: Allen Lane, 2021.

19 Sandel, M.J. *The Tyranny of Merit*. London: Penguin, 2021.

12. Food Barons, Russian Dolls and Trojan Horses

1 Garde, A. and Zrilic, J. 'International Investment Law and Noncommunicable Disease Prevention'. *Journal of World Investment and Trade*, Vol. 21 (2020), pp. 649–73.

2 Monbiot, G. 'The Hunger Gap', 9 March 2023. <https://www.monbiot.com/2023/03/09/the-hunger-gap/>

3 Kiezebrink, V. and Heitland, M. 'Hungry for Profits', 30 January 2024. <www.somo.nl/hungry-for-profits/>; Harvey, F. 'Record Profits for Grain Firms Amid Food Crisis Prompt Calls for Windfall Tax'. *The Guardian*, 23 August 2022; Murphy, S. et al. 'Cereal Secrets: The World's Largest Grain Traders and Global Agriculture'. *Oxfam Research Reports*, August 2012; Putz, A. 'The ABCDs and M&A: Putting 90 per cent of the global grain supply in fewer hands'. *Pitchbook*, 21 February, 2018.

4 Kneen, B. *Invisible Giant: Cargill and Its Transnational Strategies*. London: Pluto Press, 2002.

5 Howard, P. and Hendrickson, M. 'The State of Concentration in Global Food and Agriculture Industries'. In: Hans Herren and Benedikt Haerlin, *Transformation of Our Food Systems: The Making of a Paradigm Shift*, IAASTD, 2020; Clapp, J. and Purugganan, J. 'Contextualizing Corporate Control in the Agrifood and Extractive Sectors'. *Globalizations*, Vol. 17, No. 7 (2020), pp. 1265–75.

6 ETC Group. *Food Barons: Crisis Profiteering, Digitalization and Shifting Power*, 20 September 2022.

7 Wood, B. et al. 'Behind the "creative destruction" of human diets: An analysis of the structure and market dynamics of the ultra-processed food manufacturing industry and implications for public health'. *Journal of Agrarian Change,* 23 (2023), pp. 811–843.

8 Wood, B. et al. 'What Is the Purpose of Ultra-Processed Food? An Exploratory Analysis of the Financialisation of Ultra-Processed Food Corporations and Implications for Public Health'. *Globalization and Health*, Vol. 19 (2023), p. 85.

9 WHO/UNICEF. *How the Marketing of Formula Milk Influences Our Decisions on Infant Feeding.* Geneva: World Health Organization and the United Nations Children's Fund, 2022.

10 ETC Group, *Food Barons*, 2022.

11 SAPEA. 'A Sustainable Food System for the European Union'. *Evidence Review Report.* Berlin: Science Advice for Policy by European Academies, 2020.

12 Wood et al. 'What Is the Purpose of Ultra-Processed Food?', p. 85.

13 Mazzucato, M. *The Value of Everything: Making and Taking in the Global Economy.* New York: PublicAffairs, 2018.

14 Clapp, J. and Isakson, S.R. 'Risky Returns: The Implications of Financialization in the Food System'. *Development and Change*, Vol. 49, Issue 2 (March 2018), pp. 437-460.

15 Saladino, D. *Eating to Extinction: The World's Rarest Foods and Why We Need to Save Them.* New York: Farrar, Straus and Giroux, 2022.

16 Wilson, Bee. *The Way We Eat Now.* London: Fourth Estate, 2019, p. 37.

17 IPES-Food. *Who's Tipping the Scales? The Growing Influence of Corporations on the Governance of Food Systems, and How to Counter It*, April 2023; Clapp, J. 'Mega-Mergers on the Menu: Corporate Concentration and the Politics of Sustainability in the Global Food System'. *Global Environmental Politics*, Vol. 18, No. 2 (2018), pp. 12–33.

18 Keenan, L. et al. 'Hungry for Power: Financialization and the Concentration of Corporate Control in the Global Food System'. *Geoforum*, Vol. 147 (2023), p. 103909.

19 Allen, L.N. et al. 'Corporate Profits Versus Spending on Non-Communicable Disease Prevention: An Unhealthy Balance'. *Lancet Global Health*, Vol. 7, No. 11 (November 2019), pp. e1482–e1483.

20 Wunsch, N-G. 'Nestlé Group marketing spend 2015-2022', 8 March 2024. <https://www.statista.com/statistics/685708/nestle-group-marketing-spend/>; Nestlé S.A. 'Financial Statements 2022: Consolidated Financial Statements of the Nestlé Group 2022.' Vevey, 2022.

21 De Loecker, J. et al. 'The Rise of Market Power and the Macroeconomic Implications'. *Quarterly Journal of Economics*, Vol. 135, Issue 2, 15 November 2019. <https://www.janeeckhout.com/wp-content/uploads/RMP.pdf>

22 Inman, P. 'Greedflation: corporate profiteering "significantly" boosted global prices, study shows'. *The Guardian*, 7 December 2023. <https://www.theguardian.com/business/2023/dec/07/greedflation-corporate-profiteering-boosted-global-prices-study>

23 Lukes, S. *Power: A Radical View*. London: Red Globe, 2015; Fuchs, D. et al. 'Power: The Missing Element in Sustainable Consumption and Absolute Reductions Research and Action'. *Journal of Cleaner Production*, Vol. 132 (2016), pp. 298–307.

24 Fakhri, M. et al. 'The UN Food Systems Summit: How Not to Respond to the Urgency of Reform'. Grain, 23 March 2021. <https://grain.org/en/article/6639-the-un-food-systems-summit-how-not-to-respond-to-the-urgency-of-reform>

13. The Dark Arts

1 Gillespie, Stuart. 'Beyond Reasonable Doubt: Avoiding Conflict of Interest in Nutrition Research'. ANH Academy, 28 September 2023; Brandt, A.M. 'Inventing Conflicts of Interest: A History of Tobacco Industry Tactics'. *American Journal of Public Health*, Vol. 102, No. 1 (January 2012) pp. 63–71.

2 Lacy-Nichols, J. and Williams, O. '"Part of the Solution": Food

Corporation Strategies for Regulatory Capture and Legitimacy'. *International Journal of Health Policy and Management*, Vol. 10 (December 2021), pp. 845–56.

3 Brownell, Kelly D. and Warner, Kenneth E. 'The Perils of Ignoring History: Big Tobacco Played Dirty and Millions Died. How Similar Is Big Food?' *The Milbank Quarterly*, Vol. 87, No. 1 (March 2009), pp. 259–94.

4 UNICEF. Webinar 1: Addressing food and beverage industry interference in policy-making. (3 March 2022). <https://www.unicef.org/media/142236/file/UNICEF%20GHAI%20Webinar%201%20-%20Industry%20Interference%20Summary%20of%20Key%20Points%20and%20Resources.pdf>

5 Brownell and Warner, 'Perils of Ignoring History', 2009.

6 Lauber, K. et al. 'Commercial Use of Evidence in Public Health Policy: A Critical Assessment of Food Industry Submissions to Global-Level Consultations on Noncommunicable Disease Prevention'. *BMJ Global Health*, Vol. 6 (2021), e006176.

7 Radden Keefe, P. *Empire of Pain*. London: Picador, 2021.

8 Chavkin, S. et al. 'As Obesity Rises, Big Food Pushes "Anti-Diet" Advice'. *Washington Post*, 3 April 2024. <https://www.washingtonpost.com/wellness/2024/04/03/diet-culture-nutrition-influencers-general-mills-processed-food/>

9 Besancon, Stephane et al. 'A Study Is 21 Times More Likely to Find Unfavorable Results About the Nutrition Label Nutri-Source If the Authors Declare the Conflict of Interest or the Study Is Funded by the Food Industry'. *BMJ Global Health*, Vol. 8 (2023), e011720. Sacks, Gary et al. 'The Characteristics and Extent of Food Industry Involvement in Peer-Reviewed Research Articles from 10 Leading Nutrition-Related Journals in 2018'. *PLOS ONE*, Vol. 15, No. 12 (2020), e0243144. Lundh, Andreas et al. 'Industry sponsorship and research outcome'. *Cochrane Database System Review*, Vol. 2, No. 2 (16 February 2017); Fabbri, Alice et al. 'The Influence of Industry Sponsorship on the Research Agenda: A Scoping Review'. *American Journal of Public Health*, Vol. 108, No. 11 (September 2018), pp. e9–e16.

10 Lesser, L. et al. 'Relationship Between Funding Source and

Conclusion Among Nutrition-Related Scientific Articles'. *PLOS Medicine*, Vol. 4 (2007), e5.

11 Goldberg, D. 'COI Bingo'. *BMJ*, Vol. 351 (2015), h6577. <https://www.bmj.com/content/351/bmj.h6577>

12 Sahara Salt Consulting. 'Nestlé Nutrition South Africa Stakeholder Mapping'. Nestle ESAR, 11 December 2012. <nestle_11122012update.pdf (nestle-esar.com)>

13 Nestle, Marion. 'The Academy of Nutrition and Dietetics responds to the Washington Post'. *Food Politics*, 4 October 2023. <https://www.foodpolitics.com/2023/10/the-academy-of-nutrition-and-dietetics-responds-to-the-washington-post/?lctg=9072588>

14 Carriedo, A. et al. 'The corporate capture of the nutrition profession in the USA: the case of the Academy of Nutrition and Dietetics'. *Public Health Nutrition*, Vol. 25, No. 12 (2022), pp. 3568–3582.

15 Mensendiek, Hana et al. 'Full Disclosure: Assessing Conflicts of Interest of the 2025 Dietary Guidelines Advisory Committee'. US Right to Know, October 2023.

16 Percival, Rob. 'Sticky Fingers of Food Industry on Government Ultra-Processed Food Review'. *Soil Association*, 11 July 2023. <https://www.soilassociation.org/blogs/2023/july/11/sticky-fingers-of-food-industry-on-government-ultra-processed-food-review/>

17 Transparency International, Access Info Europe, Sunlight Foundation and Open Knowledge International. International Standards for Lobbying Regulation: Towards Greater Transparency, Integrity and Participation, 2022. <https://lobbyingtransparency.net/>

18 Allen, L.N. et al. 'Assessing the Association Between Corporate Financial Influence and Implementation of Policies to Tackle Commercial Determinants of Non-Communicable Diseases: A Cross-Sectional Analysis of 172 Countries'. *Social Science & Medicine*, Vol. 297 (2022), 114825.

19 Goswami, O. and Stillerman, K.P. 'Cultivating Control: Corporate Lobbying on the Food and Farm Bill'. Union of

Concerned Scientists, 13 May 2024. <https://www.ucsusa.org/resources/cultivating-control>

20 Chung, H. et al. 'Mapping the Lobbying Footprint of Harmful Industries: 23 Years of Data from OpenSecrets'. *The Millbank Quarterly*, 2024.

21 Brownell, K. and Nestle, M. 'The Sweet and Lowdown on Sugar'. *New York Times* Opinion, 23 January 2004.

22 Means, Calley. 2 January 2023. <https://twitter.com/calleymeans/status/1609929026889711617?lang=en>; Nutrition Insight. 'CSPI Report Criticizes "Big Soda" Philanthropy', 20 March 2013. <https://www.nutritioninsight.com/news/cspi-report-criticizes-big-soda-philanthropy.html>

23 Leatherman, T.L. and Goodman, A. 'Coca-Colonization of Diets in the Yucatan'. *Social Science & Medicine*, Vol. 61, No. 4 (Aug 2005), pp. 833–46.

24 Gómez, Eduardo J. 'Coca-Cola's Political and Policy Influence in Mexico: Understanding the Role of Institutions, Interests and Divided Society'. *Health Policy and Planning*, Vol. 34, No. 7 (September 2019), pp. 520–28.

25 Chung et al. 'Mapping the Lobbying Footprint', 2024.

26 Cullerton K. and Patay D. 'Inside a Corporate Affairs Conference: The Race for a Social License'. *Frontiers in Communication*, Vol. 9 (2024), 1419959.

27 Giridharadas, A. 'The Danger of Side Salads'. *The Ink*, 21 August 2020. <https://the.ink/p/how-corporate-good-deeds-make-things>

28 World Food Programme. 'Our Private Sector Partners'. <https://www.wfp.org/partners/private-sector>

29 CGIAR. Code of Conduct for Governance Officials. Approved by the CGIAR System Board as a CGIAR Policy with effect from 3 November 2020 (Decision Reference SB/M17/EDP11).

30 Erzse, A. et al. 'A Realist Review of Voluntary Actions by the Food and Beverage Industry and Implications for Public Health and Policy in Low- and Middle-Income Countries'. *Nature Food*, 3 (2022), pp. 650–63.

31 Campbell, N. et al. 'Ultraprocessed Food: The Tragedy of the

Biological Commons.' *International Journal of Health Policy and Management,* Vol. 12 (2023), p. 7557.

32 Campbell, D. 'Tories and Labour Urged to Show Courage to Act on Unhealthy Food'. *The Guardian,* 16 March 2024. <https://www.theguardian.com/society/2024/mar/16/tories-and-labour-urged-to-show-courage-to-act-on-unhealthy-food>

33 WHO. *Commercial Determinants of Noncommunicable Diseases in the WHO European Region.* Copenhagen: WHO Regional Office for Europe, 2024, p. 19.

34 Brandt. 'Inventing Conflicts of Interest', pp. 63–71.

35 Greenhalgh S. 'Inside ILSI: How Coca-Cola, Working Through Its Scientific Nonprofit, Created a Global Science of Exercise for Obesity and Got It Embedded in Chinese Policy (1995–2015)'. *Journal of Health Politics, Policy and Law,* Vol. 46, No. 2 (April 2021), pp. 235–76.

36 Malkan, S. 'Food Industry Lobby Group ILSI Rebrands (Again) to Duck Critical News Coverage'. US Right to Know, 7 June 2022. <https://usrtk.org/industry-pr/ilsi-rebrands-again/>

37 Slater, S. et al. 'Corporate Interest Groups and Their Implications for Global Food Governance: Mapping and Analysing the Global Corporate Influence Network of the Transnational Ultra-Processed Food Industry'. *Global Health,* Vol. 20, No. 16 (2024). <https://globalizationandhealth.biomedcentral.com/articles/10.1186/s12992-024-01020-4>

38 War on Want. 'Secrets and Fries: McDonald's £295 Million Tax Dodge, 17 March 2022. <https://waronwant.org/news-analysis/secrets-and-fries-mcdonalds-ps295-million-tax-dodge>

14. Do-Nothing Politics

1 Bhutta, Z.A. et al. 'Evidence-based Interventions for Improvement of Maternal and Child Nutrition: What Can Be Done and at What Cost?' *The Lancet,* Vol. 382, No. 9890 (August 2013), pp. 452–77.

2 Karreman, Nancy et al. 'Understanding the Role of the State in Dietary Public Health Policymaking: A Critical Scoping Review'. *Health Promotion International,* Vol. 38, No. 5 (October 2023).

3 Gillespie, Stuart. 'Nutrition Policy and Practice: Unpacking the Politics'. In: Andrew Marble and Heidi Fritschel (eds), *Global Food Policy Report*, Washington DC: IFPRI, 2013, pp. 75–86.

4 IPES-Food. *Who's Tipping the Scales? The Growing Influence of Corporations on the Governance of Food Systems, and How to Counter It*, April 2023.

5 Dimbleby, Henry and Lewis, Jemima. *Ravenous: How to Get Ourselves and Our Planet into Shape*. London: Profile Books, 2023. p. 214.

6 Food, Farming & Countryside Commission. 'So, What Do We Really Want from Food?' January 2024. <www.ffcc.co.uk>

7 Thaler, R.H. and Sunstein, C.R. *Nudge*. London: Penguin, 2009.

8 Steele, Margaret and Finucane, Francis. 'Philosophically, Is Obesity Really a Disease?' *Obesity Reviews*, Vol. 24, No. 8 (August 2023), e13590. <doi:10.1111/obr.13590>

9 Thanarajah, Sharmili Edwin et al. 'Habitual Daily Intake of a Sweet and Fatty Snack Modulates Reward Processing in Humans'. *Cell Metabolism*, Vol. 35, No. 4 (2023), pp. 571–84.

10 Vitale, M. et al., 'Ultra-Processed Foods and Human Health: A Systematic Review and Meta-Analysis of Prospective Cohort Studies'. *Advances in Nutrition*, Vol. 100121 (2023). <https://doi.org/10.1016/j.advnut.2023.09.009>

IV TRANSFORMATION

15. Regulate

1 Hawkes, C. et al. 'Double-duty Actions: Seizing Programme and Policy Opportunities to Address Malnutrition in All Its Forms'. *The Lancet*, Vol. 395, No. 10218 (January 2020), pp. 142–55.

2 Drake L. et al. 'School Feeding Programs in Middle Childhood and Adolescence'. In: D.A.P. Bundy et al. (eds), *Child and Adolescent Health and Development*, 3rd edition, Washington DC: World Bank, 20 November 2017.

3 Muiruri, P. 'Lunch Is Served'. *The Guardian*, 10 November 2023.

4 Kiru, E. and Gelli, A. 'Kenya's New Urban School Meal Plan'.

The Conversation, 18 September 2023. <https://theconversation.com/kenyas-new-urban-school-meal-plan-is-ambitious-it-could-offer-lessons-for-scaling-up-213158>

5 Venkateswaran, J. and Mehta, C. 'Food for Thought'. In: S. Hinde and V. Francis (eds), *Food: Responding to the Global Crisis*, London College of Communication, 2023, pp. 4–8. <https://www.artefactmagazine.com/category/global-food-crisis/>

6 Impact on Urban Health. 'Investing in Children's Future: A Cost Benefit Analysis of Free School Meal Provision Expansion', 2022. <https://urbanhealth.org.uk/wp-content/uploads/2022/10/FSM-Executive-Summary.pdf>

7 Simoes, M.L. 'Tackling Malnutrition in an Era of Political Uncertainty: The Case of Brazil'. Peoples Dispatch, 12 October 2023.

8 Dimbleby, Henry and Lewis, Jemima. *Ravenous: How to Get Ourselves and Our Planet into Shape*. London: Profile Books, 2023. p. 261.

9 Kiru and Gelli, 'Kenya's New Urban School Meal Plan', 2023.

10 NCD Alliance. 'Selling a sick future: countering harmful marketing to children and young people across risk factors for NCDs', October 2023. <https://ncdalliance.org/sites/default/files/Selling_a_sick_future-explainer-ENG.pdf>

11 Dillman Carpentier, F.R. et al. 'Restricting Child-Directed Ads Is Effective, But Adding A Time-Based Ban Is Better: Evaluating A Multi-Phase Regulation To Protect Children From Unhealthy Food Marketing On Television'. *International Journal of Behavioral Nutrition and Physical Activity*, Vol. 20, No. 62 (2023).

12 Taillie, L.S. et al. 'Changes in food purchases after the Chilean policies on food labelling, marketing, and sales in schools: a before and after study'. *The Lancet Planetary Health*, Vol. 5, No. 8 (2021), pp. e526-e33; Fretes, G. et al. 'Changes in children's and adolescents' dietary intake after the implementation of Chile's law of food labeling, advertising and sales in schools: A longitudinal study'. *International Journal of Behavioral Nutrition and Physical Activity*, Vol. 20, No. 1 (2023) p. 40.

13 Colchero, M.A. et al. 'In Mexico, Evidence of Sustained Consumer Response Two Years After Implementing a Sugar-

NOTES

Sweetened Beverage Tax'. *Health Affairs,* Vol. 36 (2017), pp. 564–71; Roache, S.A. and Gostin, L.O. 'The Untapped Power of Soda Taxes: Incentivizing Consumers, Generating Revenue, and Altering Corporate Behavior'. *International Journal of Health Policy and Management,* Vol. 6 (2017), pp. 489–93; Taillie, L.S. et al. 'An evaluation of Chile's Law of Food Labeling and Advertising on sugar-sweetened beverage purchases from 2015 to 2017: A before-and-after study.' *PLOS Medicine,* Vol. 17 (2020), e1003015.

14 Dorlach, T. and Mertenskötter, P. 'Interpreters of international economic law: corporations and bureaucrats in contest over Chile's nutrition label'. *Law & Society Review,* Vol. 54, No. 3 (2020), pp. 571–606.

15 Nowell, C. 'Latin America Labels Ultra-Processed Foods. Will the US Follow?' *The Guardian,* 21 May 2024. <https://www.theguardian.com/environment/article/2024/may/21/latin-america-food-labels-processed-foods?CMP=share_btn_url>

16 Nowell, C. 'The US Food Industry Has Long Buried the Truth About Their Products. Is That Coming to an End?' *The Guardian,* 20 May 2024.<https://www.theguardian.com/environment/article/2024/may/20/food-companies-nutrition-labels-truth>

17 Gomez, E. 'Government Response to Ultra-Processed and Sugar Beverages Industries in Developing Nations: The Need to Build Coalitions Across Policy Sectors'. In: D. Resnick and J. Swinnen, *The Political Economy of Food System Transformation,* Oxford University Press, 2023, pp. 133–48.

18 Barquera, S. et al. 'Mexico Attempts to Tackle Obesity: The Process, Results, Push Backs and Future Challenges'. *Obesity Reviews,* Vol. 14, Supplement 2 (November 2013), pp. 69–78.

19 Donaldson, E. 'Advocating for Sugar-Sweetened Beverage Taxation: A Case Study of Mexico'. Baltimore: Johns Hopkins Bloomberg School of Public Health, 2015, p. 17.

20 Gomez, 'Government Response to Ultra-Processed and Sugar Beverages Industries', 2023.

21 Crosbie E. et al. 'Hollow threats: transnational food and beverage companies' use of international agreements to fight

front-of-pack nutrition labeling in Mexico and beyond'. *International Journal of Health Policy and Management*, Vol. 11, No. 6 (2022), pp. 722–5.

22 Barquera, S. et al. 'The Obesogenic Environment Around Elementary Schools: Food and Beverage Marketing to Children in Two Mexican Cities'. *BMC Public Health*, Vol. 18 (2018), p. 461.

23 Batis C. et al. 'Comparison of dietary intake before vs after taxes on sugar-sweetened beverages and nonessential energy-dense foods in Mexico, 2012 to 2018'. *JAMA Network Open*, Vol. 6, No. 7 (2023), e2325191.

24 Donaldson, 'Advocating for Sugar-Sweetened Beverage Taxation', 2015, p. 18.

25 Gilmore, A.B. et al. 'Defining and Conceptualising the Commercial Determinants of Health'. *The Lancet* (March 2023), pp. 1–20.

26 Gilmore et al., 'Defining and Conceptualising the Commercial Determinants of Health', 2023.

27 World Cancer Research Fund International. *Building Momentum: Lessons on Implementing a Robust Sugar Sweetened Beverage Tax*, 2019.

28 Abdool Karim, Safura et al. 'Industry Strategies in the Parliamentary Process of Adopting a Sugar-Sweetened Beverage Tax in South Africa: A Systematic Mapping'. *Globalization and Health,* Vol. 16, No. 1 (2020), p. 116.

29 Stacey, N. et al. 'Changes in Beverage Purchases Following the Announcement and Implementation of South Africa's Health Promotion Levy: An Observational Study'. *The Lancet Planetary Health,* Vol. 5 (April 2021), pp. e200–208.

30 Burgaz, Celia et al. 'The Effectiveness of Food System Policies to Improve Nutrition, Nutrition-Related Inequalities and Environmental Sustainability: A Scoping Review'. *Food Security*, Vol. 15 (August 2023), pp. 1313–44.

31 Pedroza-Tobias, A. et al. 'Food and Beverage Industry Interference in Science and Policy: Efforts to Block Soda Tax Implementation in Mexico and Prevent International Diffusion'. *BMJ Global Health*, Vol. 6 (2021), e005662.

32 Hattersley, L. and Mandeville, K.L. 'Global Coverage and Design of Sugar-Sweetened Beverage Taxes'. *JAMA Network Open*, Vol. 6, No. 3 (1 Mar 2023), e231412.

33 NYU College of Global Public Health, and Tufts' Friedman School. 'Junk Food Tax Is Legally and Administratively Viable, Finds New Analysis', January 2024.

34 Taylor, Luke. 'Colombia Introduces Latin America's First Junk Food Tax'. *BMJ*, Vol. 383 (November 2023), p. 2698.

35 Pongutta, S. et al. 'Lessons from the Thai Health Promotion Foundation'. *Bulletin of the World Health Organization*, Vol. 97, No. 3 (2019), pp. 213–220.

36 In March 2023, the Food Research Collaboration (FRC) published a policy brief: *The Food Marketing Environment: A Force for or Against Human and Planetary Health?* in which they showed how few of these recommendations made it into the ensuing Government Strategy (GFS).

37 Gomez, 'Government Response to Ultra-Processed and Sugar Beverages Industries', 2023.

38 Burgaz et al., 'The Effectiveness of Food System Policies', 2023.

39 Monteiro, C.A. et al. 'Ultra-processed Foods, Diet Quality, and Health Using the NOVA Classification System'. UN FAO, 2019; Health Canada. 'Canada's Food Guide', 2021. <https://food-guide.canada.ca/en/>; Koios, D. et al. 'Representations of Ultra-Processed Foods: A Global Analysis of How Dietary Guidelines Refer to Levels of Food Processing'. *International Journal of Health Policy Management*, Vol. 11, No. 11 (2022), pp. 2588-2599; Monteiro, C.A. et al. 'Dietary Guidelines to Nourish Humanity and the Planet in the Twenty-first Century. A Blueprint from Brazil'. *Public Health Nutrition.*, Vol. 18 (2015), pp. 2311–22.

40 WHO/UNICEF. *How the Marketing of Formula Milk Influences Our Decisions on Infant Feeding*. Geneva: World Health Organization and the United Nations Children's Fund, 2022.

41 Gillespie, S. et al. 'Evidence to Action: Highlights from Transform Nutrition Research (2012–2017)'. *Food and Nutrition Bulletin*, Vol. 39, No. 3 (September 2018), pp. 335–60.

42 Neves, J.A. et al. 'The Brazilian Cash Transfer Program (Bolsa Família): A Tool for Reducing Inequalities and Achieving Social Rights in Brazil'. *Global Public Health,* Vol. 17, No. 1 (Jan 2022), pp. 26–42.

43 Trussell Trust. 'Record Number of Emergency Food Parcels Provided to People Facing Hardship by Trussell Trust Food Banks in Past 12 Months', 26 April 2023. <https://www.trusselltrust.org/2023/04/26/record-number-of-emergency-food-parcels-provided-to-people-facing-hardship-by-trussell-trust-food-banks-in-past-12-months/>

44 Gillespie, S. et al. (eds). 'Stories of Change in Nutrition: Special Issue'. *Global Food Security,* Vol. 13 (June 2017), pp. 1–88.

45 Millstone, E. and Lang, T. 'An Approach to Conflicts of Interest in UK Food Regulatory Institutions'. *Nature Food*, Vol. 4 (January 2023), pp. 17–21.

46 Wood, B. et al. 'Conceptualising the Commercial Determinants of Health Using a Power Lens: A Review and Synthesis of Existing Frameworks'. *International Journal of Health Policy and Management,* Vol. 11 (2021), pp. 1251–61.

47 IPES-Food. *Who's Tipping the Scales? The Growing Influence of Corporations on the Governance of Food Systems, and How to Counter It*, April 2023.

48 Robins-Early, N. 'Google broke law to maintain online search monopoly, US judge rules'. *The Guardian*, 6 August 2024. <https://www.theguardian.com/technology/article/2024/aug/05/google-loses-antitrust-lawsuit?CMP=share_btn_url>

49 Shaxson, N. 'Food giants are strangling Britain's farmers and consumers. What's the solution? Break them up'. *The Guardian*, Opinion, 22 July 2024. <https://www.theguardian.com/commentisfree/article/2024/jul/22/big-supermarkets-strangling-farmers-shoppers-solution-break-them-up?CMP=share_btn_url>

16. A Tale of Four Cities

1 Venditti, B. 'Cities and Urbanisation'. World Economic Forum, 26 April 2022. <https://www.weforum.org/agenda/2022/04/global-urbanization-material-consumption/>

2   FAO. 'Strengthening Urban and Peri-Urban Food Systems to Achieve Food Security and Nutrition in the Context of Urbanization and Rural Transformation'. *Global Forum on Food Security and Nutrition, Consultation No. 185*. Rome: FAO, 2023, p. 70.

3   Halliday, J. et al. 'A Menu of Actions to Shape Urban Food Environments for Improved Nutrition',. GAIN, MUFPP and RUAF, 2019.

4   Yau, A. et al. 'Changes in Household Food and Drink Purchases Following Restrictions on the Advertisement of High Fat, Salt, and Sugar Products Across the Transport for London Network: A Controlled Interrupted Time Series Analysis'. *PLOS Medicine,* Vol. 19, No. 2 (2022), e1003915.

5   Bernhardt, F. 'It's the Right Thing to Do: Five Years of Local Healthier Food Advertising Policies'. Sustain, 20 February 2024. <https://www.sustainweb.org/blogs/feb24-five-years-local-advertising-policies/>

6   MUFPP (2023). Milan Pact Awards, 2022.

7   The Food Foundation Podcast. 'Pod Bites: Global Food Justice Toolkit Launched', 22 September 2023. <https://foodfoundation.org.uk/podcast/pod-bites-global-food-justice-toolkit-launched>

8   Birmingham City Council. 'Birmingham Food System Strategy 2022–30'. <https://www.birmingham.gov.uk/info/50279/food_revolution/2602/birmingham_food_system_strategy>

17. Activate

1   Green, D. *How Change Happens*. Oxford: Oxford University Press, 2016.

2   Benton, T. 'Academics Can Do More to Disrupt and Reframe the Solution Space for Food System Transformation'. *Nature Food,* Vol. 4, No. 11 (Nov 2023), pp. 928–30.

3   Baksi, C. 'Landmarks in Law: McLibel and the Longest Trial in British Legal History'. *The Guardian*, 8 July 2019.

4   Northcutt, Wayne. 'José Bové vs. McDonald's: The Making of a National Hero in the French Anti-Globalization Movement'. *Journal of the Western Society for French History,* Vol. 31, 2003.

5   Osborn, Samuel. 'Coca-Cola Loses Billions After Cristiano

Ronaldo Removes Bottles and Says "Drink Water"'. *The Independent*, 16 July 2021.

6 Buse, K. et al. 'Let's end corporate sponsorship of sporting events'. *BMJ* (August 2024), p. 386.

7 Gayle, Damien. 'Spoof Billboard Ads Take Aim at BMW and Toyota over "Going Green" Claims'. *The Guardian*, 19 January 2023.

8 Beckett, A. 'British Cycling Targeted by Anti-Shell Billboards'. *Cycling Weekly*, 15 May 2024. <https://www.cyclingweekly.com/news/british-cycling-targeted-by-anti-shell-billboards>

9 Oxfam. 'Behind the Brands: Food justice and the "Big 10" food and beverage companies'. 26 February 2013. <https://policy-practice.oxfam.org/resources/behind-the-brands-food-justice-and-the-big-10-food-and-beverage-companies-270393/>

10 Eno, B. 'Foreword'. In: J. Alexander, *Citizens,* London: Canbury Press, 2022, p. 9.

11 Green, *How Change Happens,* p. 229.

12 Klein, N. *No Is Not Enough.* London: Allen Lane, 2017, p. 238.

13 Patel, Raj and Moore, Jason W. 'How the Chicken Nugget Became the True Symbol of Our Era'. *The Guardian*, 8 May 2018.

14 Swinburn, Boyd, et al. 'The Global Syndemic of Obesity, Undernutrition, and Climate Change'. *The Lancet*, Vol. 393, No. 10173 (February 2019), pp. 791–846.

15 Wood, B. et al. 'What is the purpose of ultra-processed food? An exploratory analysis of the financialisation of ultra-processed food corporations and implications for public health.' *Globalization and Health,* Vol. 19 (2023), pp. 1–20.

16 Alexander, J. *Citizens.* London: Canbury Press, 2022, p. 196.

17 Gillespie, S. et al. (eds). 'Stories of Change in Nutrition: Special Issue'. *Global Food Security*, Vol. 13, (June 2017), pp. 1–88.

18 McNeill, Kirsty. 'It's Time for a Leadership Revolution'. *Medium*, 16 December 2021. <https://medium.com/@kirstyjmcneill/its-time-for-a-leadership-revolution-4e73cd6bb9b8>

19 Krznaric, Roman. *The Good Ancestor: How to Think Long-Term in a Short-Term World*. London: Penguin, 2021.

18. Decolonise

1 Hirsch, Lioba A. and Martin, Rebecca. *LSHTM and Colonialism: A Report On the Colonial History of the London School of Hygiene & Tropical Medicine (1899–c.1960)*. Project Report. London: London School of Hygiene & Tropical Medicine, 2022.

2 Abimbola, S. 'On the Meaning of Global Health and the Role of Global Health Journals'. *International Health,* Vol. 10, No. 2 (2018), pp. 63–65.

3 Nixon, Stephanie. 'The Coin Model of Privilege and Critical Allyship: Implications for Health'. *BMC Public Health,* Vol. 19, No. 1637 (2019).

4 Mosse, D. *Cultivating Development: An Ethnography of Aid Policy and Practice*. London: Pluto Press, 2005.

5 Keshavjee, Salmaan. *Blind Spot: How Neoliberalism Infiltrated Global Health*. Oakland: University of California Press, 2014.

19. Illuminate

1 Gillespie, S. et al. 'Scaling Up Impact on Nutrition: What Will it Take?' *Advances in Nutrition,* Vol. 6 (2015), pp. 440–51.

2 IFPRI. 'Stories of Change in Nutrition'. <https://www.ifpri.org/project/stories-change-nutrition>

3 Green, D. 'Pracademics: Just a Clunky New Word or Something More Significant/Substantial?' From Poverty to Power, 9 Nov 2023. <https://frompoverty.oxfam.org.uk/pracademics-just-a-nasty-new-word-or-something-more-significant-substantial/#:~:text=Poverty%20to%20Power-,Pracademics%3A%20just%20a%20clunky%20new%20word,or%20something%20more%20significant%2Fsubstantial%3F&text=Pracademics.>

4 Hutchens, G. 'Economics Is in "Disarray", Having Placed Efficiency Before Ethics and Human Wellbeing, Says Nobel Laureate'. ABC, 17 March 2024. <https://www.abc.net.au/news/2024-03-17/> nobel-prize-winning-economist-criticises-economics-profession/103582032?utm_campaign=abc_news_web&utm_content=mail&utm_medium=content_shared&utm_source=abc_news_web >

5 Walls, H. et al. 'Addressing Malnutrition: The Importance of Political Economy Analysis of Power'. *International Journal of Health Policy and Management*, Vol. 10, No. 12 (2021), pp. 809–16.

6 HLPE. 'Reducing Inequalities for Food Security and Nutrition'. Rome: CFS HLPE-FSN, 2023.

7 Hinde, S. and Francis, V. (eds). *Food: Responding to the Global Crisis*. London College of Communication, 2023, pp. 34–41 <https://www.artefactmagazine.com/category/global-food-crisis/>

20. Innovate

1 Sayid, R. 'Exploited Female Cocoa Farm Workers Are Paid Just 23p a Day'. *Daily Mirror*, 24 February 2020. <https://www.mirror.co.uk/news/world-news/exploited-female-cocoa-farm-workers-21569248>

2 Whoriskey, P. 'Supreme Court weighs child-slavery case against Nestlé USA, Cargill'. *Washington Post,* 1 December 2020. <https://www.washingtonpost.com/business/2020/12/01/cocoa-supreme-court-child-labor/>

3 Whoriskey, 'Supreme Court weighs child-slavery case', 2020.

4 Nordhagen, Stella. 'Reaching Lower-Income Consumers with Nutritious Foods: Increase value through convenience'. GAIN, 14 November 2023.

5 2SCALE. 'Bop Marketing and Distribution', January 2024. <www.2scale.org>

6 Bruyeron, Olivier et al. 'Marketing Complementary Foods and Supplements in Burkina Faso, Madagascar, and Vietnam: Lessons Learned from the Nutridev Program'. *Food and Nutrition Bulletin*, Vol. 31, No. 2, Supplement (2010), pp. S154–67.

7 Walt, V. 'A Top CEO Was Ousted . . .' *Time*, 21 November 2021. <https://time.com/6121684/emmanuel-faber-danone-interview/>

8 Van Gansbeke, F. 'Sustainability and the Downfall of Danone CEO Faber'. *Forbes,* 6 May 2022. <https://www.forbes.com/sites/frankvangansbeke/2021/03/20/sustainability-and-the-downfall-of-danone-ceo-faber-12/?sh=4d10d1755b16>

9 Dimbleby, Henry and Lewis, Jemima. *Ravenous: How to Get Ourselves and Our Planet into Shape*. London: Profile Books, 2023.

10 UK National Food Strategy, 2021. <https://www.nationalfoodstrategy.org/the-report/>

11 Food Foundation. 'Plating Up Progress'. <https://foodfoundation.org.uk/initiatives/plating-up-progress>

12 Food Foundation. 'The Investor Coalition on Food Policy'. <https://foodfoundation.org.uk/initiatives/investor-coalition-food-policy>

21. Unite

1 Cornia, Giovanni Andrea et al. *Adjustment with a Human Face*. Oxford: Clarendon Press, 1987.

2 Akselrod, S. et al. 'Multisectoral Action to Address Noncommunicable Diseases: Lessons from Three Country Case Studies'. *Frontiers in Public Health,* Vol. 12 (2024), 1303786.

3 WHO. *Diet, Nutrition, and the Prevention Of Chronic Diseases: Report of a Joint WHO/FAO Expert Consultation*. Geneva: World Health Organization, 2003.

4 Hawkins B. and Holden C. 'A Corporate Veto on Health Policy? Global Constitutionalism and Investor–State Dispute Settlement'. *Journal of Health Politics, Policy and Law*, Vol. 41, No. 5 (2016), pp. 969–95.

5 Schram A. et al. 'A Conceptual Framework for Investigating the Impacts of International Trade and Investment Agreements on Noncommunicable Disease Risk Factors'. *Health Policy Plan,* Vol. 33, No. 1, (2018), pp. 23–36.

6 Thow, A.M. et al. 'Will the Next Generation of Preferential Trade and Investment Agreements Undermine Prevention of Noncommunicable Diseases? A Prospective Policy Analysis of the Trans-Pacific Partnership Agreement'. *Health Policy,* Vol. 119 (2015), pp, 88–96.

7 Barlow, P. and Allen, L.N. 'US and EU Free Trade Agreements and Implementation of Policies to Control Tobacco, Alcohol,

and Unhealthy Food and Drinks: A Quasi-Experimental Analysis'. *PLOS Medicine*, 20 (2023), e1004147.

8 Food Tank. 'WTO and Food Security: Biting the Hand That Feeds the Poor'. Op-ed. <https://foodtank.com/news/2017/12/india-wto-food-security-part1/>

9 Wise, T. 'US Misuses Trade Agreements to Undermine Food Sovereignty.' *Inter-Press Service*, Opinion, 11 December 2023. <https://www.ipsnews.net/2023/12/u-s-misuses-trade-agreements-undermine-food-sovereignty/>

10 UN. *Transforming our World: The 2030 Agenda for Sustainable Development*. United Nations, 2015.

11 UN. Global Compact. <https://unglobalcompact.org/>

12 WHO. 'Safeguarding Against Possible Conflicts of Interest in Nutrition Programmes'. Executive Board EB142/23, 4 December 2017.

13 PAHO. 'Preventing and Managing Conflicts of Interest in Country-level Nutrition Programs: A Roadmap for Implementing the World Health Organization's Draft Approach in the Americas', 2021.

14 WHO. 'Supporting member states in reaching informed decision-making on engaging with private sector entities for the prevention and control of noncommunicable diseases: a practical tool'. Geneva: World Health Organization, 2024.

15 UNICEF. 'Engaging with the Food and Beverage Industry: UNICEF Programme Guidance'. United Nations Children's Fund, 2023.

16 WHO. 'Framework Convention on Tobacco Control'. World Health Organization, 2005.

17 Swinburn, Boyd, et al. 'The Global Syndemic of Obesity, Undernutrition, and Climate Change'. *The Lancet*, Vol. 393, No. 10173 (February 2019), pp. 791–846).

18 Monteiro, C. et al. 'Reasons to Avoid Ultra-Processed Food'. *BMJ*, Vol. 384 (2024), q439.

19 Jolly, R. et al. *UN Ideas That Changed the World*. Bloomington: Indiana University Press, 2009.

22. Enable

1 Vogel, Jefim and Hickel, Jason. 'Is Green Growth Happening?
   An Empirical Analysis of Achieved Versus Paris-Compliant
   CO_2-GDP Decoupling in High-Income Countries'. *The Lancet
   Planetary Health*, Vol. 7, No. 9 (September 2023), pp. e759–e769.

2 Mazzucato, M. *Mission Economy: A Moonshot Guide to Changing
   Capitalism*. London: Penguin, 2021.

3 Doughnut Economics Action Lab. 'About Doughnut
   Economics', January 2024. <www.doughnuteconomics.org>

4 Hickel, J. et al. 'Degrowth Can Work: Here's How Science Can
   Help'. *Nature*, Vol. 612 (15 December 2022), pp. 400–403.

5 Monbiot, G. and Hutchison, P. *The Invisible Doctrine*. London:
   Allen Lane, 2024.

6 De Schutter, Olivier. *The Poverty of Growth*. London: Pluto
   Press, 2024.

7 Hoekstra, R. *This Is the Moment to Go Beyond GDP*. WWF,
   Wellbeing Economy Alliance, European Environmental Bureau,
   2022. <https://weall.org/this-is-the-moment-to-go-beyond-gdp>

8 Calafati, L. et al. *When Nothing Works: From Cost of
   Living to Foundational Liveability*. Manchester: Manchester
   University Press, 2023. <https://manchesteruniversitypress.
   co.uk/9781526173713/>

9 Dasgupta, P. *The Economics of Biodiversity: The Dasgupta
   Review*. London: HM Treasury, 2021. <https://www.gov.
   uk/government/publications/final-report-the-economics-of-
   biodiversity-the-dasgupta-review>

10 FAO. *The State of Food and Agriculture 2023: Revealing the True
   Cost of Food to Transform Agrifood Systems*. Rome: FAO, 2023.

11 FAO, *State of Food and Agriculture*, 2023.

12 GIST. Impact and Global Alliance for the Future of Food.
   'Natural Farming Through a Wide-Angle Lens'. *Future
   of Food*, July 2023. <https://futureoffood.org/insights/
   true-cost-accounting-of-community-managed-natural-farming-
   in-andhra-pradesh-india/>

13 World Bank. 'Trillions wasted on subsidies could help address
   climate change'. Press release, 15 June 2023.

14 Nugent, R. 'Rethinking Systems to Reverse the Global Syndemic'. *The Lancet,* Vol. 393 (February 2019), pp. 726–28.

15 Searchinger, T.D. et al. 'Revising Public Agricultural Support to Mitigate Climate Change'. *Development Knowledge and Learning.* Washington DC: World Bank, 2020.

16 Lakhani, N. 'America Is a Factory Farming Nation'. *The Guardian*, 15 February 2024. <https://www.theguardian.com/environment/2024/feb/15/us-agriculture-census-farming?lctg=9072588>

17 Gautam, Madhur et al. 'Repurposing Agricultural Policies and Support: Options to Transform Agriculture and Food Systems to Better Serve the Health of People, Economies, and the Planet'. Washington DC: World Bank, 2022. <http://hdl.handle.net/10986/36875>

18 Weldon, D. 'The Big Idea: Should We Worry About Trillionaires?' *The Guardian,* 18 March 2024. <https://www.theguardian.com/books/2024/mar/18/the-big-idea-should-we-worry-about-trillionaires?CMP=share_btn_url>

19 Oxfam. 'Richest 1 per cent Bag Nearly Twice as Much Wealth as the World Put Together Over the Past Two Years', January 2024.

20 Helm, T. 'Wealth taxes could raise £10 billion to help plug Tory budget hole, say economists'. *Observer*, 28 July 2024 <https://www.theguardian.com/politics/article/2024/jul/28/wealth-taxes-britain-10bn-tory-budget-hole-economists>

21 HLPE. 'Reducing Inequalities for Food Security and Nutrition'. Rome: CFS HLPE-FSN, 2023, p. 83; United Nations. *UN Warns of Soaring Global Public Debt: A Record $92 Trillion in 2022*. United Nations Conference on Trade and Development, 2023. <https://unctad.org/news/un-warns-soaring-global-public-debtrecord-92-trillion-2022>

22 Pfeiffer, James. 'Debt and Decolonization of Global Health'. University of Oslo, 29 November 2022; Ahmed, M. et al. 'Main Takeaways on Debt from the Annual Meetings'. Center for Global Development, 29 November 2023.

23 World Bank. International Debt Report, 2023.

24 APHA. 'A Call to Expand International Debt Relief for All

Developing Countries to Increase Access to Public Resources for Health Care', January 2024. <www.apha.org>

25 Save the Children. 'Nutrition Boost: Why the World Needs a Step Change in Finance for Nutrition and How It Can Be Achieved', 2018. <https://resourcecentre.savethechildren.net/document/nutrition-boost-why-world-needs-step-change-finance-nutrition-and-how-it-can-be-achieved/>

26 Seidelmann, Lisa et al. 'The Global Financing Facility at Five: Time for a Change?' *Sexual and Reproductive Health Matters,* Vol. 28 (2020), p. 2.

27 Development Initiatives. *Global Nutrition Report,* 2022. <https://globalnutritionreport.org/reports/2022-global-nutrition-report/>

28 Zero Hunger Coalition. 'The Zero Hunger Private Sector Pledge' <https://pledge.zerohungercoalition.org/en>

29 Zero Hunger Coalition. 'PepsiCo Inc'. <https://pledge.zerohungercoalition.org/en/pepsico-inc>

30 Oxfam, 'Richest 1% Bag Nearly Twice as Much Wealth', 2024.

31 Dyvik, Einar H. 'Billionaires Around the World'. *Statista,* 10 January 2024. <https://www.statista.com/topics/2229/billionaires-around-the-world/>

32 Schwab, Tim. *The Bill Gates Problem: Reckoning with the Myth of the Good Billionaire.* London: Penguin Business, 2023.

33 Schwab, *Bill Gates Problem,* 2023.

34 Sukumar, R. Interview with Bill Gates. *Hindustan Times.* 17 September 2024. <https://www.hindustantimes.com/india-news/ht-interview-india-continues-improving-mortality-rates-says-bill-gates-101726560722509.html>

35 Day, H. and Belay, M. 'Open Letter to USAID: Fund Sustainable Food Systems in Africa, Not Another Industrial "Green Revolution"', 18 May 2023.

36 Wise, Timothy. 'Failing Africa's Farmers: An Impact Assessment of the Alliance for a Green Revolution in Africa', 2020 <https://sites.tufts.edu/gdae /files/2020/10/20-01_Wise_FailureToYield.pdf>; *False Promises,* 2020 <https://www.rosalux.de/fileadmin/rls_uploads/pdfs/ Studien/False_Promises_AGRA_en.pdf>

37 Nestlé. 'Nestlé partners with Africa Food Prize', 9 November 2022 <https://www.nestle.com/media/news/nestle-contribute-africa-food-prize#:~:text=Nestl%C3%A9%20has%20decided%20to%20partner,livelihoods%20and%20improve%20the%20environment.>

38 Centre for Health, Science and Law, Ottawa. 'Open Letter to the Executive Board of the World Health Organization', 17 January 2017 <http://healthscienceandlaw.ca/wp-content/uploads/2017/01/Public-Interest-Position.WHO_.FENSAGates.Jan2017.pdf>.

Conclusion: Food Future

1 Béné, Christophe. 'Why the Great Food Transformation May Not Happen: A Deep-Dive into Our Food Systems' Political Economy, Controversies and Politics Of Evidence'. *World Development*, Vol. 154 (2022), p. 105881.

2 Wilson, Bee. 'We Need to Break the Junk Food Cycle: How to Fix Britain's Failing Food System'. *The Guardian*, 30 November 2021. <https://www.theguardian.com/food/2021/nov/30/break-junk-food-cycle-britain-national-food-strategy>

3 Gillespie, S. and Witten, C. 'The ultra-processed food industry has no business in sponsoring health and nutrition events'. *BMJ*, Vol. 386 (2024), q1894.

4 Kuhn, Thomas. *The Structure of Scientific Revolutions*. Chicago: University of Chicago Press, 1962.

5 Roy, Arundhati. 'The Pandemic Is a Portal'. *Financial Times*, 3 April 2020.

Acknowledgements

Half a century has gone by since I picked up *How the Other Half Dies* by Susan George. This was the book that inspired me to step onto the food, nutrition and health path. Since then, I have run into hundreds of extraordinary people – mothers in villages, front-line health workers, street vendors, activists, policymakers, revolutionaries, presidents – and learned so much from them.

First, when I started to work as a volunteer in central India in the early Eighties, I shadowed Joggaya, Ellama and Saramma – three amazing young Koya adults who showed me what was possible in a very immediate way. Many young lives were saved because of the decisions they made during my two years there.

Then there's a group of pioneers. A quarter-century after Susan George's book, Marion Nestle wrote the seminal *Food Politics*, which first opened the lid on Big Food's products and practices. Others I've been lucky to work with include Barry Popkin, Carlos Monteiro, Geoffrey Cannon, Richard Jolly, Robert Chambers, Alan Berg, Barbara Harris-White and Per Pinstrup-Andersen.

I'm immensely grateful to an inner circle of brilliant colleagues and collaborators including Olivia Yambi, Suneetha Kadiyala, Scott Drimie, Nick Nisbett, Jody Harris, Purnima Menon, Marie Ruel, Bhavani Shankar, Joe Yates, Anna Taylor, Leticija Petrovich, Chantell Witten, Phil Baker, Leah Salm, Laura Casu, Liz Kimani-

Murage, Kraisid Tontisirin, Judith Hodge, Mara van den Bold, Aulo Gelli, Danielle Resnick, Gabriel Rugalema, Alan Whiteside, Robert Greener, Michael Loevinsohn, Tim Frankenberger, Wairimu Mwangi, Meera Shekar, Ayako Ebata, Erica Nelson, John Hoddinott, Agnes Quisumbing, Namukolo Covic, Derek Headey, Rasmi Avula, Deanna Olney, Jef Leroy, Sivan Yosef, Rajul Pandya-Lorch, Vicky Sibson, Shams El Arifeen, Katherine Richards, Jane Badham, Natalie Roschnik, Samantha Reddin, Jess Meeker, Rebecca Heidkamp, Roos Verstraeten, Rebecca Pradeilles, Alan Dangour, RV Bhavani, Julia Powell, Jess Fanzo, Anne Marie Thow, Angela Carriedo, David Pelletier, Lindsay Allen, Francesco Branca, Lina Mahy, Filippo Gavazzeni, Sarah Buszard, Rebecca Tobi, Antony So, Sarah Pullen, Valarie Blue Bird Jernigan, Busiso Moyo, Nzama Mbalati, Karen Washington, David Nabarro, Bob Black, Joachim von Braun, Shweta Khandelwal, Anthony Measham, Richard Heaver, Rafa Flores, Ellen Piwoz, Rahul Rawat, Mélissa Mialon, Barrie Margetts, Anna Herforth, Nitya Rao, Devanshi Chanchani, Haris Gazdar, Megan Blake, Richmond Aryeetey, Simon Hinde, Vivienne Francis, Corinna Hawkes and Rebecca Wells.

Several colleagues and friends have since passed on. Urban Jonsson, John Mason, David Sanders, Bjorn Ljungqvist, Prakash Shetty, Hans Binswanger, MS Swaminathan, Mahabub Hossain, Arne Oshaug and David Barker all had a great impact on the world, and on me.

Next, there's an outer circle of inspirational scholars, activists and policy folk. They are . . . deep breath . . . Seye Abimbola, Madhu Pai, Michael Fakhri, Olivier De Schutter, Jeff Sachs, Boyd Swinburn, Simón Barquera, Rob Percival, Victor Aguayo, Catherine Howarth, Elisabetta Recine, Kevin Hall, Dolly van Tulleken, Erik Millstone, Tim Lang, Michael Marmot, Melissa Leach, Helen West, Anna Gilmore, Kathrin Lauber, Lucy Sullivan,

ACKNOWLEDGEMENTS

Tony Costello, Sandro Demaio, Sarah Steele, Kent Buse, Patti Rundall, Magdalena Whoolery, Nigel Rollins, Dev Sharma, Sharon Friel, Nick Rose, Jenn Lacy-Nichols, Katherine Cullerton, Ben Wood, Scott Slater, Mark Lawrence, Dominic Watters, Arun Gupta, Shalmali Guttal, Rob Ralston, Jeff Collin, Martin White, Fran Baum, Marita Hennessey, Jane Battersby, Ruby Makepeace-Somerville, Katie Cuming, Rebecca Coombes, Rosie Boycott, Luiz Inácio Lula da Silva, Caroline Lucas, Natalie Bennett, Eric Crosbie, Gary Ruskin, Duncan Green, Simon Maxwell, Eric Schlosser, Jennifer Clapp, Lorena Ibarra, Mark Petticrew, Rafael Pérez-Escamilla, Roger Mathisen, Eduardo Gómez, Cesar Victora, Juan Rivera Dommarco, Jocalyn Clark, Katerini Storeng, Harry Rutter, Jay Goulden, Kelly Brownell, Johanna Ralston, Rachel Nugent, Sue Pritchard, Sheila Dillon, Helen Walls, Lucy Westerman, Kat Jenner, Chris Béné, José Luis Vivero Pol, Million Belay, Biraj Patnaik, José Graziano da Silva, Bernie Sanders, Amandine Garde, Agnes Erzse, Nancy Karreman, Deviana Dewi, Kevin Watkins, Ed Davey, Jonathan Gorstein, Lauren Bandy, Ursula Trübswasser, Caroline Cerny, Courtney Scott, Kathy Shats, Kelly Parsons, Kim Anastasiou, Christina Zorbas, Priscilla Machado, Lindsey Smith Taillie, Linda Bauld, Lindsay Jaacks, Lisanne du Plessis, Vivica Kraak, Wilma Freire, Chris Turner, Jeff Waage, Philip McMichael, Derek Byerlee, Stephen Devereux, Julian May, Lídia Cabral, Alexander Mueller, Diarmid Campbell-Lendrum, Tim Wise, Marit Kolby, Joel Spicer, Callum Northcote, Keetie Roelen, Catherine Pereira-Kotze, Ted Greiner, Amos Laar, Andrea Freeman, Stephanie Nixon, Kate Sievert, Bronwen Gillespie, Emmanuel Faber and Marcus Rashford.

I am extremely indebted to five brilliant writers – Devi Sridhar, Chris van Tulleken, Henry Dimbleby, Tim Spector and Marion Nestle – who all wrote such generous feedback on an earlier draft of this book.

ACKNOWLEDGEMENTS

Along with theirs, books by the following luminaries influenced this one: Amartya Sen, Jean Dreze, Frantz Fanon, George Orwell, Thomas Kuhn, P. Sainath, Sathnam Sanghera, Rupa Marya, Raj Patel, Michael Moss, David Mosse, Gyorgy Scrinis, Michael Pollan, Tim Jackson, Grant Ennis, Bee Wilson, George Monbiot, Dan Saladino, Carolyn Steel, David Rieff, Yuval Noah Harari, Jared Diamond, Roman Krznaric, Tim Schwab, Anand Giridharadas, Naomi Klein, Atul Gawande, Ai Weiwei, Brian Eno, Kojo Koram, Mariana Mazzucato, Tony Barnett, Kate Raworth, Jason Hickel, Michael Sandel, David Olusoga, Ha-Joon Chang, Partha Dasgupta, Arundhati Roy, Sheila Zurbrigg, Nicholas Freudenberg, Rutger Bregman, Jon Alexander, Will Storr, Pen Vogler, James Walvin, Alex de Waal and Patrick Radden Keefe.

In the middle of a long bike ride in the summer of 2019, I realised I needed to make a change in my life. The next week, I enrolled (part-time) in the Creative Writing Programme at New Writing South in Brighton. For three years, I benefited enormously from four fabulous mentors – Holly Dawson, Hannah Vincent, Laura Wilkinson and later, Lily Dunn – along with fellow students. I'm also grateful to Lulah Ellender and Lauren Howard.

In 2021, I left my job after twenty-two great years, so I could concentrate on this other writing world. I wrote a novel and a proposal for a hybrid memoir/polemic before nervously dispatching the latter to a handful of top agents, expecting silence. The next day, I heard from Victoria Hobbs at A.M. Heath. She had seen something in the proposal which, at that time, hadn't fully crystallised for me. Working with her, it came into view. Then she set about finding the right home for the book and within a few weeks, it was on. Victoria's a gem. I would also like to thank Jess Lee at A.M. Heath for her excellent support.

ACKNOWLEDGEMENTS

My publisher, Canongate, is full of dynamic, supportive and generally wonderful people. Special thanks to my editor Helena Gonda and to CEO, Jamie Byng. Helena latched on to the proposal quickly, championed it internally, before providing some great suggestions in the structural edit. Throughout the process she was the perfect guide. As for Jamie, I was blown away by the time and attention he gave to my book, promoting it successfully in North America while giving me advice on how to further improve it. I am very grateful also to Claire Reiderman, Leila Cruickshank, Gale Winskill, Alice Shortland and Aisling Holling for their excellent work in marketing and promotion.

Huge thanks also to Jennifer Lambert and Lauren McKeon of HarperCollins for championing the book in Canada.

This book is dedicated to my family. Ciara and Rory are brilliant kids. Travelling the world with them as toddlers was occasionally terrifying, never dull.

And finally, my partner, Lindsay, for her unvarnished critique of multiple drafts and for her unwavering support. My most inspired life decision was made, forty-five years ago, when I quickly changed tack so our paths would (accidentally on purpose) cross by the jukebox at the University of Reading.

Resources

A selection of activist organisations driving change in the UK and worldwide.

United Kingdom
- Action Against Hunger
- Action on Sugar <https://www.actiononsugar.org/
- Bite Back 2030 https://www.biteback2030.com/>
- Bramble Partners <https://bramble.partners/>
- Caroline Walker Trust <www.cwt.org.uk>
- Chefs in Schools <https://chefsinschools.org.uk/
- First Steps Nutrition Trust <https://www.firststepsnutrition.org/>
- Food Equity Centre <https://www.ids.ac.uk/programme-and-centre/food-equity-centre/>
- Food Ethics Council <https://www.foodethicscouncil.org/>
- Food Foundation <https://foodfoundation.org.uk/>
- Food, Farming and Countryside Commission <https://ffcc.co.uk/
- Obesity Health Alliance <www.obesityhealthalliance.org.uk>
- ShareAction <www.shareaction.org>
- Soil Association <https://www.soilassociation.org/>

- Sustain <https://www.sustainweb.org/>
- TABLE <https://tabledebates.org/>
- Trussell Trust <https://www.trusselltrust.org/>

Worldwide

- Agriculture Nutrition Health (ANH) Academy <https://www.anh-academy.org/>
- Children In All Policies 2030 <https://cap-2030.org/>
- Collective for the Political Determinants of Health <https://www.sum.uio.no/english/research/networks/>
- Critical Takes on Corporate Power <https://criticaltakes.org/>
- ETC Group <https://www.etcgroup.org/>
- FIAN International <https://www.fian.org/
- Food Tank <www.foodtank.com>
- Global Health 50/50 <https://globalhealth5050.org/>
- Global Health Advocacy Incubator (GHAI) <https://www.advocacyincubator.org/>
- Governance, Ethics & Conflicts of Interest in Public Health Network <https://www.aub.edu.lb/fhs/Pages/GECI.aspx>
- IPES-Food <https://ipes-food.org/>
- La Via Campesina <https://viacampesina.org/>
- Milan Urban Food Policy Pact <https://www.milanurbanfoodpolicypact.org/
- People's Health Movement <https://phmovement.org/
- Vital Strategies <www.vitalstrategies.org>
- World Public Health Nutrition Association <https://www.wphna.org/>

Index

INDEX

INDEX

INDEX